REASONING with

DEMOCRATIC

VALUES 2.0,

VOLUME 1

D1205247

REASONING with

DEMOCRATIC VALUES 2.0,

VOLUME 1

Ethical Issues in American History, 1607–1865

David E. Harris
Anne-Lise Halvorsen
Paul F. Dain

TEACHERS COLLEGE PRESS

TEACHERS COLLEGE | COLUMBIA UNIVERSITY

NEW YORK AND LONDON

Published by Teachers College Press, 1234 Amsterdam Avenue, New York, NY 10027

Cover photos: Mill workers (background) via Library of Congress; engraving of Tecumseh by Benson Lossing (public domain); Winslow Homer's "The Bobbin Girl" from American Antiquarian Society; Portrait of Isaac Jefferson via Wikimedia Commons.

Library of Congress Cataloging-in-Publication Data is available at loc.gov

Names: Harris, David E., 1945- author. | Halvorsen, Anne-Lise, author. | Dain, Paul F., author. Title: Reasoning with democratic values 2.0 : ethical issues in American history / David E. Harris, Anne-Lise Halvorsen, Paul F. Dain. Other titles: Reasoning with democratic values. | Ethical issues in American history Description: New York, NY: Teachers College Press, [2018] | Includes bibliographical references and index. Identifiers: LCCN 2018004264 |
ISBN 9780807759288 (pbk. : alk. paper) |
ISBN 9780807777077 (ebook)
Subjects: LCSH: United States--History. | Decision making—Moral and ethical aspects. Classification: LCC E178.1 .L82 2018 | DDC 973—dc23
LC record available at https://lccn.loc.gov/2018004264

ISBN 978-0-8077-5928-8 (paper)
ISBN 978-0-8077-7707-7 (ebook)

Printed on acid-free paper
Manufactured in the United States of America

25 24 23 22 21 20 19 18   8 7 6 5 4 3 2 1

I know that the values and the progress that we cherish are not inevitable, that they are fragile, in need of constant renewal. I believe what Dr. King said that the "arc of the universe is long but that it bends toward justice," but I also said that it does not bend on its own. It bends because we bend it, because we put our hand on that arc and we move it in the direction of justice, and freedom, and equality, and kindness, and generosity. It doesn't happen on its own.

—President Barack Obama
John F. Kennedy Profile in Courage Award Speech, May 7, 2017

Contents

Acknowledgments

We thank professors Alan Lockwood and Fred Newmann of the University of Wisconsin who inspired this work and who taught that values are an essential part of education for citizenship in a democracy. Our students have also been a source of inspiration for this work by demonstrating the sophisticated thinking that is possible when considering ethical values.

We also thank the following individuals for their assistance: Professor Mary Beth Norton of Cornell University for her critical review of a draft of the chapter about the Salem witch trials of 1692; Jesus Trevino for providing a copy of his original screenplay for the PBS documentary about Juan Seguín; Professor Jesus de la Teja of Texas State University for sharing his scholarship about Juan Seguín; Mark Barnett for permission to reprint his original portrait of Juan Seguín; Professor Peter Knupfer of Michigan State University for his assistance in finding answers to questions about John Adams's decision to defend the British soldiers accused in the Boston Massacre, the draft during The Civil War, and the disputed presidential election of 1876; Dr. Francisco Balderrama of California State University for his guidance and insights into the history of Mexican deportation during the 1930s; Gracelaw Simmons and Mary Kathryn Menck of the Royall House and Slave Quarters Museum for their assistance in discovering information about Belinda Sutton; Margot Minardi, assistant professor of history and humanities at Reed College, for her insights into the Belinda Sutton petition; Patrick Fahey and Christian Belina, archivist technicians at the Franklin D. Roosevelt Presidential Library in Hyde Park, New York, who personally provided expert and exhaustive assistance locating primary source documents about the 1938 voyage of the *St. Louis*, especially transcripts of phone conversations between Secretary of Treasury Henry Morgenthau, Jr., and Secretary of State Cordell Hull; Louise Kashino, who kindly granted permission to reprint a family photo of her husband, Shiro Kashino; Vince Matsudaira, who furnished a copy of his splendid documentary film about Shiro "Kash" Kashino and the 442nd Regimental Combat Team; Robert Asahina for his guidance in locating sources about Japanese Americans during World War II; filmmaker George Johnston for providing a copy of his documentary film about the 442nd Regimental Combat Team; Howard Hieshima of the Chicago Nisei Post of the American Legion for assistance in locating veterans of the 442nd Regimental Combat Team; and Bonnie and John Raines for granting a lengthy personal interview about their 1971 burglary of a Pennsylvania FBI office.

We extend our appreciation to Dr. Margaret Crocco, chairperson of the Department of Teacher Education at Michigan State University, for her encouragement of this project and to the Department of Teacher Education staff for its support of our writing. Our heartfelt appreciation also goes to Amanda Slaten Frasier and Maria Siciliano for their tireless and rigorous assistance with manuscript preparation.

We are deeply grateful to the staff of Teachers College Press at Teachers College/Columbia University, in particular Carole Saltz and Peter Sclafani, for initially supporting this project and guiding us thoughtfully as it progressed.

Finally, we acknowledge the support, patience, and encouragement of our families and friends who helped to sustain us during more than 4 years of research and writing.

David Harris, Anne-Lise Halvorsen, and Paul Dain

Dear Reader,

This book is intended to enrich your study of American history. We have written true stories showing people making difficult decisions. These decisions involved basic values such as authority, the common good, diversity, equality, liberty, life, loyalty, promise keeping, property, and truth. We invite you to follow the stories of these decisions and make judgments about them.

In this volume there are 20 chapters. Each presents a story that brings you in contact with an ethical issue from U.S. history. For example, you will face the petition of freed Massachusetts slave Belinda Royall to receive income from the estate of her former owner. You will encounter lawyer John Adams's decision to defend the British soldiers accused in the Boston Massacre. You will witness Thomas Jefferson's struggle with the ethics of slavery, not only in general, but with respect to his own enslaved children. You will be a bystander as Henry David Thoreau protests the Mexican War. You will assess Juan Seguín's decision to fight on the side of Mexico against the United States. You will consider the decision to exile the Cherokees to Oklahoma. You will observe as Robert E. Lee makes a fateful decision at the outbreak of The Civil War.

Although these events took place in the past, the values continue to influence our lives. We believe that citizens of today must often make decisions involving the same values. That is why we have written this book.

Rational, responsible citizens face value issues and think carefully about them. Therefore, we have presented you with learning activities that will engage you in such thinking. Answers to these activities are presented in the Instructor's Manual for *Reasoning with Democratic Values 2.0*, available as an ebook from Teachers College Press.

More information about the Instructor's Manual, including samples of its content, and other aspects of *Reasoning with Democratic Values 2.0* is available on the website for these books at: www.rdv2.org.

We hope that you will enjoy the stories and gain a deeper understanding of the nation's remarkable history from reading and thinking about them.

Sincerely,
David Harris, Anne-Lise Halvorsen, and Paul Dain

Part I

THE COLONIAL ERA
1607–1775

CHAPTER 1

Stamp of Approval

Father Junípero Serra and the Spanish Settlement of California

United States Postal Service Airmail Stamp Issued in Honor of Father Junípero Serra

The United States Postal Service issued a commemorative airmail stamp of Father Serra on August 22, 1985. The honor was bestowed on the Spanish missionary for his contributions to the settlement of California from 1769 until his death in 1784. Father Serra, a Franciscan friar, was credited by his supporters for his missionary work with Native Americans and for laying the groundwork for the creation of nine missions that stretch from San Diego to San Francisco. Spanish missions were religious outposts designed to expand the reach of the Catholic faith and Spanish culture.

The Citizens Stamp Advisory Committee is the body that makes recommendations to the postmaster general of the United States regarding issuance of postage stamps. The postmaster general, an appointee who serves at the pleasure of the president, is the administrative head of the Stamp Advisory Committee. Criteria have been established by the postal service for determining the eligibility of persons to be honored with a commemorative stamp. These criteria recognize those who have made extraordinary contributions to American society, culture, and history. Stamps are not issued to honor religious institutions or individuals whose principal achievements were associated with religious undertakings or benefits. The committee recommended the Serra stamp to the postmaster general. The recommendation was not based on religious reasons but rather on the contributions that Father Serra had made to the settlement of California.

Of the more than 800 people featured on U.S. postage stamps since their inception in 1847, eight are religious figures. For some people, the commemorative stamp for Father Serra did have religious significance. It was seen by those who supported sainthood for Serra as an important step toward that goal. The Catholic Church bestows sainthood on men and women considered holy and who are believed to have entered heaven because of their extraordinary lives of virtue.

President Ronald Reagan's White House signaled its approval of the Father Serra stamp in 1985 and cleared the way for the stamp's issuance. As a former governor of California, President Reagan knew well the significance of Father Serra and the Spanish missions in the settlement of California. President Reagan's approval of the stamp was politically influential.

All did not agree with the issuance of a commemorative stamp for Father Serra. An organization called Americans United for the Separation of Church and State opposed the decision to issue the stamp. It argued that it would breach the wall of separation between church and state and that it was an establishment of religion in violation of the First Amendment to the Constitution.

Many Native American descendants of the California missions' inhabitants claimed that Father Serra, because of his missionary zeal, had committed cultural genocide in California. They argued that Serra led the Spanish missionaries in changing the way of life of the Native populations which, in the end, greatly reduced their population.

Father Serra was born in 1713 in the Spanish city of Petra, Majorca, an island located in the Mediterranean Sea off the coast of Spain. Shortly after his birth he was baptized as Miguel Joseph Serra. As a young boy he became interested in the local Franciscan friary (an active religious community, including a church, where Franciscan priests, known as friars, reside) at San Bernardino. The friary church was the center of life in Petra and was very close to Miguel's home. He attended primary school at the church.

The Franciscans are a Catholic religious order. The religious order adheres to the spiritual teachings of its founder, Saint Francis of Assisi. Francis became well known for his devotion to the spread of Christianity and living a life of poverty, and was canonized as a saint in 1228.

Serra excelled in primary school in Petra and at age 15 his parents enrolled him in the Franciscan school in the capital city, Palma de Majorca. At age 17, he entered into a novice year in preparation to become a Franciscan friar. Serra was inspired by friars who lived their lives with devotion and sacrifice. The friars he studied had dedicated themselves to converting pagans to Catholicism.

At the age of 24, after serving a novice year and 6 additional years of study, Miguel became a priest and changed his given name to Junípero. Father Serra decided to change his name to that of a close companion of Saint Francis, Brother Junípero, whom he considered a man of great humility and simplicity. In becoming a Franciscan friar, Father Serra took an oath of poverty, chastity, and obedience.

During the next 14 years, Father Serra distinguished himself as a tireless student and teacher. He received a doctorate in philosophy and became a highly regarded professor of theology at Lullian University at the Convento de San Francisco in Palma de Majorca. It appeared he was headed for great things within the academic and religious community. Serra wanted to deepen the religious convictions of those Catholics who were not fully engaged in Catholicism and to inspire those who were without religion to become believers.

Expected by many to be a leader at the university and friary, Serra surprised the community by taking another road. The year 1749 saw him, after much prayer and contemplation, deciding to go as a missionary to New Spain, as Mexico and California were called at the time. Serra was overjoyed to learn that his good friend and protégé Father Francisco Paulo would join him in his missionary calling to North America.

The Spanish monarchy encouraged such missionary work because it believed this work would help settle and colonize new lands for Spain, as the missionaries could help convert and pacify the Native population. By going to New Spain, Father Serra was not breaking new ground. For years, many friars from Majorca had been going as missionaries to the Americas.

Father Serra's ship left Spain in August of 1749 with 18 additional friars. They arrived in Puerto Rico in October of 1749, and the friars remained there before departing for Mexico in November.

Spain had claimed this land as well as other lands in Central and South America for over 200 years. The conquest and colonization of these lands aimed to find riches such as gold and silver, to extend the imperial reach of the Spanish monarchy, and to convert souls. The Catholic Church played a key role in these conquests by supporting the missionaries' attempts to pacify the Native population.

Centuries later, Pope Francis in his visit to Bolivia during the summer of 2016 stated: "Many grave sins were committed against the Native people of America in the name of God. I humbly ask for forgiveness, not only for the offense of the church herself, but also for the crimes committed against Native people during the so-called conquest of America."

Father Serra did not venture to New Spain to commit grave sins or to search for riches, but rather to save the souls of the Native inhabitants. Serra was not experienced, however, in trying to convert people whose religious beliefs were far removed from Christianity. Conversion would be especially difficult with those who spoke many different languages, none of which was Spanish.

Serra and the other friars traveled by ship to Veracruz, a major port city on the eastern coast of Mexico. Veracruz was strategically located on the Gulf of Mexico and had a large Spanish fort nearby. Father Serra was more interested in meeting and working with the Native population than staying in a safe location. He and Paulo soon left Veracruz for Mexico City, a 250-mile journey. On the way to Mexico City, Serra was bitten by an insect and his leg became infected. The infection hampered his ability to walk and caused an ailment from which he would suffer for the rest of his life.

While at the College of San Fernando in Mexico City, he studied the Franciscan field manual for the administration of sacraments to the Native population. The manual emphasized the need to learn their languages and also to use the whip to enforce devotion, decency, and good order on them.

Serra was told at San Fernando that the Indigenous people were like children, very superstitious, and very easily led astray by the devil. The view at the college was that they could be converted to Catholicism, but only through the adoption of European methods of agriculture that would domesticate and regulate their lives. If missionaries would keep them at the mission to work on collective fields, the priests could manage the behavior of the inhabitants.

Father Serra was appointed to preside over the missions at Sierra Gorda, several hundred miles north of Mexico City. During Serra's tenure at Sierra Gorda, agriculture improved and widespread disease was avoided. Serra also succeeded in building a number of elaborate churches in the region. Many of the Indigenous people learned construction skills and crafts necessary for building these ornate churches.

After Serra had left his position in Sierra Gorda, some Native American leaders complained to officials in Mexico City that the Indigenous people who left the mission were brutally forced by soldiers to return, under orders from the missionaries. Whipping was used to enforce rules of behavior. This corporal punishment was commonly used back in Spain as well as in the Americas by the Spaniards.

Serra's reputation would later suffer from claims of mistreatment, but in the meantime he remained highly regarded by officials in Mexico City where he waited for a new assignment.

His wait for a new assignment lasted 10 years. Finally, in 1769, Father Serra was given the opportunity he most wanted, to attempt to convert Native inhabitants from many different tribes who had little or no contact with Europeans. This opportunity came about because the Spanish monarchy was very much concerned about recent developments in New Spain. The Seven Years' War in Europe had resulted in Spain's losing its claim to Florida to the English. Further, a new threat was coming from the north. To expand their fur-trading activities from the far North, Russian hunters and traders were moving down the Pacific coast of what now are the states of Washington and Oregon. King Carlos III of Spain did not want to see the Russians lay claim to Alta California (upper California, that is, north of the Baja California peninsula). This area had been lightly explored but nevertheless claimed by Spain for over 200 years.

The King of Spain sent a visiting general to oversee the administration of New Spain and to advance Spanish interests in Alta California. The general soon realized the necessity of moving Spanish interests northward from the Baja peninsula. Missionaries from the Jesuit order had established missions in Baja for many years, but they were not successful in either converting inhabitants or in the missions being economically productive. Jesuits had also fallen out of favor with the monarchy as being too independent of the Crown. Preference shifted to the Franciscans.

Father Serra was put in charge of the Baja missions. He attempted to improve the failing missions by requiring the Native population to reside within mission settlements so they could be instructed and "civilized." This strategy was unsuccessful. The Native people were not accustomed to intense European agricultural methods, which were made much more difficult because of long hours in extreme heat and humidity.

In spite of the Baja failures, Spanish military authorities selected Serra to help lead the effort to protect Spanish interests north in Alta California. Serra's full attention was now devoted to this task. The Franciscan friars envisioned Alta California as a better place to carry on their work with the Native population. The land was better suited for agriculture and, unlike what they found in Baja, Native people had no previous experience with missionaries.

Initially, the plan was to establish three missions: present-day San Diego in the south, San Francisco in the north, and one located between them. During the 700-mile journey, Father Serra enjoyed his encounters with Native Americans. The missionaries and the Native population exchanged gifts. Through an interpreter, Father Serra assured the inhabitants that they could trust him. He was optimistic about the prospects for success in Alta California. He felt sympathy for the Native population because they had no priest to care for their spiritual needs, and he hoped that would soon be remedied.

Over the next 12 years, Father Serra established nine missions stretching from south to north. After his death in 1782, an additional 12 missions were added. These 21 missions became the basis for the settlement of what would become the state of California in 1850. The trail between the missions became known as El Camino Real—the forerunner of the California freeway system. The missions still exist and are collectively one of the largest tourist attractions in the state.

The mission system in California had interrelated goals: bring Christianity to the Native population and instruct them in Spanish culture. Having them adopt the Spanish way of life would make it more likely for them to accept the Catholic faith.

The missionary system in California lasted from 1769 to 1833. Mexico (including Alta California) achieved independence from Spain in 1822 but permitted the missionaries to retain their authority for 10 additional years. The missions became secularized beginning in 1833. Secularization meant the missions would be governed under civil authority and the missions would resemble pueblos (Native American settlements or communities).

The missions served the purpose of securing the northern frontier for Spain. In order to be successful in the wilderness, the missions had to become economically independent. Many of the missions grew into large and productive farms, ranches, and vineyards. The Native population benefited by learning the skills and agricultural methods that were necessary to make the missions economically successful for the Spanish.

Serra's work with the Indigenous people of Alta California was fraught with problems. Along the coast from north to south there were more than 60,000 inhabitants. An additional 250,000 lived in the interior. The various languages and cultural practices were as diverse as the California topography, climate, geology, and native plants and animals. It has been estimated that there were over 100 different languages. Each tribe had its own political, economic, and religious practices. The various tribes lived by hunting, fishing, and gathering (for example, acorns and sunflower seeds). European agriculture was not part of their heritage.

Although Native people did not practice agriculture, they did engage in fishing, hunting, and gathering. They managed their resources through the use of such practices as irrigation and the pruning of wild trees and plants. They set strategic fires that would later enhance growth of plant and animal resources. This land management and usage, along with fishing and hunting, resulted in the Native population enjoying a very diverse diet with the use of minimal manual labor. The Native populations in California were also master basket makers. Baskets were of great use for their own needs as well as for trading with neighboring peoples.

In spite of this richness and diversity within the native populations, Serra viewed their culture with disdain. He regarded them as primitive—often naked, lingering, and idle. He persisted in his belief that salvation for the Indigenous people could be achieved through the use of European agricultural methods that kept them confined to the missions.

His goal was to save souls. Success was limited. Baptisms did increasingly take place, and some Native people did move into missionary communities. As elsewhere in New Spain, corporal punishment was used on the Native population who did not conform to the expectations of the missionaries. This physical punishment was usually in the form of whipping (15 to 50 lashes lasting over days), sometimes to the point of death, and was administered by soldiers at the request of the friars. The whipping applied to both men and women. There is no evidence that Serra inflicted punishment by his own hand. He is credited with protecting inhabitants, especially women, from assaults by Spanish soldiers.

The Native population rebelled against mistreatment by missionaries and soldiers. At several missions there were violent uprisings resulting in deaths of soldiers, missionaries, and Native inhabitants. Father Serra would ask that any captured inhabitants who were involved in an uprising be extended forgiveness and welcomed back into the good graces of the mission.

Although not as successful as he would have liked at saving souls, Father Serra was highly successful at establishing the nine missions. Ignoring the warnings of his religious superiors back in Mexico City that he was moving too fast, he pushed ahead to establish the missions up and down Alta California.

In the final year of his life, while gravely ill with his leg ailment, Serra traveled the length of Alta California to help with the newly established missions and to baptize and confirm Indigenous people. Serra, like other missionaries, believed they would not go to heaven without conversion.

Those who objected to the commemorative stamp believed that the missionaries had organized and led a brutal system. In the view of the critics, the missionary system took prime land from the Indigenous population, forced them to work the land, mistreated those who would not conform to the mission goals, and physically abused those who fled the missions to return to their traditional way of life.

Inhabitants were not normally forced to come to the missions. Many came because they were attracted by Spanish goods such as beads, cloth, and metal. Others came after observing the knowledge and skills the Spanish possessed, including their ability to domesticate and train horses.

The original purpose of the Spanish missions was to educate the Indigenous people in Christianity and Spanish culture and then to release them to live in their own communities. Conversion was to be voluntary. The missions, however, used forced labor for the economic benefit of the Spanish. Inhabitants at the missions were not paid for their labor. They were poorly clothed and fed and did not share in the surplus of food that became abundant. Surplus food and wine were instead traded with the Spanish military and with visiting ships. The missions became dependent on the forced labor of the inhabitants and the goal of releasing them to their own settlements was never achieved while the missions were under the control of the Spanish missionaries.

Although the Native people were not enslaved the same way Africans were in North and South America, aspects of the lives of the Indigenous people at the missions were similar to the experiences of Africans who were enslaved. The friars did not intend to enslave the Indigenous population, but mission policies and practices had that effect. Although enticed, they came voluntarily to the missions, unlike enslaved Africans. They were free to leave the missions if they had not been baptized. They also knew that baptism meant a different way of life and that they would be required to remain with their families at the mission once baptized. Over time, rules were relaxed to allow the Native population who had been Hispanicized (learned the Spanish language and culture) to travel with missionary permission to other missions and presidios.

Diseases were easily spread among the Native population and between them and the Spanish. Many Indigenous people would die from diseases, some of which were brought from Europe to North America. The friars, along with civil authorities, did attempt to remedy the health problems by bringing surgeons and medicine to the missions.

Father Serra brought agriculture to the Native Americans in California. They also learned practical skills: carpentry, animal husbandry (breeding and caring for farm animals), and construction skills used in the making of mission buildings, including churches. As a result of the missions, many Native Americans of California assimilated into Spanish culture.

Although some of the Native population resisted the acculturation and religious instruction, there were those who assisted the friars in governing the missions and in pursuing and returning baptized inhabitants who had fled. It is questionable whether this cooperation was truly voluntary or the result of threats and intimidation by the friars. The Spanish settlement of California and its enduring influence are largely because of the work Father Serra did in establishing the missions.

On September 23, 2015, while in Washington, D.C., on a state visit, Pope Francis canonized Father Serra as a saint. It was a moment of happiness for many Latinos and other Californians and a source of controversy for many Native Americans. Pope Francis praised Serra for his protective treatment of Native Americans. He said Serra "was excited about blazing trails, going forth to meet many people, learning and valuing their particular customs and way of life."

Valentin Lopez, chairman of the Amah Mutsun tribal band located along the Monterey Coast, was stunned by the canonization of Father Serra. He said, "We believe saints are supposed to be people who followed in the life of Jesus and in the words of Jesus Christ. There was no Jesus Christ lifestyle at the missions."

The major sources for this chapter were:

Archibald, R. (1978). Indian labor at the California missions, slavery or salvation? *San Diego Historical Society Quarterly, 24*(2).

Castillo, E. (2015). *Crown of thorns: The enslavement of California's Indians by the Spanish missions.* Fresno, CA: Craven Street Books,

Hackel, S. (2014). *Junípero Serra, California's founding father.* New York, NY: Hill and Wang.

Steibel, W. (Director). (1989, March 17). *Junípero Serra: Saint or sinner?* [Firing Line with William Buckley, Jr.]. Columbia, SC: Southern Educational Communications Association (SECA).

LEARNING ACTIVITIES FOR "STAMP OF APPROVAL"

Facts of the Case

1. Why did Father Serra want to travel to New Spain?
2. How did Father Serra attempt to change the way of life of Native peoples?

3. How did Native Americans benefit from the work of the missionaries?
4. Why was Father Serra honored by the United States Postal Service with a commemorative postage stamp?
5. What criticisms have been expressed about Father Serra and the Spanish missions in California?

Historical Understanding

1. Explain why Spain wanted to claim land in what they called New Spain.
2. Describe how Native Americans in Alta California lived before the arrival of the missionaries.

Expressing Your Reasoning

Should the United States Postal Service have issued a commemorative stamp to honor Father Serra? Why or why not?

Key Concepts from History

What do the following have in common?

1. In 1575, Portugal began exploring and settling what is now the African nation of Angola. Travel by sea down the West Coast of Africa from Portugal to Angola was a distance of 4,500 nautical miles. Hoping but failing to discover gold and other precious metals, the Portuguese found Angola to be an excellent source for slaves. Enslaved persons could be exported to labor in other areas under the control of Portugal. Portuguese rule was characterized by the migration of Portuguese people to Angola and by the use of the Native population as forced labor. Agricultural products from Angola such as coffee and cotton were found to be economically beneficial for export to other areas of the world. The economic profits of slave and agricultural trade, along with future trade in diamonds and oil, benefitted Portuguese businesses and settlers but not the Native people. Portugal ruled most of the territory that is now Angola and formally annexed Angola as a Portuguese province in 1951. During this period, Catholicism was imposed on the population by missionaries.
2. The French occupation of Algeria began with a blockade in 1827 and continued with the invasion of Algeria in 1830. French control of what is now the independent nation of Algeria provided military protection from enemies of France. Algieria lies on the African coast across the Mediterranean Sea from France and Spain. The French imposed political rule to their advantage. They directed the economy of Algeria to agricultural cash crops that could be shipped to France across the Mediterranean. The leading export was locally produced wine. Algeria's mineral resources such as iron, oil, and natural gas were also exploited to the advantage of industries in France. Over time, there was a large

migration to Algeria by French settlers, many of whom lived in wealthy and privileged communities that were segregated. Attempts to convert the Muslim population to Christianity was met with contempt by Native inhabitants. France ruled Algeria with a military administration and later a French-appointed governor-general. The Muslim majority were treated as second-class citizens.

3. British control of India began as a result of disputes with other European trading rivals and various wars on the Asian subcontinent and evolved over many years. Through military action and trading alliances the British were able to establish their rule. The English domination of India began in 1858 and lasted until 1947. In 1858, the British East India Trading Company turned over rule of India to the British Crown. India was rich in resources, strategically located, and densely populated. Thousands of miles and several seas away from the British Isles, India provided an opportunity to expand the British Empire. The British took advantage of deep cultural and religious differences (perhaps encouraging these divisions) in order to maintain control. Many Indians were forced into labor and many were denied religious freedom. Cotton produced by Indian workers was exported to England for the economic benefit of the textile industry in England. Manufactured goods were exported to India, again, for the economic benefit of the British. Limited self-rule by wealthy Indians was gradually introduced, but the final authority remained with the British administrators.

Historical Inquiry

European settlement of the North American continent brought explorers, missionaries, and settlers from Spain, France, and England. Did these three countries treat the Native Americans differently?

Using online and other sources, test the hypothesis that the Spanish, French, and British treated Native Americans differently. Compose a short essay in which you accept or reject the hypothesis. Use evidence to support your decision. To begin your investigation, the following search items will be helpful:

- Treatment of Native Americans
- European colonization in North America
- Spanish colonization in North America
- British colonization in North America
- French colonization of North America and New France

CHAPTER 2

The Blame and Shame of It

Salem Witch Trials

Portrait of Judge Samuel Sewall and Mural Illustrating the Public Repentance of Judge Samuel Sewall in 1697

1697· DAWN OF TOLERANCE IN MASSACHUSETTS PUBLIC REPENTANCE OF JUDGE SAMUEL SEWALL FOR HIS ACTION IN THE WITCHCRAFT TRIALS

The hardships faced by the early American colonists are hard for us to imagine. Severe weather, difficulties in cultivating land for crops, conflicts with the Native inhabitants, and disease, made survival from 1 year to the next an achievement.

The first English attempt to establish a colony in North America was a complete failure. When supply ships arrived in 1590 at Roanoke (located in what is now Virginia), not a single survivor of the 1585 settlement could be found.

Settled in 1607, the Jamestown colony (also in Virginia) struggled to endure. Conflict with the local Powhatan Indians, on whose hunting grounds the settlement was built, disease and famine soon brought the colony to the brink of failure. During 1609–1610, more than 80% of the settlers perished from starvation and sickness. The colony did not manage to thrive economically until tobacco was cultivated with enslaved labor brought from Africa.

A decade after the settlement of Jamestown, other English colonists settled in present-day Massachusetts. The Pilgrims landed in Plymouth from the *Mayflower* in 1620. Ten years later, 700 colonists arrived north of Plymouth, near present-day Boston and Salem, to become the Massachusetts Bay Colony. Migration continued, and by 1640 there were more than 20,000 colonists in Massachusetts.

Unlike the Jamestown colonists, the largest group of early Massachusetts settlers were Puritans. Religion was deeply important to the Puritans. They were a group of English Reformed Protestants who sought to purify the established Church of England (the Anglican Church). English King Charles I was hostile to the Puritans' religious beliefs, and Anglican Church officials tried to repress their dissenting views during the 1620s and 1630s. This resulted in some Puritans seeking refuge in North America.

The Puritans rejected all Roman Catholic practices. They also opposed many of the traditions of the Anglican Church, including use of the *Book of Common Prayer*, the use of priestly vestments (cap and gown) during services, the use of the Holy Cross during baptism, and kneeling during the sacrament, all of which they believed constituted *popery* (doctrines, practices, and ceremonies associated with the Pope or Roman Catholicism). The social and legal systems of the Puritan colonists were closely tied to their religious beliefs.

The supernatural was considered part of everyday Puritan life. They believed that Satan (the devil) was present and active on earth. In his writings, leading New England Puritan minister Cotton Mather tried to prove that "demons were alive." Witchcraft persecutions became common, as some Puritans were suspected by their neighbors of associating with the devil.

The Puritans did not tolerate those who did not follow their religious beliefs. They pursued conformity to the teaching of the Bible down to the smallest detail. They believed that human beings existed for the glory of God, that the first concern in life was to do God's will. Church attendance was required, and absolute obedience to the stern morality of the church was expected of everyone. Ministers preached powerful sermons on the wonders of God, and on the frightful prospects of damnation—burning for eternity in the horrors of hell. They believed that the devil would do evil works and that believers had to be on guard against Satan.

One group of Puritans settled in Salem Village, just west of Salem Town (present-day Danvers, Massachusetts), a seaport settlement about 20 miles northeast of Boston.

In Salem Village, life was governed by the precepts of the church. Instrumental music, dancing, and celebration of holidays such as Christmas and Easter were strictly forbidden. The only music allowed was the unaccompanied singing of religious hymns. Folk songs were thought to glorify human love and nature and were rejected as antithetical to God. Toys, especially dolls, were forbidden, as play was considered a frivolous waste of time. Salem children received an education that emphasized religion and the need for strict piety to prevent their eternal damnation. Villagers were expected to go to the meetinghouse for 3-hour sermons every Wednesday and Sunday.

Salem Village was a quarrelsome place in the late 17th century. There were many conflicts and disputes between Salem Village and adjacent Salem Town. Original land titles had been canceled, and others not yet secured. There were arguments over property lines and grazing rights. Further, the residents were divided about their local minister, Samuel Parris. Complaints about his privileges were rife.

The political climate in the colony as a whole was one of turmoil. The original royal charter for Massachusetts Bay Colony was revoked in 1684 and its governor was ousted. In 1689, when Protestants replaced Catholics on the English throne, the colony's former leaders resumed their posts as governor and deputy governor of Massachusetts. There was doubt, however, about their authority until the spring of 1692. It was not until then that word reached the colony that a new charter unifying the entire colony as the Province of Massachusetts had been approved in London.

During this anxious time, struggles between European colonial powers France and England over control of the New England northeastern frontier added to the anxiety. There were clashes between English colonists and French-supported Indians. After 1688, during what locals called the Second Indian War and historians have termed King William's War, Wabanaki Indians attacked English settlements along the New England coast, killing settlers and causing survivors to flee their homesteads. Many refugees fled to Essex County where Salem Village was located. County residents were near the front lines of an armed conflict.

Historian Mary Beth Norton argues that "assaults from the visible and invisible worlds became closely entwined in New Englanders' minds." Fear of Indians was to merge with fear of witches. Salem villagers did not believe that Indians were witches, or that witches were Indians. Their fear of one, however, heightened their fear of the other. Norton writes that the frontier Indian wars did not cause the unique crisis over witchcraft that erupted in Salem, "but rather that the conflict created the conditions that allowed the crisis to develop as rapidly and extensively as it did."

Massachusetts Bay had been established as "a city upon a hill," but many came to fear that the Puritan experiment was in danger of failure. A unique convergence of several factors, including a new charter and government, a lethal frontier war, an economic decline, and a decrease in Puritan religious fervor, caused a witch hunt that started in Salem and spread across the region. It began during the cold, dark winter of 1691–1692 with a grim episode in the parsonage of the local Salem minister, Reverend Samuel Parris.

Elizabeth ("Betty") Parris, age 9, and her cousin Abigail Williams, age 11, lived in the parsonage. Betty was Reverend Parris's daughter and Abigail was a niece being raised by Parris and his wife. (It is not known by historians whether Abigail was actually the Parrises' niece or possibly some other relation.) In late January 1692, Betty began behaving oddly. She screamed, cried out in pain, uttered strange sounds, crawled under furniture, barked like a dog, twitched, and spun around. Soon after, her cousin Abigail started showing similar symptoms.

The two cousins complained of bites and pinches by "invisible agents." Betty fell mysteriously ill. She seemed in a trance, stared blankly into space, and babbled.

Reverend Parris tried prayer and home remedies to cure the girls, but nothing worked. He called in a local doctor and a minister for a diagnosis. Unable to find anything wrong with the girls, they both agreed that Betty and Abigail were bewitched (under the "evil hand" of the devil).

One day in late February, as they were preparing to be away from Salem Village for a short while, Reverend Parris and his wife asked a neighbor woman to look in on the girls. The neighbor conducted an experiment involving a "witch cake" intended to uncover the mystery of the girls' torment. It was believed that a witch's cake had the power to reveal whether witchcraft was afflicting a person with symptoms of illness. Such a cake or biscuit was made with rye flour and the urine of the afflicted person. The cake was then fed to a dog. If the dog exhibited the same symptoms, the presence of witchcraft was "proven."

As a result of the experiment, Betty and Abigail were deemed afflicted by witches. The girls claimed that local witches had afflicted them and named them.

At about the same time that Betty and Abigail claimed they were bewitched, two other Salem Village girls, one age 12 the other 16, showed symptoms of affliction by witches. They shuddered, convulsed, and choked, claiming they had been pinched and pummeled.

A few days later, in Salem Town, formal charges for suspicion of witchcraft were pressed against three women named as witches by the girls. The three were then arrested by the local constable. One of the women, probably accused by Abigail, was Tituba, an Indian woman brought by Rev. Parris as a slave from Barbados to Massachusetts. She resided in the parsonage with the Parris family. Betty and Abigail were fond of Tituba, and she felt affection for the two girls.

Hearings were held for the three accused women, one at a time, in the dark meetinghouse of Salem Village. Local justices of the peace presided over the hearings and interrogated the accused. The four afflicted girls were present in the meetinghouse for the hearings, and they wailed and moaned in the front row of pews. The first two accused women denied the charges and claimed that they had been falsely accused. Tituba was the third of the accused to face interrogation.

At first, Tituba denied the charge, but when pressed by the local magistrates she eventually confessed: "The devil came to me and bid me serve him." She went on to offer vivid descriptions of her witchcraft. During her interrogation, Tituba named the two other accused witches as her accomplices in consorting with the devil to harm the girls. All three women were manacled and taken to jail to await trial.

Tituba's testimony gave officials the proof they wanted of a witch conspiracy operating in their midst. She testified that other witches were present in the community. The Salem witch hunt would now begin in earnest.

Other young women in the village seemed to become afflicted, variously falling into trances; crawling while barking like a dog; flapping their arms like birds;

having convulsive fits. The girls claimed that ghosts of local women had appeared before them. It was believed that the devil could assume any shape, except that of an innocent person. It followed that if someone's ghost, or disembodied spirit, was observed doing ill, that person was considered a witch.

Some of the girls said that the devil had pressed them to sign his book. It was widely believed that Satan carried a black book in which he induced his followers to write their names in their own blood.

Soon, many of the townspeople believed that the devil was at work in Salem. Additional women were accused of witchcraft and jailed. A cold wave of terror washed over Salem Village. The girls began accusing more and more people. Some of the most respected members of the community were identified as witches. Even Rebecca Nurse, a 71-year-old woman regarded as one of the most upstanding churchwomen, was accused. If such highly esteemed people could be witches, then anybody could be a witch. Church membership was no protection from accusation.

At this time, belief in witchcraft as a tool of the devil was widespread. Leading thinkers of the day, including Isaac Newton and John Locke, believed in witches. So did all the judges of the colonial courts as well as leading Puritan theologian Cotton Mather. Witchcraft was understood as the exercise of magical powers through supernatural beings other than God and his angels. Witches, it was believed, owed their powers to having made a pact with the devil. Witchcraft was devil worship—the greatest of all sins.

On May 27, 1692, colonial governor William Phips ordered the establishment of the Court of Oyer and Terminer, a special court to hear the cases of those accused of witchcraft. The Court convened in Salem on June 2. Lieutenant Governor William Stoughton served as its chief magistrate. A panel of nine judges served on the Special Court. Five of them had to be present for the court to sit. When the special court convened, the total number of accused in custody was 62.

Following an accusation of witchcraft, there was a hearing for the accused. If suspicion persisted, the accused was brought before a grand jury. If the grand jury issued an indictment (a formal charge), the accused was tried by a jury in the Court of Oyer and Terminer. Those convicted could be sentenced to death by the judges. Unlike today, the prosecutor did not question either the accused or the witnesses. That work, as well as sentencing, was the responsibility of the judges. The accused had no counsel to defend them.

Bridget Bishop was the first to be found guilty and condemned to death by the judges. On June 10, 1692, she was hanged on what was later called Gallows Hill. Giles Corey, whose wife had been condemned to death and hanged as a witch by the Special Court, refused to enter a plea. In an attempt to make him enter a plea, the judges applied a form of torture in which stones were piled on his chest to crush him until he could no longer breathe. After 2 days, Corey died without entering a plea. Some claim his last words were "more weight."

Of the nine judges who served on the Special Court, one of them, Nathaniel Saltonstall, resigned at the beginning of the trials when Bridget Bishop was condemned to hang. Judge Saltonstall said that he disapproved of the judicial proceedings.

During the trials, several methods were used to determine guilt. The "touch test" was used in some of the later trials. If the accused "witch" touched the victim while the victim was having a fit, and the fit then stopped, that meant the accused was the person who had afflicted the victim. Although it was doubted by some and not relied upon exclusively for a conviction, "spectral evidence" was also used by the court. An afflicted person would allege that the accused appeared as a "specter" (ghost) of some sort of monster or distorted animal and, as such, afflicted the unfortunate victim. When this occurred in the courtroom, the alleged witch's specter seemed to harm the afflicted, who then writhed and shrieked in pain in response to spectral attacks invisible to the jury and the rest of the court.

Other evidence included confessions of the accused; testimony by a confessed witch who identified others as witches; the discovery of poppets (small dolls supposedly used in sorcery), books about palm reading, horoscopes, or pots of ointments in the possession or home of the accused; and observation of "witches' teats," moles or blemishes somewhere on the body that were sensitive to touch. (Discovery of such insensitive areas was considered evidence of witchcraft.)

The court's policy was to spare those who confessed (including Tituba). No one who confessed to being a witch was executed, with the exception of one man who recanted his confession.

As the trials continued, some began to doubt whether the accusers should be believed. A local farmer and innkeeper, John Proctor, was one of the doubters. He said that if there were any devils in the area, they were the girls. One of the girls, who was Proctor's servant, admitted to him that what the girls were doing was "for sport."

Proctor's wife, Elizabeth, was accused of being a witch. Proctor accompanied his wife to her hearing. At the hearing, the girls wailed and moaned, and Proctor himself was accused by one of them as a man with magical powers working with the devil. He was tried, convicted, and condemned to be hanged by the Special Court.

In 1953, eminent playwright Arthur Miller wrote the now classic play *The Crucible* about the Salem witch trials. The play was intended as an allegory for the zealous injustices of the anti-Communist persecutions during the 1950s in the United States. Not meant to be an accurate historical portrayal, the play partially fictionalizes events and characters to serve Miller's dramatic purposes.

John Proctor could have saved his life by confessing, as many of those accused of witchcraft did. Arthur Miller's powerful play captures Proctor's anguish. In the final scene of the play, Proctor is trying to decide whether to confess. He is talking with his pregnant wife, Elizabeth, who has been condemned as a witch but whose sentence had been commuted until after she gives birth. Judge Danforth of the Special Court tries to persuade Proctor to confess:

Proctor, with great force of will but not quite looking at her: I have been thinking I would confess to them, Elizabeth. *She shows nothing.* What say you? I give them that?

Elizabeth: I cannot judge you, John.

Pause

Proctor, simply—-a pure question: What would you have me do?

Proctor: Then who will judge me? *Suddenly, clasping his hands* God in heaven, what is John Proctor, what is John Proctor? *He moves as an animal, and a fury is riding in him, a tantalized search.* I think it is honest, I think so; I am no saint. *As though she had decided this, he calls angrily at her.* Let Rebecca go like a saint; for me it is fraud!

Danforth: Mr. Proctor. When the Devil came to you, did you see Rebecca Nurse in his company? *Proctor is silent.* Come, man, take courage—did you ever see her with the Devil?

Proctor almost inaudibly: No. *Danforth, now sensing trouble, glances at John and goes to the table and picks up a sheet—the list of condemned.*

Danforth: Did you ever see her sister, Mary Easty, with the Devil?

Proctor: No, I did not.

Danforth (his eyes narrow on Proctor): Did you ever see Martha Corey with the Devil?

Proctor: I did not.

Danforth: Mr. Proctor—

Proctor: I have three children—how may I teach them to walk like men in the world, and I sold my friends?

Danforth: Then explain to me, Mr. Proctor, why you will not let—

Proctor (with a cry of his whole soul): Because it is my name! Because I cannot have another in my life! Because I lie and sign myself to lies! Because I am not worth the dust on the feet of them that hang! How may I live without my name? I have given you my soul; leave me my name!

John Proctor refused to confess and was hanged with the others.

During the summer of 1692, the pace of accusations quickened. In August and September, formal charges were brought against another 40 alleged witches. By the fall of 1692, however, the hysteria in Salem began to abate. Increasing numbers of townspeople realized that innocent people were being accused. Some accusers were retracting their accusations. Some of the judges doubted spectral evidence as well as the girls' hysterical fantasies.

On October 29, the colonial governor dissolved the Special Court, dismissed its judges, freed most of the accused, and halted all future indictments. Those accused remaining in custody, however, continued to be prosecuted by another court until May of the next year. The last legal proceeding took place on May 9, 1693 when a grand jury refused to indict Tituba, the enslaved Indian woman who had been the first to confess 15 months earlier. After her release, she disappears from the historical record.

The infamous episode of madness in Massachusetts came to a close more than 16 months after it had begun. In Salem, the death toll was 25: 19 people hanged, 14 of them women; one man tortured to death; and five who died in prison.

One of the judges, Samuel Sewall, served for the entire term of the Special Court. Sewall was born in England in 1652 and moved to Massachusetts with his parents when he was 9 years old. He spent 6 years and earned two degrees at Harvard College studying for the ministry. He was a devoutly religious Puritan. He lived his daily life in strict accordance with his faith in the Bible. On the Sabbath, from sundown Saturday until sundown Sunday, he attended public worship with his family, foregoing all work, recreation, and frivolity. Devout families like the Sewalls regularly observed silence during scripture study at home.

Samuel Sewall, like many other Puritans, believed that their Massachusetts Bible commonwealth was the contemporary equivalent of the Promised Land, a place specially chosen by God for his people in the New World.

Sewall combined piety with worldly success. By his thirties, he had risen rapidly in Boston society and become one of New England's most prominent men. He married into a wealthy family and soon afterward abandoned his career as a minister to become his father-in-law's junior business partner. He amassed great wealth engaging in trade, managing large sums of money, and collecting vast tracts of real estate on both sides of the Atlantic. He was also an elected member of the Massachusetts governing council and an overseer of Harvard College.

When 44-year-old Samuel Sewall was appointed to be a judge of the Special Court for witchcraft in Salem, he did not question whether to serve. He viewed the appointment as a way to serve his country and to advance himself.

As one of the judges of the special court, Sewall sentenced many to death. He attended some of the hangings. For example, he stood by with townspeople as Sarah Good, whose recent pregnancy had ended with a stillbirth while she was in jail, climbed the ladder to the gallows. He saw the hangman place the rope around her neck and listened to her last words called out to her accuser in the crowd: "I am no more a witch than you are a wizard."

For Samuel Sewall, the witchcraft trials served as a stepping-stone for his career. The colonial governor rewarded him for his service on the Special Court by appointing him to the highest court of the colony, which survives today as the Supreme Judicial Court of Massachusetts.

Judge Sewall's conscience, however, was burdened. Years after the Special Court was disbanded, he felt guilty about his role as a judge during the witchcraft trials and wanted to repent for what he now thought were his sins. He sought to be reconciled with God for condemning those accused of witchcraft. He still believed that witches were real and in league with Satan, but he thought many of those accused had been innocent.

On a Sunday morning in January 1697, the congregation of the Third Church of Boston was greeted with an extraordinary confession of guilt. The minister gave way to Judge Sewall who had prepared a statement of repentance for his part in the Salem witchcraft Special Court. In the judge's statement, made openly that day in church, he desired to "take the blame and shame of it," and asked that both God and men pardon his sin.

Around this time Sewell began wearing sackcloth, a biblical symbol of penance. He realized that true repentance was not momentary. It would be a long process of many steps, including contrition, confession, compensation to those wronged, and a change of heart. Guided by his ardent faith, he was determined to take all of these steps.

Judge Sewall also began to take bold steps in professing radical social ideas. He admonished his fellow Englishmen to treat Indians better. He and his wife hosted several Indian boys who lived with the Sewalls while preparing for Harvard. Samuel delivered the youths to college and paid for their educations. At the time, few Englishmen viewed Native Americans as their equals. In a society that rejected racial equality, Samuel, as a member of the colonial governing council, argued that Indians had the same right to religion and life as Englishmen.

Samuel also decided to attack slavery at its foundation. He wrote in 1700 that all men "have equal right unto liberty and all other outward comforts of life." This belief was also extremely radical for the time. Though Samuel owned no slaves, roughly one in five New England families did in the 17th century. He openly condemned the enslavement of Africans. In 1700, he expressed his opposition to slavery in a published pamphlet.

He also wrote an essay in which he addressed "the right of women," a most unusual phrase in the early 18th century.

Samuel Sewall authored America's first antislavery tract, which set him at odds with every other prominent man of his time. He portrayed Native Americans not as savages, the standard view of his time among colonists, but as worthy of the grace of God. In a period when women were widely considered inferior to men, he wrote an essay affirming the fundamental equality of the sexes. He was, and would always be, a Salem witch judge. Yet he acknowledged his misjudgment and never ceased his efforts to make amends.

The major sources for this chapter were:

Baker, E. W. (2015). *A storm of witchcraft: The Salem trials and the American experience.* New York, NY: Oxford University Press.

LaPlante, E. (2007). *Salem witch judge: The life and repentance of Samuel Sewall.* New York, NY: HarperCollins.

Miller, A. (1995). *The crucible*. New York, NY: Penguin. (Originally published 1953)

Norton, M. B. (2002). *In the devil's snare: The Salem witchcraft crisis of 1692*. New York, NY: Alfred A. Knopf.

Schiff, S. (2015). *The witches: Salem, 1692*. New York, NY: Little, Brown and Company.

LEARNING ACTIVITIES FOR "THE BLAME AND THE SHAME OF IT"

Facts of the Case

1. What were some of the tensions faced by the residents of Salem Village in 1692?
2. How did the matter of witchcraft arise in Salem Village?
3. Describe the behavior of the girls of Salem Village who claimed to be afflicted by witches.
4. What was the touch test?
5. What was spectral evidence and how was it used during the Salem witch trials?
6. Who was Samuel Sewall and what was his role during the Salem witch trials?
7. How did Judge Sewall attempt to repent for serving as a judge during the Salem witchcraft trials?

Historical Understanding

1. Who were the settlers of Massachusetts Bay Colony?
2. Describe the religious beliefs of the Puritans.

Expressing Your Reasoning

1. Should John Proctor have confessed to being a witch? Why or why not?
2. Should Samuel Sewall have been forgiven for what he did as a judge during the Salem witchcraft trials? Why or why not?

Key Concepts from History

What do the following have in common?

1. The Puritans established a government in Massachusetts Bay Colony that limited the vote to church members. The elected legislature, called the General Court, sought to prevent any independence of religious views. Those with other religious beliefs, such as Roger Williams and Anne Hutchinson, were banned, and laws were passed persecuting Quakers. In 1638, the General Court required all freemen and non-freemen to pay a tax to support the commonwealth and the church. The law required that church members pay the salary of their Puritan minister.

2. Israel, the only country with a majority Jewish population, is defined in several of its laws as a Jewish state. Although Israel describes itself as a Jewish state, all religious groups have freedom to practice their faiths. Religious schools in Israel receive public funding. The chief rabbis in Israel are elected by a religious body whose members receive salaries from the government. Under Israeli law, marriage and divorce can only occur in a religious ceremony. Only Jews have the obligation of military service. There are laws governing observance of the Jewish Sabbath. Any Jew who immigrates to Israel may obtain Israeli citizenship.
3. Islam is the state religion of Saudi Arabia. Almost all Saudis are Muslims. Religious minorities do not have the legal right to practice their religions. No churches, temples, or other non-Muslim houses of worship are permitted. Under Saudi law, conversion by Muslims to another faith carries the death penalty. Islamic schools and mosques are funded by the Saudi government.

Historical Inquiry

Arthur Miller's play *The Crucible* was written during the time of the House of Representatives Un-American Activities Committee (HUAC) hearings in the United States. Is there a relationship between Miller's play about the Salem witch hunt and what some have called an anti-Communist "witch hunt" during the 1950s in America?

Using online and other sources, test the hypothesis that there is a relationship between *The Crucible* and HUAC, and compose a short essay in which you accept or reject the hypothesis. Use evidence to support your decision. To begin your investigation, the following search terms will be helpful:

- The Crucible
- HUAC
- McCarthyism
- Red Scare

CHAPTER 3

Defending the Redcoats

John Adams and the Boston Massacre

Paul Revere, "Bloody Massacre"

The decade of the 1760s was a period of increasing tension between the British Crown and its American colonies. By defeating France in the French and Indian War (1754–1763), Britain had secured its control of the colonies. The war, however, left England with enormous debt. Desperate for money, England thought the Americans should help fund the costs of the British Empire, particularly the costs of maintaining an army in the American colonies. England's various attempts to tax the American colonists triggered events that led to revolution.

England tried to raise revenue in the colonies by collecting customs duties, or tariffs, which were taxes on the goods the colonists imported from abroad. To avoid paying the tariffs, some Americans became smugglers. They snuck, or smuggled, foreign goods into the colonies without paying the customs duties. Customs officials of the British Crown obtained written court orders, called Writs of Assistance, that authorized general searches for smuggled goods. Although a group of Massachusetts merchants challenged the Writs of Assistance in court, they lost their case. Nevertheless, smuggling continued.

In 1764, the British Parliament passed the Sugar Act. The act levied a new tax on molasses, sugar, and other products imported by the American colonies from the West Indies. Smugglers in the colonies had previously evaded customs duties on molasses. To ensure that the new tax would be collected, the Sugar Act established special courts in the major American seaports. In cases of suspected smuggling, judges examined the evidence, determined guilt or innocence, and passed sentence on those found guilty. There were no jury trials. Strict enforcement of the act angered the colonists because, among other things, as the risk and danger of molasses smuggling increased, the cost of sugar also greatly increased.

In addition to the economic cost, the colonists protested the Sugar Act because it gave a foreign legislature power over their trade and their right to govern themselves. These protests led to the now famous slogan "No taxation without representation" that summarized a major reason for the American Revolution.

A year after the Sugar Act, in the quest for more revenue, Parliament passed the Stamp Act, placing a direct tax on many printed materials produced in the colonies. Colonists were required to purchase stamped paper (paid for in British money) that was made in England. Stamped paper was used for many items in the colonies, including newspapers, leases, playing cards, legal documents, advertisements, and other items.

The colonists' response to the Stamp Act was swift and violent. On August 14, 1765, a group of colonists formed a mob and hung an effigy of the Crown-appointed stamp collector, Andrew Oliver, on a huge elm tree in the Boston Common in Boston, Massachusetts. The tree became known as the Liberty Tree. That evening, the mob burned the effigy on a hill behind Oliver's elegant townhouse, then broke into the house, destroying furniture and terrorizing Oliver and his family. The Loyal Nine, a group of colonists, forced Oliver to resign from his position as stamp collector. Protests against the stamp tax spread to other cities in the colonies.

Prominent Bostonians rejected the authority of Parliament to tax the colonies without their consent. A group of protesters, led by Samuel Adams, formed a group called the Sons of Liberty whose aim was to turn mob violence into political action. They organized boycotts of British imports to put pressure on British merchants and manufacturers.

When the colonists' boycotts of British goods following the Stamp Act began to affect British trade, Parliament passed the Declaratory Act on March 18, 1766, at the same time that it repealed the Stamp Act. The Declaratory Act gave

Parliament full power to make laws for the colonists of America "in all cases what-soever." The colonists, who were outraged, began to demand self-government.

Next, beginning in 1767, Parliament passed a series of acts called the Town-shend Acts. The first act was the Revenue Act of 1767 that placed more customs duties on various imports to the colonies. These products included paint, tea, pa-per, lead, and glass. The act stated that the colonists, who did not produce these products, were allowed to buy them only from Britain. These taxes were to be used to pay the salaries of colonial governors. The colonists had previously paid these salaries directly; they realized this change removed any power they had over the governors. The Sons of Liberty and their supporters insisted that the power to levy and collect taxes belonged to the colonial assemblies and not to the British Crown.

Some merchants in the colonies refused to import British goods until the taxes levied by the Townshend Acts were repealed. In Boston, where the re-action was extremely strong, the anti-tax violence renewed. In response, the British government tried to exert military control over Boston by sending four regiments of royal troops to the city in 1768. Their responsibility was to protect the Crown-appointed colonial governors. A foreign army now occupied a major American city and confrontations between citizens and soldiers seemed certain.

Lord North, the prime minister of England, had little sympathy for the colo-nists and their complaints. He described the protesters as "the drunken ragamuf-fins of a vociferous mob." He said, "I can never acquiesce in the absurd opinion that all men are equal." The Founding Fathers later rejected Lord North's posi-tion in the American Declaration of Independence (July 4, 1776) that famously states, "All men are created equal."

The British soldiers (the Redcoats), wearing their bright red uniform jackets, marched through the Boston streets, carrying the British flag, to the sound of drums and fifes. The colonists called them "Lobsterbacks" and made them the objects of their anger and bitterness.

Hostilities between citizens and soldiers flared repeatedly. On February 22, 1770, Christopher Snider, age 12, joined other boys in protests outside the Bos-ton home of Ebenezer Richardson, a customs employee. When Richardson fired his musket into the crowd of boys, Christopher Snider, sometimes remembered as the first victim of the American Revolutionary War, was killed. John Adams, who was a cousin of Samuel Adams, attended the boy's funeral on the following day.

John Adams was a talented young lawyer and author and a leader among the colonists. Although not as radical in his views on the problems of the American colonies as Samuel Adams, he was sympathetic to the cause of the Sons of Liberty. At age 30, he published an unsigned essay called *A Dissertation on the Canon and the Feudal Law* (1765) in the *Boston Gazette*, which revealed his strong convic-tions about the importance of guaranteeing the rights of citizens. In the essay, he wrote, "liberty must at all hazards be supported."

In the same year, Adams wrote the *Braintree Instructions* that the town meet-ing in Braintree sent to its representative in the Massachusetts legislature. The document instructed the representative to oppose the Stamp Act because it taxed the colonists without their consent and denied them the right to a jury trial by their peers. Adams wrote, "In these courts, one judge presides alone! No juries have any concern there!" Forty other towns in Massachusetts adopted the *Braintree Instructions.*

In 1768, Adams and his family moved from their small farm in Braintree to a house on Brattle Street in Boston where he could be closer to his law practice. When he rode the circuit court as a traveling judge or walked the streets of Boston, he was recognized as a "patriot" lawyer.

The early months of 1770 were a melancholy time for John Adams and his wife, Abigail. Their 1-year-old daughter, Susanna, died in February. Abigail, who was expecting a baby in May, was unusually quiet and listless. Normally she was strong, active, and capable, but now she often sat in the dark looking out the window. Both parents grieved for Susanna, although they still had two other children, Abigail, age 5, and John Quincy, age 3.

In Boston, under military occupation, clouds of discontent continued to gather over the city. The colonists regarded British soldiers as bullies and criminals rather than as "His Majesty's Dignified Regulars." The colonists jeered at the soldiers with the cry of "Lobsters for sale . . . lobsters, who'll buy?" The soldiers responded with curses and cries of "Yankees!"

On the morning of March 4, 1770, someone nailed a poster to a wall near the Boston waterfront:

> This is to inform the rebellious people in Boston that the soldyers in the 14th and 29th regiments are determined to join together and defend themselves against all who shall oppose them.
>
> Signed
> The soldyers of the 14th and 29th Regiments

Some suspected that the Sons of Liberty rather than the British soldiers had posted the warning, possibly to provoke an incident or to unite Bostonians against the British.

The next day, March 5, 1770, a street fight broke out in Boston between the colonists and a squad from the 29th Regiment. Private Hugh White, a sentry at the Customs House, was patrolling his solitary post in the snow on King Street, now known as State Street. Private White reprimanded Edward Garrick, a young wigmaker's apprentice, for his insolence in criticizing Captain Lieutenant John Goldfinch for not paying his wigmaker's bill. After angry words were exchanged, White knocked down young Garrick with his musket butt. A crowd assembled and began to throw snowballs, ice chunks, and lumps of coal at White. White ran to the Customs House to take shelter, but the door was locked. The crowd chanted, "Kill him, kill him!" Henry Knox, a bookseller and later a general in the Revolutionary War, yelled, "If he fired he must die for it."

As a nearby church bell tolled, the usual signal for fire, more than 50 Bostonians, led by Crispus Attucks (some say he was a runaway slave; others say he was a freedman) rushed into the streets and challenged White to fire his weapon. Captain Thomas Preston, the British officer in charge, heard the uproar and led a relief party of eight soldiers to White's rescue.

In response to the crowd's taunts and thrown objects, the soldiers fired their muskets. When the smoke cleared, five citizens were dead, including Attucks, and six citizens were injured. After Captain Preston ordered the soldiers to withdraw across the street, the wounded and dead were carried away.

Suddenly, all over Boston, church bells rang the alarm. More and more men appeared on the streets carrying weapons. As cries of "To arms!" echoed through the streets, Governor Thomas Hutchinson came immediately to King Street. Calling for calm, he said, "Let the law settle this thing! Let the law have its course. I myself will live and die by the law. Let you also keep to this principle. Blood has been shed; awful work was done this night. Tomorrow there will be an inquiry." By three o'clock in the morning, the crowd had disappeared.

Before sunrise, a court of inquiry issued warrants for the arrest of Captain Preston and his soldiers. They were jailed to await their trial for the deaths of the five civilians. Samuel Adams described the killings as a "bloody butchery" and the incident as "the Horrid Massacre." The Boston citizens called this night "the Boston Massacre." The British called it "the Incident on King Street."

The day after the Boston Massacre, John Adams, who had heard the sounds of the conflict the night before, went to his law office as usual. There he met James Forest, a British loyalist and friend of Captain Preston. When Adams asked Forest his purpose, Forest begged Adams to represent Captain Preston and his men. "His life is in danger," claimed Forest (and his men). "He has no one to defend him. Mr. Adams, would you consider—will you take his case?"

Forest explained that he could find no other lawyer to take the case. He also said he knew of Adams's reputation as a fair and honest man. Skeptics would later claim Adams was bribed to take the case, but because he charged only 18 guineas (just enough to buy a gold watch), this charge seems unfounded.

Adams was in a situation with very serious implications. Other lawyers thought that defending the Redcoats could ruin Adams's legal and possible political career as well as put his life and the lives of his family in grave danger. Yet Adams strongly supported the ideals of impartial justice, the rule of law, and due process. He thought the trial would be as important a case as any yet tried in the colonies.

The fears for his safety were underlined when a group from the Sons of Liberty stopped him on the street and warned him against defending "those murderers." However, some Tories (those colonists loyal to the British Crown) in Boston urged him to take the case. "Nine Tories out of ten," John told Abigail gloomily, "are convinced I have come over to their side." He was greatly disturbed at the thought that his friends in the Sons of Liberty would scorn him for taking the case, especially if the Loyalists hailed him a hero. If he took the case, people might look on him as a Loyalist sympathizer acting on behalf of the British monarch, King George III. Indeed, after he took the case, someone threw rocks through the window of his house.

Adams learned that Governor Hutchinson was determined, if a jury convicted the accused, to request a king's pardon for the eight men. Yet the governor was also aware that Adams might persuade the jury to bring a verdict of not guilty. The governor preferred a verdict of not guilty to a royal pardon.

The case was certain to be difficult. Of the 96 witnesses prepared to testify, 94 blamed the soldiers for the shootings. Furthermore, it would take Adams a great deal of time to prepare challenges to their testimony. The trial itself would last a long time, and could pose an enormous emotional and physical burden on him and his family.

Clearly, the case would also mean a financial loss for Adams. He would have little time for the other legal work that supported his family. He also suspected his career would change in unpredictable ways if he took on the defense of the Redcoats. For example, the case could damage the career in politics he was considering. Would voters elect him to the legislature if he had defended British soldiers?

On the other hand, would his defense of the Redcoats add to his reputation as a fair-minded lawyer? Politicians and jurists, certainly in England and perhaps in all Europe, would follow the trial. Adams remarked to friend and fellow lawyer Josiah Quincy, "It will serve our enemies well if we publish proof that the people's cause in America is led by a mere mob, a riotous and irresponsible waterfront rabble." Adams had a stake in demonstrating to the world that the colonists supported due process and the rule of law.

As Adams thought about the pros and cons of taking the case, he reminded himself of his protest in the *Braintree Instructions* when he criticized the denial of a jury trial to the accused. Finally, with the assistance of his friend Josiah Quincy, he decided to defend the British soldiers. Years later, he said that this case was "one of the most gallant, generous, manly and disinterested actions of my whole life, and one of the best pieces of service I ever rendered my country." In his defense of the British soldiers, he argued, "The reason is, because it's of more importance to community, that innocence should be protected, than it is, that guilt should be punished."

The jury acquitted Captain Preston on the basis of "reasonable doubt" and acquitted six of the eight soldiers. Two soldiers were found guilty of manslaughter and thus escaped the death penalty. In later years, Adams served as the American ambassador in Great Britain, and was elected as the first vice president of the United States and as the second president.

The major sources for this chapter were:

Adams, J. (1770). Argument in defense of the soldiers in the Boston Massacre Trials. Available at http://www.bostonmassacre.net/trial/acct-adams1.htm

Adams, J. Q., & Adams, C. F. (1871). *The life of John Adams*. Philadelphia, PA: J. B. Lippincott.

Bowen, C. (1950). *John Adams and the American revolution*. Boston, MA: Little, Brown.

McCullough, D. (2001). *John Adams*. New York, NY: Simon & Schuster.

Russell, F. (1976). *Adams, an American dynasty.* New York, NY: American Heritage.

Shepard, J. (1975). *The Adams chronicles.* Boston, MA: Little, Brown.

Zobel, H. B. (1996). *The Boston massacre.* New York, NY: W. W. Norton & Company.

LEARNING ACTIVITIES FOR "DEFENDING THE REDCOATS"

Facts of the Case

1. Identify two events that led to violence on King Street in Boston on the night of March 5, 1770.
2. Why was John Adams worried about his family before the Boston Massacre?
3. Why did James Forest ask John Adams to be the defense lawyer for the British soldiers accused of murder?
4. What did Adams want the trial to demonstrate to people in other countries?

Historical Understanding

1. What did the Writs of Assistance, the Sugar Act, the Stamp Act, and the Townshend taxes have in common?
2. Explain the Sons of Liberty's slogan, "No taxation without representation."
3. Why were British troops sent to Boston?
4. Describe the Boston Massacre.

Expressing Your Reasoning

1. Should John Adams have defended the British soldiers? Why or why not?
2. Although Adams was convinced of the soldiers' innocence and right to defend themselves, suppose he thought the soldiers were guilty of murder and/or manslaughter. Should he have accepted the case? Why or why not?

Key Concepts from History

What do the following have in common?

1. On April 19, 1995, the Alfred P. Murrah Federal Building in Oklahoma City, Oklahoma, was bombed, killing 168 people and injuring 684. Timothy McVeigh, who was charged with the bombing, was indicted on 11 federal counts, including conspiracy to use a weapon of mass destruction, destruction by explosives, and eight counts of first-degree murder. Stephen Jones was McVeigh's defense attorney in a trial that lasted 28 days. McVeigh pleaded not guilty. After deliberating for 23 hours, the jury convicted McVeigh of all 11 counts of the federal indictment and recommended the death penalty. The judge sentenced him to death. Following his several unsuccessful appeals and his

refusal to ask President George W. Bush for clemency, McVeigh was executed by lethal injection on June 11, 2001.

2. On August 9, 2014, in Ferguson, Missouri, Darren Wilson, a White Ferguson police officer, shot and killed 18-year-old Michael Brown, an African American. Brown was unarmed. On August 20, 2014, a grand jury consisting of three African American jurors and nine White jurors (seven men and five women) began hearing testimony in the case of *State of Missouri v. Darren Wilson*. The grand jury's charge was to determine whether to indict Darren Wilson. The prosecutor presented the jury with more than 5,000 pages of testimony from 60 witnesses. James P. Towey, Jr., an experienced criminal defense attorney who had represented the St. Louis Police Officers Association for more than 20 years, represented Wilson. The grand jury found insufficient evidence to indict Wilson.

3. On June 4, 2003, the U.S. government indicted the American businesswoman Martha Stewart on nine counts related to insider trading, including securities fraud and obstruction of justice. She pleaded not guilty at her trial, where she was represented by Robert Morvillo, a veteran criminal defense attorney. After the 6-week trial, Stewart was found guilty of felony charges of conspiracy, obstruction of an agency proceeding, and of making false statements to federal investigators. She received a sentence of 5 months, to be served in a federal correction facility, the minimum sentence allowed by law. The Second Circuit Court of Appeals upheld her conviction on appeal. Her former stockbroker, Peter E. Bacanovic, was also sentenced to 5 months in prison.

Historical Inquiry

Not all Massachusetts colonists supported the Sons of Liberty. Using online and other sources, research the question: Did more Massachusetts colonists favor the Sons of Liberty or the Crown?

Using online and other sources, test the hypothesis that more Massachusetts colonists favored the Sons of Liberty than the Crown. Compose a short essay in which you accept or reject the hypothesis. Use evidence to support your decision. To begin your investigation, the following search terms will be helpful:

- Sons of Liberty
- British loyalists
- American patriots
- Choosing sides during U.S. Revolution

CHAPTER 4

A Luxury We Can't Afford

Thomas Jefferson and Slavery

Isaac Granger Jefferson, a Slave at Monticello (Library of the University of Virginia)

Thomas Jefferson stands out as one of the most distinguished leaders in American history. The list of his achievements in government is impressive. He was a delegate to the Virginia colonial legislature, author of the Declaration of Independence, governor of the state of Virginia, member of the Continental Congress, U.S. minister to France, secretary of state, and both vice president and president of the United States. He is one of the Founding Fathers of the Republic; his ideas form a cornerstone of American democracy. His brilliant intellect has been admired from the colonial era to the present time. A more recent president, John F. Kennedy, honored him in 1962. Speaking before a group of Nobel Prize recipients being honored at a White House dinner, Kennedy said: "I think this the most extraordinary collection of talent, of human knowledge, that has ever been gathered together at the White House, with the possible exception of when Thomas Jefferson dined alone."

To many it seems odd that Jefferson, a champion of democracy and foe of tyranny, arose from a society based on slavery. He was immersed in the practice of slavery from cradle to grave. His first memory was of being carried on a pillow by a slave. A slaveowner when he died, Jefferson was buried in a coffin made by an enslaved carpenter.

Early in his career, Jefferson called the institution of slavery an "abominable crime," a "moral depravity," a "hideous blot," and a "fatal stain." Yet his slaveholdings were among the largest of his time. When he wrote in the Declaration of Independence of mankind's inalienable right to liberty, he owned more than 100 slaves. Throughout his career he was troubled by the existence of slavery in America. A statement he made in 1820 reveals the continuing dilemma it posed for him. In reference to slavery, he said: "We have the wolf by the ears; and we can neither hold him, nor safely let him go. Justice is in one scale, and self-preservation in the other."

The story of Jefferson's internal struggle over the morality and value of slavery begins in Virginia. He was born there in 1743 and until his death was a member of its upper class. During the American Revolution, when Jefferson said "my country," he meant Virginia. His ancestors had lived there for three generations before him. All of his formal education took place there. By age 40, he had spent less than a year outside the borders of Virginia.

In the year 1757, when Jefferson was 14, his father died. Jefferson inherited an estate near Charlottesville, Virginia, including 30 slaves. This inheritance made him a member of the Virginia aristocracy.

Jefferson's father had wanted his son to be well schooled. His dying instruction was that the boy receive a thorough classical education. Jefferson later said that he was more grateful for this than all the other privileges his father placed within his reach. From private tutors he learned Greek and Latin. Later, he attended the College of William and Mary in Williamsburg, the colonial capital. He loved books as much as he hated laziness and applied himself eagerly to his studies. After college he became a law student in Williamsburg. In 1765, Thomas Jefferson officially became a lawyer. His father's wish had been satisfied. The boy was well schooled and refined in manners. Socially, in all respects, he was considered a gentleman.

Jefferson's education had made him a student of the Enlightenment. Enlightenment thinkers believed that humankind was emerging from the shackles of darkness. In their view, the time had come for people to be forward-looking and free of old superstitions and myths.

Enlightenment philosophers believed that the path of reason and science would lead to discovery of natural laws that governed the universe. Out of this natural law doctrine came the political idea of natural rights. One such right was liberty. To Jefferson, liberty meant freedom from both tyranny and oppression.

Two years after he began the practice of law, Jefferson took (without fee) the case of Samuel Howell. Both Howell's mother and grandmother had been slaves who were freed. Howell sued for freedom from the master to whom he had been sold before his mother received her freedom.

Jefferson argued that Virginia laws did not extend slavery to offspring of slaves who had been set free. His argument in court went beyond the laws of Virginia. He invoked the "law of nature." Under that law, he said, "We are all born free." The Virginia court ruled against him. Such Enlightenment ideas carried no weight with a practical-minded judge in a slave-owning society. In Virginia, the enslaved were considered property and not people. They were essential to the cheap production of cotton and tobacco crops of Virginia plantations.

Following a brief period of practicing law, Jefferson entered the political arena. In 1769, the freeholders (White landowners) of Albemarle County met in the Charlottesville courthouse to elect their representative to the Virginia House of Burgesses, the colonial legislature. They chose as their burgess 26-year-old Thomas Jefferson. While a burgess, Jefferson regarded himself a loyal subject of the Crown. He drank toasts to the king and the royal governor. From the beginning, however, he defended colonial rights against the Crown, strongly opposing the taxes England placed on the colony.

Just when colonial rights were becoming a major issue in 1772, Jefferson married a widow, Martha Wayles Skelton. For the time being, he put public affairs aside and tended to personal matters.

He arranged for the leveling of the little mountain on the estate he inherited from his father. He translated "little mountain" into Italian, and Monticello became the name of the plantation to which Jefferson devoted a lifetime of building. His house at Monticello, designed by Jefferson and built by local masons and carpenters assisted by enslaved people, is today a famous architectural and historic monument. Beyond Jefferson's family, there were hundreds of enslaved men, women, and children who resided at Monticello over the course of his very long life. Monticello was the place where Jefferson enjoyed domestic life and dreamed of his hopes for the future of a new nation. It was also a slave plantation where human beings under Jefferson's dominion had the status of property, in seeming contradiction of his stated ideals. In his 1781 book, *Notes on the State of Virginia*, the apostle of liberty expressed the contradiction of slavery: "The whole commerce between master and slave," he wrote, was "a perpetual exercise of the most boisterous passions, the most unremitting despotism on the one part, and degrading submissions on the other."

Upon the death of his father-in-law, 2 years after Jefferson married, his wealth doubled. Included in his wife's inheritance were 135 slaves. This brought the total of those enslaved at Monticello to 187, making Jefferson the second largest slaveholder in Albemarle County.

Compared to other slaveholders, Jefferson was at the time considered a kinder master. A French nobleman visiting Monticello claimed that Jefferson's slaves were nourished, clothed, and treated as well as White servants could be. Jefferson rewarded hard work with extra rations of food and time off for slaves to work their own gardens. On occasions when he leased his slaves to work on neighboring plantations, Jefferson allowed them to keep as wages a portion of what was paid for their labor. He allowed members of his family to teach some of those enslaved at Monticello to read. Although he generally discouraged teaching the enslaved to write, he corresponded with a very small number of his most favored slaves. He once described Monticello as a place "where all is peace and harmony, where we love and are loved by every object we see."

In 1811, Jefferson wrote of "the moral duties which [the master] owes to the slave, in return for the benefits of his service, that is to say, of food, clothing, care in sickness, & maintenance under age & disability, so as to make him in fact as comfortable, & more secure than the laboring man in most parts of the world."

Jefferson never personally applied the lash, and he directed that overseers whip those enslaved at Monticello only in extreme cases. He always preferred to sell disobedient slaves rather than to flog them. When selling such slaves, unlike other masters, Jefferson favored disposing of families as a unit. He tried not to separate parents and children, husbands and wives.

In addition to growing tobacco and cotton, Jefferson had nails manufactured at Monticello. They were sold in Richmond for a handsome profit. The enslaved boys and teens who worked in the nailery shared in this prosperity. They received a pound of meat a week, a dozen herrings, a quart of molasses, and a peck of meal. Those who turned out the most nails were rewarded with a suit of red and blue cloth.

Some of the enslaved at Monticello who did not share Jefferson's perception that "all was peace and harmony" there fled when the Revolutionary War broke out. About 30 of Jefferson's slaves escaped and fought with the British Army. Later during the war, when Jefferson was governor of Virginia, British soldiers occupied his plantations. Dozens of slaves left with the invaders. Others, however, actively protected their master's possessions and aided his escape from the enemy.

Soon after Jefferson settled down with Martha at Monticello, the growing conflict between colonies and the Crown sharpened. In 1774, colonial leaders in Virginia suggested that representatives of all the colonies meet in Philadelphia to draft a joint protest. This meeting launched the First Continental Congress. In 1775, Virginians sent Jefferson as one of their delegates to the Second Continental Congress in Philadelphia. From this date onward Jefferson's story becomes a key part of the history of the republic.

The Virginia delegates were instructed to propose to the Continental Congress that the united colonies be declared free and independent states. Jefferson had come to support this proposal because of recent acts of the British Parliament. In his view, trade with all parts of the world was a natural right of the colonies. The acts of Parliament that restricted colonial trade were void, he wrote, because "the British Parliament has no right to exercise authority over us."

In response to the Virginia proposal, the Second Continental Congress appointed a committee of five to prepare a declaration. John Adams of Massachusetts, Benjamin Franklin of Pennsylvania, and Thomas Jefferson of Virginia were members of the drafting committee.

Jefferson was asked to draft the declaration. What he wrote was presented to the whole Congress on June 28, 1776. Members of the Congress debated the document before voting on it. According to the rules, the vote had to be unanimous for the resolution to be adopted. Several changes were made before the final vote was taken. The most heated conflict occurred in the debate over Jefferson's words about slavery. The delegates from South Carolina and Georgia objected to the passage in Jefferson's draft that condemned King George for the slave trade. That passage read:

> He [King George III] has waged cruel war against human nature itself, violating its most sacred rights of life and liberty in the persons of a distant people who never offended him, captivating and carrying them into slavery in another hemisphere or to incur miserable death in their transportation thither. This piratical warfare . . . is the warfare of the Christian King of Great Britain.

Scene seven of the play *1776* by Peter Stone and Sherman Edwards presents a dramatic account of the debate over this passage by members of the Continental Congress. The characters in this part of the play are:

Edward Rutledge: Delegate from South Carolina
John Hancock: President of the Continental Congress
Charles Thompson: Secretary of the Continental Congress
Thomas Jefferson: Delegate from Virginia
John Adams: Delegate from Massachusetts
Stephen Hopkins: Delegate from Rhode Island
Benjamin Franklin: Delegate from Pennsylvania

Hancock: If there are no more changes, then, I can assume that the report of the Declaration Committee has been—
Rutledge (deliberately): Just a moment, Mr. President.
Franklin (to John): Look out.
Rutledge: I wonder if we could prevail upon Mr. Thompson to read again a small portion of Mr. Jefferson's Declaration— the one beginning "He has waged cruel war—"?
Hancock: Mr. Thompson?
Thompson (reading back rapidly to himself): ". . . He has affected . . . He has combined . . . He has abdicated . . . He has plundered . . . He has constrained . . . He has excited . . . He has incited . . . He has waged cruel war! Ah. (*He looks*

up.) Here it is. (*He clears his throat and reads.*)" He has waged cruel war against human nature itself, in the persons of a distant people who never offended him, captivating and carrying them into slavery in another hemisphere. Determined to keep open a market where men should be bought and sold, he has prostituted—

Rutledge: That will suffice, Mr. Thompson, I thank you, Mr. Jefferson, I can't quite make out what it is you're talkin' about.

Jefferson: Slavery, Mr. Rutledge.

Rutledge: Ah, yes. You're referrin' to us as slaves of the King.

Jefferson: No sir, Black slaves.

Ruthledge: Ah, Black slaves. Why didn't you say so, sir? Were you tryin' to hide your meanin'?

Jefferson: No, sir.

Rutledge: Just another literary license, then?

Jefferson: If you like.

Rutledge: I don't like at all, Mr. Jefferson. To us in South Carolina, black slavery is our peculiar institution and a cherished way of life.

Jefferson: Nevertheless, we must abolish it. Nothing is more certainly written in the Book of Fate than that this people shall be free.

Rutledge: I am not concerned with the Book of Fate right now, sir. I am more concerned with what's written in your little paper there.

John [Adams]: The "little paper there" deals with freedom for Americans!

Rutledge: Oh, really! Mr. Adams is now callin' our black slaves Americans. Are-they-now?

John: They are! They're people and they're here—if there is any other requirement, I've never heard of it.

Rutledge: They are here, yes, but they are not people, sir, they are property.

Jefferson: No, sir! They are people who are being treated as property. I tell you the rights of human nature are deeply wounded by this infamous practice!

Rutledge (*shouting*): Then see to your own wounds, Mr. Jefferson, for you are a—practitioner—are you not? (*A pause, Rutledge has found the mark.*)

Jefferson: I have already resolved to release my slaves.

Rutledge: Then I'm sorry, for you have also resolved the ruination of your personal economy.

John: Economy. Always economy. There's more to this than a filthy purse string, Rutledge. It's an offense against man and God.

Hopkins: It's stinking business, Mr. Rutledge—a stinking business.

Rutledge: Is it really, Mr. Hopkins? Then what's that I smell floatin' down from the North—could it be the aroma of hypocrisy? For who holds the other end of that filthy purse-string Mr. Adams? (*To everyone*) Our northern brethren are feelin' a bit tender toward our slaves. They don't keep slaves, no-o, but they're willin', for the shillin'— (*rubbing his thumb and forefinger together*)—or haven't y'heard, Mr. Adams? Clink! Clink! . . .

Gentlemen! You mustn't think our northern friends merely see our slaves as figures on a ledger. Oh no sir! They see them as figures on the block! Notice the faces at the auctions, gentlemen—white faces on the African wharves—New England faces, seafaring faces: "Put them in the ships, cram them in the ship, stuff them in the ships!" Hurry, gentlemen, let the auction begin! . . .

. . . Mr. Adams, I give you a toast! Hail, Boston! Hail, Charleston! Who stinketh the most?!?!? (*He turns and walks straight out of the chamber. Hewes of North Carolina follows, and Hall of Georgia is right behind them. Others leave the chamber. Only Franklin, Jefferson, Hancock, and Thompson remain.*)

Franklin: We've no other choice, John. This slavery clause has to go.

John: Franklin, what are y'saying?

Franklin: It's a luxury we can't afford.

John: A luxury? A half-million souls in chains, and Dr. Franklin calls it a luxury! Maybe you should have walked out with the South!

Franklin: You forget yourself, sir! I founded the first anti-slavery society of this continent.

John: Don't wave your credentials at me! Perhaps it's time you had them renewed!

Franklin (angrily): The issue here is independence! Maybe you've lost sight of that fact, but I have not! How dare you jeopardize our cause when we've come so far? These men, no matter how much we disagree with them, are not ribbon clerks to be ordered about; they're proud, accomplished men, the cream of their colonies—and whether you like it or not, they and the people they represent will be part of the new country you'd hope to create! Either start learning how to live with them or pack up and go home—but in any case, stop acting like a Boston fishwife!

Adams was finally persuaded that the antislavery passage in the Declaration should be removed. Jefferson reluctantly agreed to delete the passage from his draft. With it remaining, there could be no unanimous vote for independence. The passage was removed, and the Declaration of Independence was unanimously adopted by the delegates meeting in Philadelphia.

For Thomas Jefferson, slavery was not the main issue in the debate over the Declaration. Although Jefferson opposed slavery, his main concern was independence from England and new principles of government for the colonies. Deleting the slavery passage from the Declaration, he thought, was a small price to pay for his broader goals. Once independence was achieved, the slavery issue could be raised again. Jefferson would repeatedly have to decide what to do about slavery in light of his most memorable words from the Declaration: "We hold these truths to be self-evident: that all men are created equal; that they are endowed by their creator with certain unalienable rights; that among these are life, liberty and the pursuit of happiness."

Jefferson did not forget that he had offered a creed for himself and the new republic. The challenge for him would be to make this creed a living reality. He went back home to Virginia to take a major hand in the drafting of a new constitution and new laws for his native state. A major issue for the new social and political order in the revolutionary colonies was slavery. Jefferson was convinced that slavery was an intolerable wrong. But he believed that after emancipation

Blacks and Whites would be unable to live in peace under the same government. Deep-seated prejudices ingrained in Whites and the memory of injuries suffered by Blacks would produce violent uprisings. He thought it would be better to send former slaves, once freed, to Africa, where they could set up a colony of their own.

Upon his return to Virginia, Jefferson tried to translate his hatred of slavery into state law. In his 1776 draft of a new state constitution, he introduced a clause prohibiting future importation of slaves. He later proposed freedom for the children of all Virginia slaves born after 1800. Freedom, he said, was "the birthright of all men regardless of their color or condition." His fellow Virginians did not share his views on freedom for slaves. They rejected both of his proposals.

It became clear to Jefferson that the time had not arrived for the government to abolish slavery. Nonetheless, he could still act personally to free his own slaves. A sense of guilt beset him. Setting his own slaves free, however, posed several obstacles for Jefferson. Because he was often burdened by debt, he hired out some of his slaves to raise money. Outright selling of his slaves would have been the quickest way to raise cash to pay his creditors, but to do so would have deprived him of the labor force upon which his income depended and would have had a detrimental effect on his comfortable style of living. Without slaves, a Virginia plantation like Monticello could not function.

Another obstacle to freeing those he enslaved was the law of Virginia, under which a master who took a slave to the county court to gain his or her release had to certify that the slave had a skill and a place to use it. It was unlawful to free a slave without first providing for his or her support. This would have been extremely difficult for the master of Monticello, because he owned so many slaves. Colonial Virginia was organized around the great plantations. There was no place, off the plantation, for large numbers of freed slaves to settle. Freed slaves were not welcome in other states, several of which excluded their entry by law. Further, beginning in 1806, Virginia law required that freed slaves leave the state within a year. At that time, Jefferson wrote, "The laws do not permit us to turn them loose."

Jefferson did, however, help limit the spread of slavery in the United States. In 1787, Congress passed the Northwest Ordinance. It covered all of the modern states of Ohio, Indiana, Illinois, Michigan, and Wisconsin, as well as the northeastern part of Minnesota. Jefferson helped shape this historic law, including its prohibition of slavery in the territory and the states to be created from it.

Jefferson had personal misgivings about freedom for slaves. In a letter written in 1789 he said, "To give liberty to, or rather, to abandon persons whose habits have been formed in slavery, is like abandoning children." He considered himself like a father to those enslaved at Monticello, the patriarch of a family.

Abolitionists (those arguing for the ending of slavery) urged Jefferson to set an example by freeing his own slaves. They encouraged the patriarch of Monticello to put the full weight of his immense prestige on the side of the antislavery movement. Jefferson, they said, was in a position to set an example that would lead other Virginia planters to free their slaves.

The famed Black mathematician Benjamin Banneker believed that Jefferson was violating his own principles by holding Black people as slaves. In a 1791 letter to Jefferson, Banneker denied earlier claims by Jefferson that Blacks were intellectually inferior to Whites. In the letter, Banneker also asked Jefferson to reconcile his "created equal" phrase from the Declaration with his practice of "detaining by fraud and violence so numerous a part of my brethren, under groaning captivity."

In a polite reply to Banneker, Jefferson expressed hope for the appearance of "such proofs as you exhibit" that nature had endowed Blacks with "talents equal to those of the other colours of men" and that their apparent absence among Blacks was only the result of "the degraded condition of their existence, both in Africa and America." Jefferson made no promise to free his slaves in his reply to Banneker's letter.

Jefferson feared that if enslaved Black people were freed within the United States, they would initiate a race war to exact revenge for what had been done to them, and he called for deportation of freed slaves to Africa. He did not favor integration of the races and once wrote that he wanted freed slaves "beyond the reach of mixture." Ironically, in his own lifetime, reports circulated that he practiced such mixture of Blacks and Whites at Monticello.

Among the slaves Jefferson inherited in 1773 from his father-in-law, John Wayles, was Elizabeth (Betty) Hemings. She was the daughter of an African American woman and a White sea captain. (As the child of an enslaved woman, Betty was by law born a slave herself, despite having a White father.) Betty became the enslaved mistress of John Wayles after his third wife died, and bore him six children, who were, like her, born enslaved. Such open relationships between White planters and their female slaves were not uncommon. When Wayles died, all seven members of the Hemings family were among the slaves that went to Monticello as the inheritance of his daughter Martha.

Because they were related to Jefferson's wife, the Hemingses were treated quite differently from others enslaved at Monticello. They were like a caste apart. The women worked as house servants and never in the fields. The men worked as valets, cooks, and skilled craftsmen. Jefferson paid wages to some of them and allowed a few to live in nearby Charlottesville or Richmond and to keep the wages they earned there.

Jefferson's wife, Martha, died in 1782, and, as he had promised her, he never married again. In 1787, 14-year-old Sally Hemings accompanied Jefferson's young daughter Polly from Virginia to Paris, where Jefferson was serving as minister to France. Sally Hemings, as the daughter of John Wayles and Betty Hemings, was Martha Jefferson's half-sister, and therefore Jefferson's half-sister-in-law.

According to the 1873 memoir of Madison Hemings, one of Sally Hemings's sons, at some point after Sally Hemings arrived in Paris, she and Thomas

Jefferson, 30 years her senior, became intimately involved. Madison Hemings claimed to be one of their seven children, three of whom died in infancy.

After serving as minster to France, Jefferson eagerly returned to plantation life at Monticello. In a letter he wrote in 1793, he said, "I have my house to build, my field to farm, and to watch for the happiness of those who labor for mine."

Most historians now acknowledge that Thomas Jefferson was the father of Sally Hemings's known children, born from 1795 to 1808. The four who survived were enslaved, along with their mother, at Monticello. Jefferson's daughter Martha Jefferson Randolph and her children consistently denied any liaison between Jefferson and Hemings as well as his paternity of her children. They never openly acknowledged their father or grandfather's relationship with Sally Hemings, in the face of persistent accusations in the newspapers and despite family resemblances that startled visitors at Monticello.

Reports of Sally Hemings as Jefferson's enslaved mistress first became public in 1802, while Jefferson was president. James Callender published a sensational article in a Richmond newspaper. He wrote that President Jefferson "keeps, and has for many years past, has kept, as his concubine, one of his own slaves. Her name is SALLY." Sally was described as "decidedly good looking with very light skin and long straight hair down her back." Jefferson made no public comment about the matter. His friend James Madison denounced Callender and dismissed his story as incredible. Nevertheless, the scandalous story spread across the country and has fueled controversy ever since.

Although there are no records left by Thomas Jefferson or Sally Hemings regarding their relationship, Madison Hemings claims that his father (Jefferson) promised his mother that her children would be granted freedom when they reached age 21. According to Madison Hemings, Jefferson made this pledge in order to persuade Sally to return from Paris to Monticello. Had she chosen to remain in France, under French law she would have been a free woman.

Jefferson certainly took a special interest in these children. He allowed two of them, daughter Harriet and son Beverly, ages 21 and 24, respectively, to leave Monticello in 1822. Very light-skinned, they chose to live out their lives as White people. The other two surviving children of Sally Hemings, Madison and his brother Eston, were freed by Jefferson's will. In response to a request in the will, the Virginia legislature waived the law that would have required Madison and Eston Hemings to leave the state.

All of the Monticello slaves known to have gained their freedom in Jefferson's lifetime or in his will were Betty Hemings's children or grandchildren. At Jefferson's death, Sally Hemings, though not legally freed, was permitted to live out her life in freedom in Virginia with her two freed sons, Madison and Eston.

For those still enslaved at Monticello, Jefferson's death in 1826 was a catastrophe. The flyer announcing the auction of his estate identified its contents, including "130 VALUABLE NEGROES." To settle his enormous debts, his possessions, among them his slaves, were sold at the auction block. The families he had long tried to keep intact were destroyed.

Jefferson came to take the position that emancipation was an idea whose time had not yet come. He thought it would be a mistake to try to hasten its coming. His aim was gradually to place slavery in the course of ultimate extinction. He was awaiting the "ripening" of public opinion. He believed a premature effort against slavery would result in an irreversible setback. He did not want to get so far in advance of public opinion that he lost his political followers. A successful reformer, he thought, ought not rush in where revolutionaries might fear to tread. Overeager zealots might set the cause back.

Thomas Jefferson died on July 4, 1826. Though some of his contemporaries freed their slaves during and after the Revolution, he did not. The "Sage of Monticello," during his lifetime, freed only eight of more than 600 people he held in bondage. At the time of his death, he had one of the largest holdings of slaves in Virginia.

If Jefferson had freed his slaves late in life or in his will, he would have left his family with monumental debt. If he had freed his slaves as a young man, he would have suffered financially and jeopardized his political career. As an advocate for the abolition of slavery, it is unlikely that he would have been chosen as a delegate to the Continental Congress where he drafted the Declaration of Independence. Absent that distinction, he probably would not have been elected governor of Virginia, chosen as secretary of state, or elected both vice president and president of the United States. Not until 1860 was a man actively opposed to the spread of slavery elected to the presidency.

The major sources for this chapter were:

Davis, D. B. (1970). *Was Thomas Jefferson an authentic enemy of slavery?* Oxford, UK: Oxford University Press.

Finkleman, P. (1993). Jefferson and slavery: Treason against the hopes of the world. In P. S. Onuf (Ed.), *Jeffersonian legacies* (pp. 181–221). Charlottesville, VA: University of Virginia Press.

Gordon-Reed, A. (1997). *Thomas Jefferson & Sally Hemings: An American controversy.* Charlottesville, VA: University of Virginia Press.

Gordon-Reed, A. (2008). *The Hemingses of Monticello: An American family.* New York, NY, and London, UK: W. W. Norton & Company.

Meacham, J. (2012). *Thomas Jefferson: The art of power.* New York, NY: Random House.

Miller, J. C. (1977). *The wolf by the ears.* New York, NY: The Free Press.

Stanton, L. (2012). *"Those who labor for my happiness": Slavery at Thomas Jefferson's Monticello.* Charlottesville, VA: University of Virginia Press.

Stone, P., & Edwards, S. (1964). *1776.* New York, NY: Viking Press.

LEARNING ACTIVITIES FOR "A LUXURY WE CAN'T AFFORD"

Facts of the Case

1. How were those enslaved at Monticello treated differently from slaves on most other plantations?
2. Why did Jefferson believe that freed Blacks and Whites could not live peacefully together in the United States?
3. Why were Jefferson's antislavery proposals rejected by Virginia lawmakers?
4. How would freeing his slaves have affected Jefferson financially and politically?
5. What did Virginia law require of masters who wished to free those they enslaved?
6. What was the relationship between Jefferson and both Madison and Eston Hemings?

Historical Understanding

1. How did the Enlightenment influence Jefferson's view of slavery?
2. What did Jefferson mean when he said, "We have the wolf by the ears, and we can neither hold him, nor safely let him go"?
3. For what purpose did the First Continental Congress meet?
4. Why was the antislavery passage deleted from Jefferson's draft of the Declaration of Independence?
5. How did some New Englanders benefit from slavery?

Expressing Your Reasoning

1. Should Thomas Jefferson have freed his slaves? Why or why not?
2. Should Jefferson have agreed to delete the antislavery passage from his draft of the Declaration of Independence? Why or why not?

Key Concepts from History

What do the following have in common?

1. In his 1781 book entitled *Notes on Virginia*, Thomas Jefferson compared Black people to White people. Of Blacks, he wrote: "Comparing them by their faculties of memory, reason, and imagination, it appears to me, that in memory they are equal to the whites; in reason much inferior, as I think one could scarcely be found capable of tracing and comprehending the investigations of Euclid; and that in imagination they are dull, tasteless, and anomalous." After The Civil War and well into the 20th century, these views of Black inferiority found their way into what is called the Jim Crow era in the American South. In the states of the former Confederacy, Whites segregated African Americans by

law. They were required to attend separate schools and churches, were buried in separate cemeteries, and were even compelled to drink from separate drinking fountains. Black and White people were not allowed to travel together and Blacks were excluded from public facilities, including hotels and restaurants. Black people were denied the vote and excluded from juries. They were also denied admission to public colleges and restricted to low-paying jobs requiring manual labor.

2. During the Third Reich in Germany (1933–1945), the country was ruled by totalitarian dictator Adolf Hitler and his Nazi Party. The Nazis believed that a master "Aryan race" should rule over all other peoples, whom they considered inferior. According to the Nazis, the "Nordic race" comprising the Germanic peoples was the purest stock of the Aryan race. Nazi ideology stressed the superiority of the White (Caucasian) Nordic race and stereotyped their physical characteristics: fair skin, blond hair, blue eyes, long head, smooth straight nose, and tall stature. Nazi policy discriminated against those they considered inferior, including Slavs, Poles, Roma (Gypsies), Africans, Asians, and especially Jews. In 1935, the Nazis announced new laws to institutionalize many of their racial theories. These laws excluded German Jews from citizenship and prohibited them from marrying or having sexual relations with persons of "German or related blood." Ultimately, Nazi race policies were extended to countries conquered by Germany and resulted in mass murder, including six million European Jews.

3. Following the defeat of the Boers (Dutch settlers) in the Anglo-Boer or South African War (1899–1902), the Union of South Africa was created as a dominion of the British Empire. In 1961, the country became a sovereign state, the Republic of South Africa. A policy called *apartheid* was introduced in 1948. Apartheid (an Afrikaans word meaning "separateness" or "the state of being apart") was a system of racial segregation in South Africa enforced through legislation by the National Party, the governing party from 1948 to 1994. Under apartheid, the rights, associations, and movements of the majority Black inhabitants and other ethnic groups were curtailed, and White minority rule was maintained. Legislation classified inhabitants into four racial groups: "Black," "White," "Colored," and "Indian," and residential areas were segregated. From 1960 to 1983, the government removed 3.5 million Black South Africans from rural areas designated as "White" to "homelands" (called Bantustans) and sold their land at low prices to White farmers. Non-White political representation was abolished in 1970, and starting in that year Black people were deprived of their citizenship.

Historical Inquiry

There is disagreement over whether Thomas Jefferson fathered children with Sally Hemings, a woman enslaved at Monticello. Using online and other sources, test the hypothesis that the couple had children together, and compose a short essay in which you accept or reject it. Use evidence to support your decision. To begin your investigation, the following search terms will be helpful:

- The Hemingses of Monticello
- Sally Hemings
- Madison Hemings
- Eston Hemings

Part II

THE NEW NATION
1776–1800

CHAPTER 5

Not One Morsel

Petition of an Enslaved African Woman

Belinda Royall's Petition to the Commonwealth of Massachusetts

Belinda Royall was born in 1712 in West Africa in what is now the nation of Ghana. While walking hand in hand with both of her parents, she was taken with force by a gang of European men whom she described as having faces as white as the moon. The year was 1724, and she was 12 years old. Belinda was captured and enslaved along with 300 other Africans. They were chained on board a slave ship in horrific conditions. The kidnapped Africans were crammed tightly below decks amid filth and without adequate food or water. Aboard such ships, diseases such as dysentery (an intestinal inflammation that can lead to severe diarrhea) were rampant, and many of the victims did not survive the crossing to the Americas. Suicide and rebellion on the ships was not uncommon.

Belinda was transported first to Antigua, an island in the Caribbean, where she was purchased by the Royall family; she was later shipped by Isaac Royall, Jr. to the city of Medford, near Boston in the Province of Massachusetts, a British Crown colony at the time. Royall kept Belinda on his relatively new estate. There she would reside for 52 years at the Royall family slave quarters. Her mother and father were left behind in Antigua because they were not seen as young enough to have the energy to be good workers. Younger Africans were more valuable on the slave market because they could work for many years. Once she left Antigua, Belinda never saw her parents again. Little is known about how Belinda served her slave master. Perhaps she worked in the fields, cooked, took care of children, or served as a maid.

The African slave trade began in the beginning of the 16th century and lasted through most of the 19th century. Europeans found a ready market, first in Europe and then in both North and South America, where there was a great demand for enslaved persons to provide the labor for field work on plantations, carpentry, cooking, clothes-making, blacksmithing, farming, mining, and working as house servants.

In what is called the Triangular Trade, European goods were shipped to Africa in exchange for Africans who were kidnapped and enslaved. African leaders, especially in West Africa, captured and sold Africans to European traders. The enslaved were transported to various Caribbean islands or America, from where sugar, rum, and molasses were shipped to Europe.

Portugal, Spain, England, France, and Holland all participated in the slave trade. Some slave ships sailed to all three corners of the triangle, while others went back and forth between Africa and the Americas. As many as 10 million Africans were shipped into slavery in North and South America. It is estimated that two to three million Africans died because of the brutal conditions of the transatlantic journey.

In 1641, Massachusetts became the first American colony to legalize slavery formally and, 140 years later, the first state in which it became illegal. Abolition was accomplished not by legislation but rather by court rulings based on the Massachusetts Constitution's provision of 1780 that declared "all men are born free and equal."

Slavery is often mistakenly thought to be solely a feature of the South. In reality, it existed in the Northeast as well and was an integral part of the economy of that region. There were, however, fewer enslaved persons in the New England colonies (Massachusetts, Rhode Island, Connecticut, and New Hampshire) than in the southern colonies, because harsh weather conditions in the North were not conducive to having large plantations. Further, the large plantations of the South required more labor. It was also more difficult in the North to grow enough food for the enslaved.

Although slave holding was smaller in scale in New England, the slave trade provided a major source of income in the region. Slaveholder Isaac Royall, Jr. was the wealthiest man in Medford. His wealth was based on slave and sugar trading. He and his family lived a lavish lifestyle. They never had the worry of paying his enslaved servants and estate workers for their labor. There is no personalized record of Belinda's life as an enslaved person, but the hardship, frustration, and hopelessness of living a life in slavery is well documented. The enslaved had no control over their existence. Belinda endured the conditions of her life while observing the opulence enjoyed by the master's family.

Things changed for both Isaac, Jr. and Belinda in 1775, just prior to the American Revolution in 1776. Isaac was loyal to the British Crown. Those with the same loyalty were called Loyalists or Tories. After the Battle of Lexington and Concord, Isaac, as a Loyalist fearing for his own and his family's safety, tried to flee to the family's Caribbean estate in Antigua. Unable to book passage on a ship, they fled instead to Nova Scotia in Canada, which was then part of the British Empire. Those enslaved by Royall were left behind in Massachusetts.

He tried over the years to keep control of his Medford properties by making generous gifts of land to Harvard University. Eventually, this land was used to fund the establishment of Harvard Law School. Isaac Royall made provision in his will for the dispersal of his properties, which included the Africans he had enslaved, to family members. Another provision in his will called for Belinda's freedom and an allowance of money for her following his death. In the end, however, he, like other Loyalists, had his estate confiscated by the state, so there would be no allowance for Belinda.

However, once Royall's estate was confiscated, Belinda and the others were no longer enslaved. They were able to claim their legal freedom because Royall's properties were seized by the Province of Massachusetts after Royall fled to Canada. Her freedom was not the result of the manumission provided for in Isaac's will that was proved after his death in 1781. (Manumission is the act of a slave owner freeing an enslaved person.) In his will, Royall had provided for the manumission of Belinda so long as she had the money to take care of herself. His concern was not for the well-being of Belinda or her son and daughter. Rather, he did not want to burden the city of Medford with the expense of caring for Belinda and the children. (There is no record identifying the father of the children.) Being a freed enslaved person was not like being a free White person. Freed enslaved persons were subject to being kidnapped and sold back into slavery in other states. They also often faced other obstacles—for example, finding a way to earn a living and coping with nighttime curfews.

Belinda was not free financially. She was unable to support herself and her daughter. There is no record of Belinda's son, but it is known that her daughter was with her at the time of Isaac Royall's flight to Nova Scotia.

In 1783, at age 70, likely with the help of a local abolitionist, Belinda petitioned the Massachusetts General Court (the official name of the new Massachusetts state legislature) for payment of a pension of 15 pounds per year. Unable either to read or write, Belinda signed the petition only with her mark, which was an *X*. The money was to be paid from the confiscated Royall property. Because the Commonwealth of Massachusetts had seized the property it was necessary for Belinda to ask the state for the payment of what might considered to be a pension. This was the first known public demand for reparation by a former enslaved person. Belinda was old and weary and needed financial assistance to care for herself and her disabled daughter. Her petition describes her cruel capture in Africa, her horrific voyage on a slave ship, and her 52 years of enslavement by Isaac Royall, Jr. The petition was in part a plea for sympathy. Below is the actual wording of the petition:

The Petition of Belinda an Afffrican, humbly shews: that seventy years have rolled away, since she on the banks of the Rio de Valta received her existence— the mountains Covered with spicy forests, the valleys loaded with the richest fruits, spontaneously produced; joined to that happy temperature of air to exclude excess; would have yielded her the most compleat felicity, had not her mind received early impressions of the cruelty of men, whose faces were like the moon, and whose Bows and Arrows were like the thunder and the lightning of the Clouds.—The idea of these, the most dreadful of all Enemies, filled her infant slumbers with horror, and her noontide moments with evil apprehensions!—But her affrighted imagination, in its most alarming extension, never represented distresses equal to what she hath since really experienced.

An obstacle to Belinda's petition was the patriarchal nature of the society in which she lived. At the time, men dominated and controlled life in their families and in their businesses. It was not unusual for enslaved women to face sexual assault by their slave masters. Belinda's petition asked for consideration from a male-dominated government in Massachusetts and from the estate of her master, also a male.

Belinda's petition went beyond sympathy, though. It appealed to the spirit of the American Revolution and to the ideal of all people having natural rights. In the Declaration of Independence, Thomas Jefferson largely based colonial independence from England on the natural rights doctrine that "all men are created equal; that they are endowed by their Creator with certain unalienable Rights; that among these are Life, Liberty, and the pursuit of Happiness." Belinda supported the Revolution and hoped her petition would resonate with its call for individual freedom and justice, even for those people who had been enslaved.

It is not known whether the descriptions of Belinda's life in Africa or her kidnapping at age 12 were exaggerated in her petition in order to advance her cause. Her strategy was to gain approval of her petition by references to her past suffering and by appeals to the revolutionary fervor in America. The petition's appeal to unalienable rights was inspiring, but its representation of Belinda being old, weary, and in need of assistance for her and her children was compelling.

One of the elements of capitalism is wage labor. In exchange for their labor, workers receive compensation in the form of wages or a salary, and owners receive the profits that are generated by the labor. Belinda's petition asserted her claim to wages under the American economic system. It stated: "The face of your petitioner, is now marked with the furrows of time, and her frame feebly bending under the oppression of years, while she, by the Laws of the Land, is denied enjoyment of one morsel of that immense wealth, a part whereof hath been accumulated by her own industry, and the whole ugmented [*sic*] by her servitude." Belinda was seeking a pension that she felt was due to her for her uncompensated labor.

The petition was widely circulated in newspapers in Massachusetts and New Jersey. Later, her story would find its way to Europe where it was greatly exaggerated by publishers as a way of both selling newspapers and exposing the hypocrisy of a new nation founded on liberty while embracing slavery.

Not exaggerated was the role Black women played in building America. Enslaved women served and cared for the families of their masters, contributed manual labor leading to the creation of wealth for their masters, and provided a steady stream of new slaves by giving birth. The latter was especially true after the importation of slaves was banned in 1808 as provided by the United States Constitution. Some have argued that America's economic strength and power was built in large measure by Black women.

In 1980, Rita Dove, later to become poet laureate of the United States, put Belinda's petition to verse:

Belinda's Petition (Boston, February 1782)

To the honorable Senate and House
of Representatives of this Country,
new born: I am Belinda, an African,
since the age of twelve a Slave.
I will not take too much of your Time,
but to plead and place my pitiable Life
unto the Fathers of this Nation.

Lately your Countrymen have severed
the Binds of Tyranny. I would hope
you would consider the Same for me,

pure Air being the sole Advantage
of which I can boast in my present Condition.

As to the Accusation that I am Ignorant:
I received Existence on the Banks
of the Rio de Valta. All my Childhood
I expected nothing, if that be Ignorance.

The only Travelers were the Dead who returned from the Ridge each Evening. How might I have known of Men with Faces like the Moon who would
ride toward me steadily for twelve Years?

"Belinda's Petition" from *The Yellow House on the Corner*, Carnegie Mellon University Press, Pittsburgh,
PA ©1980 by Rita Dove

Faced with the petition, the Massachusetts legislature was expected to re-
spond. A decision to pay Belinda from the confiscated estate of Loyalist Isaac
Royall might be acceptable to the Massachusetts legislators. With the end of slavery in Massachusetts, however, approval of Belinda's petition might prompt others who were enslaved to demand reparations from former slave masters who had
been Patriots.

Further, under the law, enslaved people had been considered property of their
slave masters. The Massachusetts legislature would have to consider whether slave
owners ought to be compensated for their lost property once slavery was abolished, especially if reparations had to be paid to those they had enslaved.

Famed revolutionary leader Samuel Adams was a member of the Massachusetts legislature in 1783. At the same time another famous Patriot, John Hancock,
was serving as the state's governor. Samuel Adams vowed never to own a slave.
John Hancock was a slave owner and had been a slave trader. Both of these heroes
of the American Revolution had proclaimed its ideal of natural rights.

The state legislature had discovered examples of former enslaved persons
farming on estates confiscated from Loyalists and had allowed that practice to
continue. The Massachusetts legislature had already decided that old and ill former slaves could be provided for out of the confiscated properties of Loyalists
who fled the country. Belinda's petition, however, was asking the legislature to
go further.

It took only 4 days for the Massachusetts state legislature and governor to approve Belinda's petition. The approval was signed by both State Senator Samuel
Adams and Governor John Hancock.

There is no known record of the vote count on approving the petition in the
Massachusetts legislature. Nor is there any record of the reasoning of the legislature. The payments were coming from the confiscated property of a Loyalist

and not from taxes. Previous petitions for compensation by other freed slaves had been denied when there was no confiscated property that would yield money for payment. Issac Royall had not met his responsibility to provide for a former enslaved person. The state of Massachusetts could argue that it was doing so within the boundaries of the laws governing slavery and not as reparation payment.

Belinda was awarded an annual payment of 15 pounds and 12 shillings. The payments were not consistently forthcoming and Belinda had to continue to make requests of the state for the annual pension. The last such approved request was in 1787. No later documentation tells us what became of Belinda and her daughter. There are records of Belinda filing at least four additional petitions in order to receive the annual payment. The newly discovered petitions show her name as Belinda Sutton.

In 1796, the Massachusetts Supreme Judicial Court decided that slave masters had no obligation to support those who had been enslaved. The court agreed with the prevailing view of former slave masters that if those enslaved were free of bondage then the masters were free of any obligations for the well-being of the former slaves.

The major sources for this chapter were:

Adams, C., & Pleck, E. H. (2010). *Love of freedom: Black women in colonial and revolutionary New England*. New York, NY: Oxford University Press.

Minardi, M. (2004). The poet and the petitioner: Two Black women in Harvard's early history. In L. Ulrich (Ed.), *In yards and gates: Gender in Harvard and Radcliffe history* (pp. 53–68). New York, NY: Palgrave Macmillan.

Minardi, M. (March 2006). *Pure air being the sole advantage: The limited freedom of Belinda, an African New Englander*. Paper presented at the Consortium on the Revolutionary Era, Georgia State University, Atlanta, GA.

The Royalls. (December 2015). *Royall House and Slave Quarters*. Available at http://www.royallhouse.org/the-royalls

LEARNING ACTIVITIES FOR "NOT ONE MORSEL"

Facts of the Case

1. Why did Belinda come from Africa to America?
2. How did Belinda contribute to the wealth of Isaac Royall, Jr.?
3. How was Belinda's freedom obtained?
4. Why did Belinda petition the Commonwealth of Massachusetts?
5. How did the Commonwealth of Massachusetts act upon Belinda's petition?

Historical Understanding

1. Why was slavery less prevalent in New England than in the South?
2. Describe the Triangular Trade.
3. What was the argument of former slaveholders against reparations?
4. What did American revolutionaries mean by natural rights?

Expressing Your Reasoning

Should the Commonwealth of Massachusetts have granted reparations to Belinda Royall? Why or why not?

Key Concepts from History

What do the following examples have in common?

1. Japanese Americans were interned in camps during World War II. Against their will, thousands of Japanese Americans living mostly on the West Coast of the United States were removed under presidential order from their homes and placed in internment camps. They were seen as threats to the homeland because the United States was at war with Japan. Later, the government of the United States distributed over $1.6 million in payments to 82,219 Japanese Americans who had been interned and their heirs.
2. Millions of European Jews were forced into slave labor by the Germans before and during World War II. Their property was confiscated and six million Jews were murdered in what is called the Holocaust. In 2013, the German government agreed to pay over $1 billion to 56,000 Holocaust survivors.
3. Many Native Americans lost their tribal lands by force and coercion during settlement of the United States. Native Americans also suffered gross mismanagement of lands and monies that were being managed by the United States Department of the Interior. In 2012, the federal government and American Indians finalized a $3.4 billion payment settlement over government mismanagement of tribal lands and trust fund accounts.

Historical Inquiry

The Three-Fifths Compromise is found in Article I, Section 2, Paragraph 3 of the U.S. Constitution: "Representatives and direct Taxes shall be apportioned among the several States which may be included within this Union, according to their respective Numbers, which shall be determined by adding to the whole Number of free Persons, including those bound to Service for a Term of Years, and excluding Indians not taxed, *three fifths of all other Persons.*"

Did the Three-Fifths Compromise affect the American political system? Using online and other sources, test the hypothesis that the Three-Fifths Compromise affected the American political system. Compose a short essay in which you accept or reject the hypothesis. Use evidence to support your decision. To begin your investigation, the following search terms will be helpful:

- Slave state representation
- Presidential election of 1800
- Southern voting bloc
- Sectional interests
- Connecticut Compromise
- Thomas Pickering

CHAPTER 6

Washington for the British

Harry Washington and a Question of Loyalty

Certificate of Freedom Issued to Black Loyalists in 1783

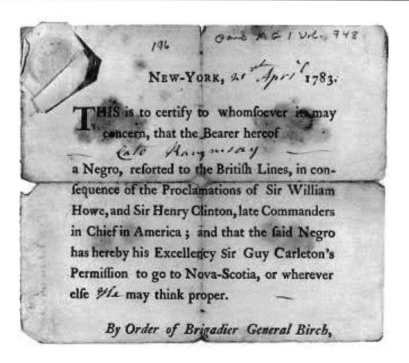

Harry Washington was a "saltwater slave," a person not born into slavery but rather kidnapped in Africa and shipped to North America by slave traders. Harry was born in 1740, on the Gambia River in West Africa, and was sold into slavery in 1760. His birth name is not known. He was first bought by a lower Potomac River plantation owner, Daniel Tibbs, in the colony of Virginia and later purchased by George Washington in 1763. He was given the name "Harry" and assumed the last name of the slave owner, a standard practice in naming enslaved persons.

Harry was purchased by Washington to work as part of a group of slaves who were assigned to dig a ditch (three feet deep by ten feet wide) covering five miles to a lake in order to drain a large swamp named the Great Dismal Swamp. After working in the mosquito-infested swamp for 2 years, Harry was taken to George Washington's plantation, Mount Vernon. Mount Vernon was a 7,000-acre estate in Fairfax County, Virginia.

Once at Mount Vernon, Harry worked as a servant in and around the house. Eventually, he was assigned to care for George Washington's horses. In 1773, Harry ran away from Mount Vernon and was captured and returned several weeks after George Washington posted a reward for his capture. This attempt at freedom would not be Harry's last.

The American Revolutionary War began in 1775 when fighting broke out between the Massachusetts militia and British regular troops at Lexington and Concord. The Continental Congress appointed George Washington to command the militia units that were besieging the city of Boston. Later, Washington was selected by the Continental Congress to serve as the commander of American forces during the entire war. (The Continental Congress was the legislative body that supervised the conduct of the war.)

On July 2, 1776, the Continental Congress formally voted for independence; it issued the Declaration of Independence on July 4. The Declaration of Independence, whose primary author was Thomas Jefferson, accomplished three important things: It stated that all men are created equal and have certain inalienable rights, including life, liberty, and the pursuit of happiness; it specified the wrongs that the British monarch was inflicting on the colonists; and it formally declared the United States to be an independent nation.

Heated debate over revolution, war, independence, and the natural rights of man took place in all the colonies. Those enslaved, working in households like Mount Vernon, heard the talk, and discussion of such topics found its way into slave living quarters. Did Jefferson really mean that "all men are created equal" or did he mean all free White males who owned property? When Jefferson listed the grievance that the king "had excited domestic insurrections amongst us," he was referring to British efforts to have Native people fight on behalf of the Loyalists.

Slave owners expressed grave concerns about the possibility of slaves fleeing for their freedom to the British side. The economic and military implications were far-reaching. Who would work the fields and in the households? Who would care for the farm animals and maintain the farming tools and equipment? Thousands of slaves fighting for the British might also mean the difference in the war's outcome. George Washington expressed his concern to his cousin, Lund Washington, whom he had put in charge of Mount Vernon while he was commanding American forces. General Washington thought many slaves would escape, which would have the effect of "a snowball rolling." Although he did not agree with his cousin at the time, Lund would later think differently after losing many slaves. He explained the defection with the words, "liberty is sweet."

Communication among those enslaved was extensive and intricate. The slave quarters on plantations housed families in close proximity, permitting the sharing of stories, gossip, and speculation about the future. Some plantation owners also permitted their slaves to visit with slaves at other plantations. This talk extended beyond plantations. Political information was exchanged at Saturday town markets where the enslaved came to sell produce from their own small plots. Slaves were aware of the political situation and were very much aware of the arguments for and against remaining loyal to their slave masters.

In 1775, John Murray, fourth Earl of Dunmore, the royal governor of Virginia, fearing for his life from threatening Patriots, fled to a British warship in the Chesapeake Bay. Once there, he issued a proclamation granting freedom to any enslaved person who would fight for the British. The proclamation enticed hundreds of enslaved persons to escape to the safety of British ships.

Virginia law spelled out punishments for runaways who defected to Dunmore. Whipping, execution, or a sentence to work in dangerous lead mines were all punishments that were sometimes used. The law also provided for pardons to those runaways who voluntarily returned. The enslaved knew full well the risks of fleeing to the British.

In spite of these great risks, hundreds of enslaved persons fled to Lord Dunmore's ships in the Chesapeake. During the war overall, thousands of the enslaved fled to the British: One estimate puts the number at 100,000; Thomas Jefferson estimated 30,000 slaves fled to the British from Virginia during the war. Thousands of others remained in slavery, with many fighting on the side of the Patriots.

It is not certain whether more enslaved persons fought for the Patriots or for the Loyalists. It is estimated that as many as 9,000 Black Patriots, both free Blacks and slaves, served in the American army, navy, or one of the state militias. The promise of winning freedom by enlisting in the military was appealing to many. Both Loyalists and Patriots made promises of freedom to runaway slaves serving in the military. However, after the war, British and American law (including that of individual states), as well as the peace treaty, posed obstacles to the granting of freedom to runaway slaves who fought in the war. The peace treaty following the war attempted to prevent the British from keeping their promise of freedom to runaways. Many American slave owners believed that slaves who fought for the Patriots were still their property and, at the war's end, should be returned.

Harry Washington, aware of both the risks and rewards, decided to leave Mount Vernon. He had been enslaved by George Washington for 13 years and knew well what it was like to work in the fields of the plantation, as a household servant, and as a trusted hostler (a person who takes care of horses and stable). He also knew what kind of slave owner he had in George Washington.

George Washington became a slave owner at age 11 when his father, Augustine, died and left George 10 slaves in his will. Washington later acquired additional slaves, totaling 318 upon his death in 1799. Historians dispute how he treated his slaves. Some claim that he treated them more severely than other nearby slave owners, while others maintain that his treatment was far more humane. There is agreement that punishments at Mount Vernon did include whipping, although not at the hand of George Washington himself. The most severe punishment Washington personally used, and rarely, was to sell a disobedient slave away from his or her family to a buyer in the West Indies, thereby ensuring the family would never be reunited.

Another indicator of treatment by a slave owner could be the degree to which enslaved persons were cooperative and compliant. Resistance to ill treatment could reveal itself in a variety of ways. Some, including servants to both George and Martha Washington, decided to flee. Others at Mount Vernon resisted by performing tasks slowly or poorly, feigning illness, sabotaging crops, or stealing equipment or food.

Washington may have viewed the enslaved as inherently inferior; it is hard to be sure, as his beliefs and regrets regarding slavery were seldom publicly expressed. He did address the paradox of being a strong believer in liberty and natural rights while at the same time denying liberty and rights to those enslaved at Mount Vernon. He said, "This may seem a contradiction but it is neither a crime nor an absurdity. When we profess, as our fundamental principle, that liberty is the inalienable right of everyman, we do not include madmen or idiots; liberty in their hands would become a scourge. Till the mind of the slave has been educated to perceive what are the obligations of a state of freedom, the gift would insure its abuse."

On the other hand, George Washington's will provided for the freeing of his slaves upon the death of his wife, Martha. According to the will, the elderly and sick would be supported by the estate; following Martha's death, children would be supported by those who would teach them to read and write, and to become skilled at a trade, and would be freed at age 25. George Washington died in 1799. In 1800, Martha signed a deed of manumission (a grant of legal freedom) for the slaves she inherited. Her suspicions about the loyalty of the slaves, and concern for her personal safety, prompted her to free George's slaves in advance of her death.

In deciding whether to escape to the British, remain at Mount Vernon, or fight for the Patriots, as many of those enslaved had chosen to do, Harry Washington had to consider the risks. He had become a trusted and loyal caretaker of General Washington's horses, an important responsibility. Escaping to the British meant leaving behind family and friends, and probably never seeing them again. He could be killed, or severely punished, for escaping to the British. He could end up on the defeated side of the war. Joining the British meant fighting against black Patriots. By fighting for the British, he would be forgoing possible manumission upon the death of Washington.

Both Patriots and Loyalists were promising freedom to those slaves who helped the war effort. Harry Washington had to consider which side, Patriot or Loyalist, was his quickest and best chance for freedom. He also had to consider questions of loyalty to Washington, and loyalty to other slaves. It is not known whether he had family at Mount Vernon. Escaping to the British meant freedom in the short term (during the war), whereas freedom following the war might be less certain if the British were to lose.

We do not know what factors influenced Harry Washington's decision to escape. Perhaps he asked himself why he should owe loyalty to George Washington. Harry was an enslaved person without freedom. He could be bought and sold. He could, without his consent, be removed from his family and friends. He was treated as property and not as a person. Slavery had been abolished on English soil in 1772. The English could be better trusted to grant freedom to slaves. In 1776, it was obvious to most observers that the British would have little difficulty defeating the much weaker Patriots. It would be better to be on the winning side of the American Revolutionary War.

In 1776, Harry and several White indentured servants escaped and made their way to one of Lord Dunmore's ships in the Chesapeake Bay. (Indentured servants were men and women from European countries who signed contracts to work for a certain number of years in exchange for transportation to American colonies, as well as for food, clothing, and shelter once they arrived.) His escape was successful and he ended up serving the British in several military capacities until the war's end in 1783.

After Cornwallis's defeat at Yorktown, the battle that ended the war, Harry Washington ended up behind the British lines in New York City along with several thousand Black refugees (persons who flee their country because of war or persecution) who had also served on the British side. Cornwallis's defeat was sad news for those former slaves who had been counting on a British victory. Now they faced being returned to their slave owners and eventual punishment.

The formal treaty ending the war, the Treaty of Paris, was signed in 1783. One of its provisions was a "prohibition from carrying away any Negroes or other property of the American inhabitants." This could mean that thousands of Black refugees would have to be returned to their masters. Slave owners traveled to New York City to reclaim their enslaved property. George Washington was ordered by the Continental Congress to ensure the treaty obligations were fulfilled by the British.

In New York, the British commander, Sir Guy Carleton, defied the treaty obligation. He ordered that all former slaves who had fought for the British for at least 1 year should be issued certificates of freedom and be allowed to go wherever they chose. Carleton maintained that those who were granted certificates of freedom were no longer property and, therefore, did not have to be returned to their previous slave owners. The British made good with a document assuring what Lord Dunmore had promised in his 1775 proclamation.

Commander Carleton used a face-to-face opportunity to lecture George Washington on moral obligations. He told Washington the British government would never accept the dishonor of violating their faith to the Negroes. As a concession, Carleton did permit the Americans to inspect ships leaving New York so there could be an accurate record of the people leaving. The British agreed to compensate Americans for the loss of property, including those enslaved. The record of those leaving included their names, age, when they fled to the British, and the name of their slave owner. (Harry Washington was listed at 43 years of age and having fled Mount Vernon 7 years prior.) The record is known as Carleton's Book of Negroes and has since become a valuable historical source of information. The record was used by British General Birch after the war in issuing the certificates of freedom. One such certificate, along with Birch's name, is shown at the beginning of this chapter.

The Black refugees along with thousands of White British Loyalists left New York in 1783 aboard a number of British ships. Some left for England and others for Canada. Others were not so fortunate as to have been issued a certificate of freedom. For them, the war's end meant attempts to escape to northern states and freedom, risking recapture, or being turned over to their slave owners by the British because they did not meet the requirement (serving at least 1 year with British forces) to be issued certificates of freedom.

Harry Washington left on a British ship along with several hundred other newly freed people, bound for Nova Scotia, Canada. By 1785, more than 3,000 formerly enslaved persons migrated to Nova Scotia, joining more than 30,000 other Loyalists who settled in Canada. Harry and the others settled in Birchtown, a town named after British General Birch. Harry was accompanied by a woman named Jenny whom he had met after leaving Mount Vernon. Harry and Jenny married and started a family.

The Birchtown settlers found life very difficult in Nova Scotia. After waiting 3 years for land they had been promised, they found it unsuitable for farming. The climate was much colder than what they were accustomed to. Moreover, these newcomers were not treated as equals by the Nova Scotians. Despite these challenges, the new settlers had a lively and spirited religious life in a supportive congregation.

In 1791, a British company established by abolitionists, the Sierra Leone Company, enticed many in the congregation to move to Sierra Leone, Africa. The company was motivated in this venture by its antislavery beliefs and its expectation the enterprise would result in profitable trade between Africa and Europe. The company promised free land grants and no discrimination between Black and White settlers. Harry and his wife Jenny arrived in Sierra Leone in 1792.

As in Nova Scotia, the life in Sierra Leone also proved to be difficult and in the end a disappointment. The free Blacks settled in Newtown, which was a remote wilderness where land was difficult to clear for farming. Hostility between the residents and the company grew.

Harry Washington was able to grow subsistence crops on his farm to feed his family. However, he was very unhappy with the company's unequal treatment of Blacks and Whites and its refusal to allow people to govern themselves. Others agreed, and eventually a rebellion broke out. Harry was captured and found guilty of rebelling by a British military court. He was banished without his family to a distant settlement. Harry died within a year of his removal.

The major sources for this chapter were:

Henriques, P. (July 2001). *The only unavoidable subject of regret: George Washington and slavery.* Available at chnm.gmu.edu/courses/henriques/hist615/gwslav.htm

Lepore, J. (May 8, 2008). Goodbye Columbus. *The New Yorker.* Available at http://www.newyorker.com/magazine/2006/05/08/goodbye-columbus

Phybus, C. (2011). Mary Perth, Harry Washington, and Moses Wilkenson: Black Methodists who escaped from slavery and founded a nation. In A. F. Young, G. B. Nash, & R. Raphael (Eds.), *Revolutionary founders, rebels, radicals, and reformers in the making of a nation* (pp. 543–601). New York, NY: Alfred A. Knopf.

Phybus, C. (2016). Washington's revolution (Harry that is, not George). *Black Loyalist.* [Blog]. Available at www.blackloyalist.info/washington-s-revolution-harry-that-is-not-george

LEARNING ACTIVITIES FOR "WASHINGTON FOR THE BRITISH"

Facts of the Case

1. How did Harry Washington come to be enslaved at Mount Vernon? What work did he perform at the plantation?
2. How did enslaved persons learn about the talk of rebellion by the American colonists?
3. What ideas in the Declaration of Independence may have given hope to those enslaved?
4. How did Harry Washington end up with the British in New York City?
5. How did the British commander in New York City circumvent the Treaty of Paris?
6. What happened to Harry Washington after leaving the United States?

Historical Understanding

1. Why did the British encourage slaves to run away to the British?
2. Why were slave owners fearful of slaves fleeing to the British?

Expressing Your Reasoning

Should Harry Washington have fled to the British? Why or why not?

Key Concepts from History

What do the following have in common?

1. George Washington is referred to informally as "The Father of Our Country." He commanded American forces during the American Revolutionary War; signed the Declaration of Independence; presided over the Constitutional Convention; and became the first president of the United States, serving two terms, 1789 to 1797.

2. Molly Pitcher is a name in folklore given as a composite to women who served during the American Revolutionary War by bringing water and equipment to the men fighting. Men would yell "Molly" and then "Pitcher" as a way of asking for fresh water. Mary Ludwig Hays was born and grew up in Pennsylvania. In 1777, she married a local barber turned artilleryman during the American Revolutionary War. At the American army's winter camp at Valley Forge, PA, she joined a group of women, led by Martha Washington, known as "camp followers." They washed clothes and blankets, and helped care for the sick and wounded. Women also brought pitchers of water to the artillerymen who used the water to cool down the cannon barrels, and wet sponges used at the end of ramrods for the cleaning of sparks and gunpowder from the cannon barrels. During the Battle of Monmouth in 1778, after spending most of the day carrying water from a nearby spring, Mary noticed that her husband had collapsed from heat exhaustion or injury. He was removed from the battle to be treated. Mary went on to spend the rest of the day swabbing and loading the cannon during the heat of the battle. During one artillery exchange, a cannon ball from the British harmlessly passed between her legs. At the conclusion of the battle General Washington issued a warrant card in commemoration of her valiant service, naming her a noncommissioned officer. For the rest of her life she was known as Sergeant Molly.

3. Roger Sherman of Connecticut was the only person who signed all these four founding documents: Declaration of Independence, Articles of Association (adopted by the Continental Congress in 1774 and asserting that there would be a boycott of British goods on December 1, 1774, if the Intolerable Acts were not repealed), the Articles of Confederation, and the U.S. Constitution. Born in Massachusetts, but later moving to Connecticut upon the death of his father, Sherman went from working on his father's farm to being a shoemaker, store owner, town clerk, county surveyor, lawyer, representative to the Connecticut House of Representatives, justice of the peace, treasurer of Yale College, professor of religion, mayor, and a Connecticut delegate to the Constitutional Convention in 1787. He achieved all this though he was self-educated beyond grammar school. At the Constitutional Convention, he was known for being intelligent and influential, despite being an ineloquent speaker. He proposed the Connecticut Compromise, which became known as the Great Compromise: a Senate with equal representation for each state and a House of Representatives based on the population of each state. This adopted proposal ended the dispute between large and small states over representation in Congress.

Historical Inquiry

With a promise of freedom from some slave-owning Patriots, many enslaved persons fought on the side of the Patriots during the American Revolutionary War. After the American victory against the British, did Patriots keep their promise?

Using online and other sources, test the hypothesis that enslaved persons who fought for the Patriots during the American Revolutionary War were granted freedom following the victory by the Americans. Compose a short essay in which you accept or reject the hypothesis. Use evidence to support your decision. To begin your investigation, the following search items will be helpful:

- Slavery after the American Revolutionary War
- Plight of Black Patriots
- African Americans in the American Revolution
- Black Patriots and Loyalists

CHAPTER 7

The Power of a Fraction

James Wilson and the Three-Fifths Compromise

Graphic Illustrating the Three-Fifths Ratio

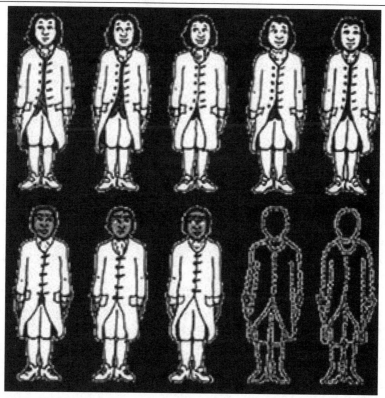

A clause included in the U.S. Constitution describing the basis of representation in the House of Representatives is known as the Three-Fifths Compromise. Article I, Section 2. Clause 3: "Representatives and direct Taxes shall be apportioned among the several States which may be included within this Union, according to their respective Numbers, which shall be determined by adding to the whole Number of free Persons, including those bound to Service for a Term of Years, and excluding Indians not taxed, three fifths of all other Persons." The last four words of this clause refer to enslaved persons.

The U.S. Constitution was preceded by the Articles of Confederation. The Articles were adopted by the Second Continental Congress in 1777 and fully ratified by all 13 states in 1781. At the time the Articles were ratified, six of the 13 states were slave states: Delaware, Maryland, Virginia, Georgia, North Carolina, and South Carolina. Northern states had much higher percentages of free labor, relied less on slave labor, and were able gradually to abolish slavery. By the end of the 18th century, all northern states had abolished slavery.

The Articles of Confederation did not effectively balance power between the new central government and the states. Each state, regardless of its size, had one vote in the unicameral (single house) legislature. The federal government could not manage disputes among states, nor could it require the payment of taxes by states. Amending the Articles required a unanimous vote of all 13 states. There was no independent executive or judicial branch of the federal government. Without a strong central government, it was as if 13 sovereign nations had agreed to a treaty that provided for limited governance.

The states disputed whether the well-being of the new nation could be managed by the Articles of Confederation. An armed uprising in Massachusetts, known as Shays' Rebellion, brought together thousands of angry citizens protesting what they believed to be unjust evictions and foreclosures on their homes and property. The rebellion demonstrated the weakness of the federal government in maintaining order within states. Politicians in Virginia and Maryland argued over how their boundaries were impacted by the Potomac River. The government of Rhode Island decided to tax all traffic on its post road (an important road designated for the transportation of mail, including mail between states). These two disputes resulted in delegates from five states meeting in what is known as the Annapolis Convention in 1786. This meeting called for a constitutional convention the following year to consider improvements in the Articles of Confederation.

The Constitutional Convention began in May 1787 in the city of Philadelphia. All states were represented except one: The legislature of Rhode Island feared its interests would not be best served by attending.

Delegates realized that modifying the Articles of Confederation would not be sufficient. An entirely new document was needed. James Madison, a delegate from Virginia who would later be called the "Father of the Constitution," introduced the Virginia Plan. This plan became the framework for the U.S. Constitution.

The delegates began their work by modifying Madison's Virginia Plan. The plan called for three branches of government: executive, legislative, and judicial. The chief executive would be chosen by the legislative branch. The legislative branch would be bicameral (two houses) and based on states' populations. The Senate members were to be selected by the state legislatures and the House of Representative members were to be elected by people eligible to vote in each state. In most states, the voting population was White land-owning adult males; in New Jersey, Pennsylvania, and Connecticut, free Black adult males owning property could vote. Women could not vote anywhere except New Jersey.

The convention spent most of its time dealing with several difficult issues: the composition and election of members to the Senate and House of Representatives; whether to have a single person with executive power serve as president; how to elect a president and the length of the term; whether the slave trade should be abolished; what to do about fugitive slaves who had escaped to a free state; and how federal judges should be selected.

The Great Compromise settled the dispute between large states, which favored proportional representation in Congress (the Virginia Plan), and small, which called for equal representation for each state in Congress (the New Jersey Plan). The compromise called for a House of Representatives based on proportional representation. A census would be conducted to determine a state's population and each state would have a representative in the House of Representatives for every 30,000 people. Because there had been no census at the time of the convention, each state was assigned a number of representatives based on its population estimates until the first national census was conducted in 1790. Members of the House would be chosen by the popular vote of those eligible to vote in a given state. Each state would have two senators in the new Senate, chosen by its state legislature, thus protecting the interests of small states. The question of who should be counted in determining a state's population was not settled.

Among the 55 delegates (25 were slave owners) who regularly attended the convention was James Wilson from Pennsylvania. Wilson was born in Scotland in 1742 and moved to America in 1765. He became a tutor at the College of Philadelphia, studied law, and was admitted to the Pennsylvania bar in 1767. In 1774, Wilson gained fame by writing an essay that was critical of the English Parliament's authority over the American colonies.

In 1775, while serving in the Second Continental Congress, Wilson was part of the Pennsylvania delegation that signed the Declaration of Independence. He became one of the most influential delegates at the Constitutional Convention. Wilson is credited with being second only to James Madison in contributing to the underlying political theory of the Constitution. He served on the convention's Committee of Detail, which produced the first draft of the Constitution.

Wilson went on to sign the new document and was an influential leader and advocate for his state's ratification of the Constitution. In 1789, he became a professor at the University of Pennsylvania, and in the same year he was appointed as one of the original justices to the Supreme Court of the United States. He died in 1798 at age 55.

The debate over determining how to base proportional representation was one of the most contentious issues at the Constitutional Convention. At issue was whether enslaved persons should be counted when determining the number of representatives a state would have in the House of Representatives, and in determining the direct tax each state would owe to the national government. The slave states wanted slaves to be counted in full. This would increase their population count and their number of representatives in the House of Representatives. Northern states with few or no slaves wanted only free persons to be counted.

The debate over this issue lasted throughout the convention and almost prevented the delegates from agreeing on a proposed constitution.

Although James Wilson was opposed to slavery, he (along with Roger Sherman of Connecticut) proposed the "Three-Fifths Compromise," whereby each slave would be calculated as three-fifths of a person. This compromise proposal seemed to recognize the legitimacy of slavery. Wilson, like a number of other delegates from northern states, was convinced that a new constitution would not be agreed to by the southern states (Georgia, Maryland, North Carolina, South Carolina, and Virginia) without counting at least three-fifths of their enslaved population in calculating representation. The less populated southern states feared they would be at a political disadvantage in protecting their economic and social interests unless enslaved people were tallied as part of their population. Without counting enslaved people at all, the five southern states would have only 41% of the seats in the new House of Representatives. If their slaves were counted in full, they would have 50% of the seats. Adoption of the Three-Fifths Compromise meant they would have 47% of the seats.

The compromise did not specifically suggest that slaves were to be valued as less than full human beings. It was a question of the allocation of political power. Having more representatives in the House of Representatives meant for a state, or region, a greater share of political power that could be used for protecting their economic and social interests. Counting a three-fifths fraction of the Black population, however, did not mean that slaves had voting rights.

The Three-Fifths Compromise provided for state representation in the House of Representatives to be based on population as well as a state's share of direct taxes to be paid to the federal treasury. This tax provision was included to deter southern states from inflating their slave populations during a census. If states inflated their slave populations, it would mean more representatives in the House, but it would also mean those states would have to pay more in federal taxes. As it turned out, however, states never paid direct taxes to the federal government.

The proposed three-fifths fraction was not an entirely new idea to the delegates. Many of them had been serving in Congress when James Madison proposed an amendment to the Articles of Confederation calling for the slave population in a state to count as three-fifths for the purpose of determining a state's taxes to be paid to the national government. Madison's proposal received majority support of the 13 states but was ultimately defeated. The amendment did not obtain the required unanimous approval of all states.

The decision to adopt the Three-Fifths Compromise was no small matter. Besides determining the number of representatives a state would have in the House of Representatives, the clause was also linked to the manner in which the president would be chosen. The convention adopted a plan called the "Electoral College." Each state would have a number of presidential electors equal to its number of representatives and senators. A majority of electors was required to elect the president. The electors were chosen in a manner determined by each state legislature. Originally, each elector had two votes to be cast for two people. The presidential candidate with the majority of electoral votes became president, while the person with the next highest number would be the vice president. The Three-Fifths Compromise would mean that the Southern states had an advantage in both the House of Representatives and in the Electoral College.

James Madison and James Wilson, as part of a committee of 11 delegates, devised the idea of the Electoral College even though Madison thought direct election of the president by a popular vote was the ideal. Madison's home state of Virginia would be at a disadvantage in electing a president by popular vote. Virginia and the other southern states did not allow slaves or other Black people to vote. Other less populated states also saw a disadvantage for them in direct election of the president.

The Electoral College formula for determining a state's number of electoral votes offset the political disadvantages of both the slave states and small states. The three-fifths count of the slave population benefited slave states by adding to their electoral votes. Each state having two senators produced an electoral vote that was not directly proportional to its population, and that benefited small states.

There were other reasons for not electing the president by a direct popular vote. The delegates did not believe transportation and communication in the country were sufficient to allow voters to make informed decisions in a popular election of the president. In addition, there was a wide difference in voter eligibility from state to state. Each state had its own voting requirements. This lack of uniformity in eligibility would put states with stringent voting requirements at a numerical disadvantage.

The advantages afforded to the slave states by the Three-Fifths Compromise were regarded by some delegates as unfair. Some argued that if the southern states could count their enslaved property as population, other types of property, such as machinery or domesticated animals, should be counted in determining population. Madison rebutted this argument by rationalizing that slaves were both people and property. Still others maintained that to give into the slave states' demands would be contrary to the value of equality expressed in the Declaration of Independence. Some suggested that it would be better for the North and South to go their separate ways and become two nations rather than to have one nation half free and half slave. Delegates from the southern states agreed that separate nations would result if no allowances were made for slavery.

One of the most outspoken opponents of the Three-Fifths Compromise was a delegate from Pennsylvania, Gouverneur Morris. He argued that if slaves were to be counted for representation:

> The inhabitant of Georgia and South Carolina who goes to the Coast of
> Africa and in the defiance of the most sacred laws of humanity tears away his

fellow creatures from their dearest connections and damns them to the most cruel bondages, shall have more votes in a Government instituted for protection of rights of mankind, than the Citizen of Pennsylvania or New Jersey who views with laudable horror, so nefarious a practice.

After many debates throughout the summer of 1787, the Three-Fifths Compromise was approved by a majority of the states and was included in the final draft of the Constitution that was ratified in June 1788 when New Hampshire became the required ninth state to ratify.

Other allowances for slavery also entered into the deliberations of the convention. In the end, they were agreed to without the words *slave* or *slavery* ever being written in the final document. The Constitution protected the importation of slaves for 20 years. Federal forces could be used to suppress domestic insurrections—a constitutional clause that could be applied to slave revolts. What is called the Fugitives from Labor Clause or the Fugitive Slave Clause in the Constitution required that escaped slaves who fled to different states be returned to their owners. Amendments to the Constitution required approval of three-fourths of the states, thus giving power to slave states over amendments that might abolish, or in any way limit, slavery or the slave trade. These provisions, along with the Three-Fifths Compromise, prompted the famous abolitionist William Lloyd Garrison to consider the Constitution "a Covenant with death, and an agreement in Hell."

The proslavery representation in the House of Representatives had historical consequences. Thomas Jefferson would not have been elected president in 1800: John Adams would have been reelected as president if there had been no Three-Fifths Compromise. Without his opponent's additional votes from the slave states, Adams would have received a majority of the electoral votes. The passage of the Missouri Compromise of 1820, allowing Missouri to enter the union as a slave state, would not have passed without the compromise. Nor in 1845 would Texas have been annexed as a slave state. The Three-Fifths Compromise also enabled passage of the Fugitive Slave Law of 1850, which made it easier to have slaves who had escaped to the North returned to their slave owners. The same was true for the passage of a law allowing slavery in Utah and New Mexico as well as the Kansas-Nebraska Act of 1854, which opened up slavery to the Great Plains and the Rocky Mountains.

During the summer of 1787, the delegates at the Constitutional Convention could not have predicted what adoption of the Three-Fifths Compromise would mean for the history of the new nation. Most believed that there would not be a new constitution without the compromise, possibly resulting in the United States muddling along under the ineffective Articles of Confederation. Another possibility could have been that the North and South parted and formed two new nations. In that case, it is likely that slavery would have lasted in the South beyond its abolition by The Civil War beginning in 1861 and the passage of the Thirteenth Amendment to the Constitution in 1865.

It was not realistic to believe that the delegates from the slave states would support a constitution that did not protect their economic and social way of life. Even if the delegates at the Constitutional Convention had conceded to the demands of the free states, there was little chance of the new Constitution being ratified by the necessary three-fourths (nine) of the states.

Some of those opposed to slavery who supported the compromise believed that the institution of slavery was doomed and its end would be quickened by the adoption of the Constitution. They believed a new, more powerful central government would eventually be able to abolish slavery. Northern states were gradually abolishing slavery, and many believed its continuation as a political and economic system could not be sustained. Others suspected that the South was bluffing with its threat not to support a new national Constitution absent the proposed slavery safeguards. They believed that the South could not thrive economically without the industry, markets, and transportation systems of the North, which were required to make cotton, tobacco, and rice profitable crops.

The major sources for this chapter were:

Finkelman, P. (2013, February 26). The Three-Fifths Clause: Why its taint temains. *The Root.* Available at http://www.theroot.com/articles/politics/2013/02/the_ threefifths_clause_the_compromise_over_slavery_and_its_lingering_effects/

Finkelman, P. (2014). *Slavery and the founders: Race and liberty in the age of Jefferson.* New York, NY: M. E. Sharpe, Inc.

Wilentz, S. (2015, September 16). Constitutionally, slavery is no national institution. *The New York Times.* Available at www.nytimes.com/2015/09/16/opinion/ constitutionally-slavery-is-no-national-institution

Wills, G. (2003). *Negro president: Jefferson and the slave power.* Boston, MA, and New York, NY: Houghton Mifflin Harcourt.

LEARNING ACTIVITIES FOR "THE POWER OF A FRACTION"

Facts of the Case

1. What was the Three-Fifths Compromise and why did the southern states support it?
2. Why did some delegates from northern states oppose the Three-Fifths Compromise?
3. What concessions to slavery were included in the new Constitution?
4. How did the Three-Fifths Compromise impact the number of votes each state would have in the Electoral College?

Historical Understanding

1. What were some of the effects of the Three-Fifths Compromise?
2. Why did the delegates to the Constitutional Convention choose not to have the president elected by popular vote?

Expressing Your Reasoning

Should James Wilson have proposed and supported the Three-Fifths Compromise? Why or why not?

Key Concepts from History

What do the following have in common?

1. The Patient Protection and Affordable Care Act (PPACA, also known as the Affordable Care Act, or Obamacare) was proposed by Congress in 2010. Republicans saw the proposal as too radical and as excessive government intrusion into health care. Congressional Democrats, who controlled both houses of Congress, developed the health-care proposal. Democrats in the House and Senate had many disagreements among themselves over the content of the bill. In the end, Democrats made concessions to one another that permitted the final bill to be passed and then signed into law by President Obama.

2. In 2015, Iran was committed to its program for development of nuclear weapons. The government of the United States joined the other five members of the United Nations Security Council (United Kingdom, France, Germany, Russia, and China) in negotiating a nuclear agreement with Iran curtailing the country's nuclear weapons program. The agreement was reached because the Security Council member nations wanted to prevent Iran from developing nuclear weapons, and Iran was willing to accept an end to economic sanctions against it in exchange for curtailing its nuclear program.

3. In 1820, the United States Congress adopted a federal law that regulated slavery by balancing the number of new states that would be admitted to the Union as either "free states" or "slave states." The legislation allowed for the admission of Maine as a free state and Missouri as a slave state. It prohibited slavery north of the southern boundary of Missouri except for Missouri itself. Northern states were worried about being dominated in Congress as a result of the spread of slavery into new states. Southern states worried about being overpowered in Congress by new states added to the Union as free states. This agreement between proslavery and antislavery forces in Congress contributed to delaying The Civil War.

Historical Inquiry

Enslaved persons were not allowed to vote, yet their numbers were computed in the population of a state. Did the end of slavery following The Civil War and the adoption of the Reconstruction Amendments (Thirteenth, Fourteenth, and Fifteenth) mean the right to vote had actually been extended to African Americans?

Using online and other sources, test the hypothesis that the right to vote was extended to African Americans when The Civil War ended and the Reconstruction Amendments were adopted. Compose a short essay in which you accept or reject the hypothesis. Use evidence to support your decision. To begin your investigation, the following search terms will be helpful:

- Voting rights
- Voting rights laws
- Voter suppression
- Jim Crow
- Poll tax
- Literacy test
- Voter identification laws
- Fifteenth Amendment

CHAPTER 8

A Little Rebellion Now and Then

The Whiskey Rebellion

Famous Whiskey Insurrection in Pennsylvania by R. M. Devens

Courtesy of the New York Public Library

In 1783, when the American Revolutionary War ended, the Americans were free of British rule and British taxes. Yet the country was not unified politically under a federal government. Most former colonists probably thought of themselves first as citizens of their states, and second as citizens of the new nation.

From 1781 to 1789, the Articles of Confederation, an agreement among the states, provided for a central (federal) government with the name "The United States of America." Although certain powers were delegated to the federal government (for example, the conduct of foreign and commercial relationships and the power to declare war), the Articles also recognized the states' right of self-government (sovereignty). Under the Articles, there were no office of the president or of the vice president, no executive agencies, and no federal judiciary. Moreover, no provision was made for a federal tax system. Could this new federal government solve the problems that the country faced, especially without the power to levy taxes? Could the new state governments, with "every power, jurisdiction, and right" guaranteed by the Articles, manage their own problems? No one knew the answers to these questions.

One of the most immediate problems for the federal government was how to pay for the expenses of the War, including the repayment of foreign loans. The federal government owed some $54 million (equivalent of $1.5 billion in today's currency) to its creditors, who included France, Spain, and various foreign investors. The states, which had borrowed to pay their soldiers and to buy supplies, had a collective debt of some $25 million (equivalent of $675 million). Because a major cause of the War was the unjust system of taxation, the states were reluctant to levy more taxes. The federal government had no authority to levy taxes.

In 1789, the U.S. Constitution replaced the Articles of Confederation and became the supreme law of the land. The new federal Constitution, which provided for a much stronger central government than the Articles, established the three branches of federal government under the doctrine of the separation of powers: executive, legislative, and judicial. It also gave Congress the authority to regulate trade among the states and to levy taxes. However, in its outline of the states' rights and responsibilities, the U.S. Constitution established the idea of federalism that provides for the division of power between the federal government and the state governments.

In 1789, President George Washington appointed Alexander Hamilton, a charismatic 35-year-old, as the first secretary of the treasury. As the founder of the Federalist Party, Hamilton supported a strong federal government. He had been among those who called for the Philadelphia Convention of 1787 that led to the replacement of the Articles of Confederation with the U.S. Constitution.

The role of the secretary of the treasury when Hamilton held the position was (and still is) to act as a principal advisor to the president on issues of economic and financial policy. At the request of Congress, Hamilton, as secretary of the treasury, wrote a 51-page financial plan called the *Report on Public Credit* in which he urged Congress to consolidate the federal and state debts into a single debt funded by the U.S. government. The report called for full repayment of the federal debt and for the federal government to pay the states' debts. After much debate, in July 1790, Congress approved this measure.

Money still had to be raised to repay the War loans from the various foreign countries and investors. Because Hamilton did not favor increasing duties on imported goods, he proposed the taxation of certain domestic goods, one of which was distilled spirits, including the enormously popular whiskey, which was made from corn and grain. People all over the country drank whiskey, even at church meetings and at electoral polling places. Many claimed whiskey had medicinal value. In fact, whiskey was so popular in the West (that is, in the late 18th century, regions west of the Appalachian Mountains, primarily parts of Pennsylvania, Kentucky, and Ohio) that it was used as a medium of exchange. Hamilton's tax, which became known as the whiskey tax, was levied on distilled spirits, whether produced by distilleries in the East or home-distilled by farmers in the West.

Distilled spirits, popular as they were, were considered a luxury, not a necessity like food and household items. Hamilton thought citizens would object less to a luxury tax than to a tax on essential goods. He also thought social reformers would support the tax on distilled spirits as a "sin tax." Hamilton misjudged much of the public reaction, particularly in the West, to the whiskey tax.

Despite initial opposition within Congress and from some citizens, the tax on distilled spirits passed in March 1791. The law, the "Whiskey Act," was the first federal internal revenue tax. In part, Congress passed the tax to avoid having to tax land and income. By November of that year, President Washington had established tax revenue districts and appointed tax revenue supervisors and inspectors.

The whiskey tax was enormously controversial, especially among farmers in the West. Many farmers distilled corn and grain into whiskey that could be stored almost indefinitely. Whiskey not personally consumed could be sold to neighbors (or exchanged for other items) or sold in the eastern markets. Whiskey in barrels was relatively easy to transport on wagons. Thus, the whiskey business was a profitable way to deal with surplus corn and grain. Even the leftover solids from the distilling process could be fed to farm animals. It is not surprising that farmers were outraged by the tax. In addition, not all transactions involving whiskey also involved cash. Western farmers often used whiskey to pay for private purchases using a barter system. Why, they wondered, should they be required to pay a tax on the whiskey they exchanged for cloth, tools, and other "store-bought" goods?

The western farmers also claimed the way the taxes were imposed was unfair. To levy and collect the taxes on distilled spirits, Hamilton established a system by which the various distilleries paid taxes according to their size and location. Distilleries in towns and villages (located mainly in the East), which could be rather easily visited and monitored, paid a per-gallon tax on the whiskey they produced. Distilleries in the more remote areas (which were most of the distilleries in the West) paid an annual flat fee on the gallon capacity of their stills. Western farmers, with their rural stills, did not produce whiskey year-round. Because they were farmers as well as home distillers, they thought it unjust that they had to pay an annual fee when they distilled no whiskey during the planting, growing, and harvesting seasons.

The large distilleries soon began producing more spirits in order to qualify for the two-cent tax discount Hamilton offered on every 10 gallons produced. With this tax reduction, these distilleries could lower their sales prices even as small distilleries had to raise theirs. In short, it seemed the whiskey tax favored the large distilleries. Smaller distilleries ultimately paid more than twice the amount of tax per gallon as the large distilleries. Owners of small farms and small distilleries thought the tax meant they would not be able to compete with the owners of the large farms and the large distilleries in the East. This tax was *regressive*: It charged the smaller distillers more per gallon than larger distillers.

Many farmers opposed the whiskey tax on political as well as economic grounds. Although they were represented in Congress, the farmers did not feel they had a voice in the new federal government. For them, the whiskey tax reminded the farmers of the slogan "no taxation without representation"—the very injustice that had sparked the American Revolution. Additionally, some people objected to paying taxes that would be used to settle other states' debts. Now, instead of protesting British stamp and tea taxes, their protests were turned against their new government's tax on domestic production.

Initially, resistance to the whiskey tax was peaceful. The small distillery owners and western farmers simply refused to pay the tax. Their refusal, however, was met with the federal government's demand that they appear in a Philadelphia court, in many cases some 300 miles away, at crucial times when they were plowing or harvesting. When the federal government was unresponsive to their protests, the protesters circulated petitions and resolutions against the whiskey tax. They also held meetings in which the goal was the repeal of the tax. On July 27, 1791, they selected delegates to attend a convention that was to occur in Pittsburgh in September of that year. This convention sent a petition to the Pennsylvania Assembly and the U.S. House of Representatives. In response, the House modified the law by reducing the whiskey tax by one cent per gallon.

The protesters were not satisfied. In August 1792, they met again in Pittsburgh. Most attendees were radicals; the only moderate to attend was a local politician named Albert Gallatin (who would be the secretary of the treasury from 1801 to 1814 under Presidents Thomas Jefferson and James Madison). Although Gallatin called for a peaceful response to the tax protest, the radicals at the meeting silenced him with their outcry against the tax. As had been the practice during the War, these tax protest groups raised liberty poles, formed committees of correspondence, and seized control of local militias.

Hamilton, who supported using military force to collect the taxes, called the protesters "traitors." Although President Washington also wanted to maintain the authority of the federal government, he did not want to risk alienating public opinion by using force unnecessarily. On September 5, 1792, President Washington issued a national proclamation admonishing the western farmers for their resistance to the taxes.

However, the farmers simply ignored the proclamation and became increasingly violent. Thus began the battle between "the revenuers and the moonshiners" that American folklore often describes. The farmers fired shots at the tax collectors, robbed them, branded them with irons, and tarred and feathered them. For example, when Robert Wilson tried to find work as a schoolmaster in western Pennsylvania, a group of farmers, acting on a rumor that he was a shadow inspector for the U.S. Department of the Treasury, kidnapped him, stripped him naked, and threatened to burn him with a hot iron. Ultimately, the farmers tarred and feathered him. However, it was later revealed Wilson was neither a tax collector nor a government spy. He simply supported the whiskey tax.

The federal government had little success in collecting the whiskey tax, and the violence continued. By July 1794, the violence had escalated to more dangerous levels. General John Neville, the western Pennsylvania regional excise inspector and a large-scale distiller himself (and thus a beneficiary of the tax, which favored large distilleries), was a target. On July 16, 1794, 30 militiamen surrounded his home on his sprawling plantation near Pittsburgh called Bower Hill.

Neville ordered the men off his property, and when they refused, he fired into the crowd, killing Oliver Miller, one of the rebels. He was a boy. The next day, 600 militiamen, commanded by Major James McFarlane (a Revolutionary War veteran), returned to Bower Hill to make two demands: that General Neville hand over his remaining writs and that he resign as excise inspector. There were 10 soldiers protecting Neville's Bower Hill plantation. The rebels demanded that the soldiers surrender, and when they didn't, the rebels set fire to some of the outbuildings. In the gun fighting that followed, McFarlane was shot, and in response, the rebels set other buildings on Neville's property ablaze. The soldiers protecting Neville's property then surrendered. This event is known as the Battle of Bower Hill.

Ten days later, on July 26, 1794, a lawyer, David Bradford, led a group of men in a robbery of the U.S. mail in Pittsburgh. They hoped the mail would reveal the identities of the people who opposed the farmers' protests. Bradford, who took the side of the farmers, had a radical view of the situation. He thought the protests could lead to secession of the West from the Union. Bradford and his fellow westerners even dared to create a flag with six stripes that represented the unified six counties of western Pennsylvania and northwestern Virginia.

President Washington, in meetings with his Cabinet, tried to find a solution to the crisis. Although he doubted whether they could be effective, he sent three peace commissioners to western Pennsylvania to negotiate with the farmers. At the same time, he began raising a militia army to deal with the Whiskey Rebellion.

On August 1, 1794, Bradford led men to Braddock's Field in Pittsburgh to protest the tax. Wives and children accompanied the men who were estimated to number from 5,000 to 9,000. Because most of the men were poor and owned no land, their grievance was more against U.S. financial policies that they thought favored the wealthy than against the whiskey tax in particular.

Bradford's group at Braddock's Field faced William Findley, a farmer and U.S. congressman from Pennsylvania. Like Bradford, Findley opposed Hamilton's financial policies and supported states' rights as well as the interests of the small farmers. However, Findley was less radical than Bradford and could not support the secessionist movement that Bradford advocated. Change, Findley thought, was better achieved at the ballot box than by mob protest. Findley is today remembered as the voice of reason in the eventual, peaceful end to the Whiskey Rebellion.

On August 7, 1794, President Washington issued a second proclamation calling on the tax protesters to disperse. The proclamation cited the Militia Act of 1792 that gave the Office of the President permission to suppress internal rebellions. The protesters continued to meet publicly to decide on their next action. The most important of these meetings was held on August 14–15, 1794, at Parkinson's Ferry south of Pittsburgh.

Some 240 elected delegates from Pennsylvania and Virginia and three federal commissioners appointed by the president, as well as David Bradford and Albert

Gallatin, attended the Parkinson's Ferry meeting. Gallatin spoke eloquently in his call for peace. When negotiations between a committee of protesters and the commissioners achieved nothing, the commissioners returned to Philadelphia and recommended that the federal government use force to quell the insurgency.

As military preparations authorized by the federal government began, the Parkinson's Ferry delegates continued to meet. Gallatin, an experienced politician who had revealed his opposition to Hamilton's financial policies during his brief period as a U.S. senator, continued to play a key role in convincing others to work toward a peaceful solution. Although he opposed the whiskey tax, he did not support the westerners' radical views and violent actions. Using skillful negotiation and persuasive arguments, Gallatin oversaw a 34–23 secret ballot vote (in late August 1794) in favor of peaceful submission to federal law and of a proposed reduction in the whiskey tax.

Nevertheless, President Washington continued to mobilize a militia of nearly 13,000 men. On September 19, 1794, Washington, Hamilton, and the Virginia governor, Henry "Light Horse Harry" Lee, led a militia from Philadelphia on a nearly month-long march to Bedford, Pennsylvania (this was the first and only time an American president has ever led troops in the field). On September 25, 1794, Washington issued yet another proclamation—the Proclamation of Militia Service—declaring that he would not allow "a small portion of the United States [to] dictate to the whole union."

However, when the federal militia, which had continued westward, arrived in Pittsburgh in October, they found that the insurgents had dispersed, because Gallatin had been successful in his efforts to resolve the rebellion peacefully. In a meeting with Washington and Hamilton, representatives from the Parkinson's Ferry group (including William Findley) agreed to end the rebellion, to obey U.S. laws, and to abide by the U.S. Constitution.

Eventually two tax protesters, John Mitchell and Philip Weigel, were found guilty of treason. (President Washington later pardoned them.) However, state courts in Pennsylvania convicted some protesters of rioting and assault. Washington's contemporaries generally approved of his handling of the crisis. Many historians have also praised the outcome of the Whiskey Rebellion as a success. It should be noted, however, the whiskey tax remained law for another 7 years, but continued to be difficult to enforce.

The complex financial and political issues that the whiskey tax raised resulted in a violent rebellion that threatened the legitimacy and authority of the new democracy. Yet some critics have downplayed the importance of the insurrection. In his book on the rebellion, William Findley, for example, charged that the uneducated, Scots-Irish backwoodsmen were only protesting a tax on their whiskey. Alexander Hamilton coined the term *Whiskey Rebellion* in order to smear the protesters. He also wanted to divert attention from their anger at financial policies they thought favored the wealthy and at political policies they thought favored the sovereignty of the federal government over the states and the right of the people to challenge the federal government.

The Whiskey Rebellion was, in some ways, a minor event in U.S. history. Certainly it was not comparable in length, violence and destruction, or implications for democracy to the American Revolution or to the American Civil War. However, the Whiskey Rebellion is nevertheless worthy of our attention. In suppressing the Whiskey Rebellion, the federal government strengthened its power over the states.

The Whiskey Rebellion also raised fundamental constitutional questions about the division of power between the states and the federal government. People who supported a less centralized and powerful government eventually formed a new political party, the Democratic-Republican Party, which supported states' rights. Thomas Jefferson, who was the leader of this party, became the third U.S. president in 1801. (Perhaps because of an alleged compromise with Hamilton on the re-location of the federal capital to Washington, D.C., Jefferson did not speak out against the whiskey tax during the Rebellion.)

Nevertheless, as he later wrote, Jefferson thought it was a mistake to pass the tax, to try to enforce it, and to use it to split the country. Jefferson had always supported citizens' right to rebel when unjustly governed. Jefferson also wrote that "a little rebellion now and then . . . is a medicine necessary for the sound health of government." In 1802, Jefferson signed into law the repeal of the whiskey tax, passed by Congress.

The major sources for this chapter were:

Bouton, T. (2011). William Findley, David Bradford, and the Pennsylvania regulation of 1794. In A. F. Young, G. B. Nash, & R. Raphael (Eds.), *Revolutionary founders, rebels, radicals, and reformers in the making of a nation* (pp. 233–252). New York, NY: Alfred A. Knopf.

Hogeland, W. (2010). *The Whiskey Rebellion*. New York, NY: Simon & Schuster.

LEARNING ACTIVITIES FOR "A LITTLE REBELLION NOW AND THEN"

Facts of the Case

1. Following the Revolutionary War, how much debt did the United States have, and what was the cause of this debt?
2. Why did Secretary Hamilton propose a tax on distilled spirits?
3. How did the tax on distilled spirits benefit the large-scale distilleries?
4. How did the farmers oppose the whiskey tax?
5. How did President Washington try to suppress resistance to the whiskey tax?

Historical Understanding

1. Describe the political beliefs of the Federalists, in relationship to the whiskey tax and the resulting rebellion.
2. Why did President Washington want to avoid the use of military force in the Whiskey Rebellion?

Expressing Your Reasoning

Were the farmers of western Pennsylvania justified in rebelling against the whiskey tax? Why or why not?

Key Concepts from History

What do the following have in common?

1. The federal government funded President Franklin D. Roosevelt's New Deal programs in the 1930s in the United States. However, the states administered the relief programs (for example, public works such as bridges and hospitals) and farm/rural programs (such as electrification, schools, and mechanization).
2. In the 1950s and 1960s, the federal government provided up to 90% of the cost of federal highway construction. The states built and maintained the highways.
4. The federal government has the sole power to make treaties and to declare war. The states have the sole power to issue marriage and driving licenses.

Historical Inquiry

The Revolutionary War and the Whiskey Rebellion are two examples of resistance to taxation by Americans. Using online and other sources, test the hypothesis that Americans have not resisted taxation since the Whiskey Rebellion. Compose a short essay in which you accept or reject the hypothesis. Use evidence to support your decision. To begin your investigation, the following search terms will be helpful:

- Americans' resistance to taxation
- Whiskey Rebellion

Part III

NATION BUILDING
1801–1828

CHAPTER 9

Chilling Effect

The Greenleafs and Freedom of the Press

The Masthead of the *New York Journal & Patriotic Register*

After its invention by Johannes Gutenberg in the mid-15th century, printing with moveable type spread rapidly in Europe. Printing was an important factor in the spread of Renaissance and Reformation thought, and later in facilitating the Age of Enlightenment and the Scientific Revolution. Literacy and education became more widespread. The printing press allowed for the mass communication of information and ideas, some of which proved troublesome for religious and political leaders.

In England, a 1530 royal proclamation required publishers to obtain a license from the government. Later monarchs banned criticism of the king. By 1695, requirements for publishing licenses in England were abolished, and censorship laws were eased. One could, however, still be prosecuted for defamation (statements that damage a person's good reputation). Such statements could be oral (slander) or written (libel). Further, *seditious libel* laws were enacted. They permitted prosecution of those who published criticism of the government that incited people to rebel, regardless of whether such criticism was true or false. (It was not until the middle of the 19th century that the truth of claims became an admissible defense for those accused of seditious libel in England. The accused person could attempt to prove statements were truthful, and therefore, not libelous.)

Britain's laws against seditious libel also had force in the colonies. In 1735, publisher John Peter Zenger was accused of printing stories that criticized the royal governor of New York. Zenger's attorney argued that the truth of his client's claims should be a defense against charges of libel. A jury found Zenger innocent. He continued to print attacks against colonial rule.

During events leading up to the American Revolution, publishers played a major role in communicating to the public through books, newspapers, and pamphlets. Those who printed criticism of colonial rule could find themselves on the Crown's list of enemies. One such person was Joseph Greenleaf (1720–1810). He was a prosperous farmer and a justice of the peace (a local judge) in Plymouth County, Massachusetts Colony, who wrote a strongly worded newspaper article in 1770 that attacked the tax policies imposed by the British Parliament. He quickly became famous.

Greenleaf's writing fame led him to change careers. He sold his farm and house, moved to Boston, and became a partner of Isaiah Thomas in the publication of the *Massachusetts Spy*. The well-known newspaper's office became a meeting place for rebellious colonial leaders, including Samuel Adams and John Hancock.

Publishers (*publisher* and *printer* were used as synonyms) could be held liable for what appeared in their publications. Many articles against British colonial rule were written anonymously or pseudonymously (under a false name). This would protect the authors from prosecution. Their publishers, however, could face prosecution for defaming colonial rulers.

The royal governor of Massachusetts, Thomas Hutchinson, fired Greenleaf as a justice of the peace. Hutchinson objected to a series of critical articles published in the *Massachusetts Spy*. The unintended consequence of the governor's action was to make Joseph Greenleaf better known and more popular.

In 1773, Joseph Greenleaf and his son Thomas published their own newspaper, the *Royal American Newspaper*. Printers did not have high social status. They were considered tradesmen and manual laborers. The job was physically demanding, as every page of a publication had to be hand cranked on a large and oily machine. Nonetheless, the Greenleafs found themselves in the company of famous patriots who supported revolution.

Joseph Greenleaf's publishing enterprises resulted in his being one of many who were placed on Governor Hutchinson's list of enemies. Those listed were to be rounded up and jailed. They could be executed if rebellion were to break out. When fighting broke out in the American Revolutionary War, Joseph and Thomas fled for safety.

After the War ended, the Greenleafs returned and worked for a Boston newspaper that was very critical of corruption in the nation's new government. The newspaper, *The Independent Chronicle*, was one of only a few Anti-Federalist publications in New England. During the writing of a new Constitution in 1787, and the battle over whether the new document should be ratified by the states, Anti-Federalists were those who opposed ratification. Federalists favored adoption.

The Federalists believed the United States needed a stronger national government to correct the weaknesses that existed in the nation's first formal governing document, the Articles of Confederation. The Anti-Federalists feared that a stronger national government would reduce the authority of the states and threaten individual liberties.

In 1785, Thomas Greenleaf struck out on his own when he joined the *New York Journal and Patriotic Register* (commonly referred to as the *New York Journal*). Two years later, when the paper was up for sale, Thomas purchased it. Now his own daily paper, the *New York Journal* continued its Anti-Federalist tradition and its opposition to the ratification of the new constitution.

Early newspapers largely consisted of small print advertising, speeches, government documents, letters, and political essays. Many of the papers printed items from other papers. Because newspapers were not highly profitable, their publishers could not afford to hire reporters to gather news. Often, they printed anonymous articles that were dropped off at the printer's office after business hours.

Even with the obstacles faced by publishers, newspapers became the most influential source of news and ideas. The influence of the press frightened many political leaders, including those who helped draft the proposed constitution. They feared that criticism in the press would lead to political discord and possibly to violence. A young and relatively weak government, they thought, might be torn apart by the turmoil resulting from press criticism.

The framers of the proposed constitution believed the nation would be better without political parties. They were convinced that partisan citizen involvement at the state and local level would prevent national leaders from making necessary but difficult decisions.

Many Federalists believed the nation would be best governed by a wealthy and well-educated citizenry. These Federalists were joined by farmers, tradesmen, and business owners. They were determined to have the new constitution provide the economic stability that was missing under the Articles of Confederation.

On July 26, 1788, New York became the 11th state to ratify the U.S. Constitution. (Ratification by 9 of the 13 states was required for adoption.) Celebrations took place all over New York City. Many working people saw ratification as the best way to secure prosperity and were displeased with those who opposed adoption. Thomas Greenleaf's home and publishing office were ransacked by an angry mob. Greenleaf was defiant. Within a few days, he was back to publishing his newspaper. He considered threats of punishment and violence as attempts to infringe on the freedom of the press.

Such attempts were later referred to as having had a *chilling effect* on freedom of the press—that is, as having prompted self-suppression of free speech and press through fear of violence, punishment, or legal sanction.

The Constitution was adopted in 1788, and George Washington was elected president by a unanimous vote of the Electoral College. President Washington would serve two terms (1789–1797). During his time in office, and that of his successor, John Adams, both the executive and legislative branches of the national government were controlled by the Federalists.

George Washington disapproved of political parties. He believed that they would lead to excessive arguing, with party members putting the interests of their party above the well-being of the nation. Washington avoided becoming a member of a political party, but he was sympathetic to the Federalists. The Federalist Party, led by Alexander Hamilton (the first secretary of the treasury) and John Adams (the first vice president and the second president), was the first American political party.

Adams became the only Federalist Party president to be elected. The party unsuccessfully contested presidential elections through 1816, but by the 1820s the Federalist Party all but disappeared from the political landscape.

The Anti-Federalist opposition led by Thomas Jefferson and James Madison evolved into the Democratic-Republican Party. It was often referred to as the Republican Party (not to be confused with the present-day Republican Party founded in 1854).

The Democratic-Republican Party feared a government with overly centralized power, while the Federalist Party believed a strong central government was necessary to unite the states and bring about political stability and economic prosperity.

The Republicans believed that the Washington and Adams administrations favored wealthy planters, lawyers, and merchants. They opposed Washington's invoking of executive privilege to protect presidential secrets, Hamilton's economic policies, and a foreign policy that appeared to favor Great Britain over France. Washington was accused by his partisan opponents of being like a king.

To oppose the policies identified with Washington and Adams, Jefferson and Madison encouraged newspapers to become the voice of their Republican Party. One such paper was Thomas Greenleaf's *New York Journal*. Greenleaf argued that people joining together in political parties was the only practical way of defeating those in power. He helped lead a partisan political movement that enabled Republicans at the state and local levels to have their voices heard.

Thomas Greenleaf was not a writer but rather the owner and editor of his daily newspaper, the *New York Journal and Patriotic Register*. Like other papers, the *New York Journal* printed articles from other newspapers and by anonymous writers. Greenleaf could be prosecuted for criticism of the government that ran in his paper.

In 1793, Greenleaf became a center of attention when he published an article from a frequent contributor without first reading it. The article was an attack on President George Washington that Greenleaf would later admit was distasteful. The Federalists called for a public apology and encouraged a boycott of Greenleaf's paper. He was summoned to a public meeting where he apologized for the article, but he refused to reveal the name of the article's author or to agree that he, the publisher, should be disciplined or punished. Greenleaf argued that to do so would undermine freedom of the press.

At a meeting, Greenleaf's supporters and contributors drafted a statement claiming the press should be unrestrained, that such freedom was a necessary check by the governed on those who governed them. The statement went on to state, "Though it is to be lamented that freedom of the press is sometimes abused by being the vehicle of licentious scurrility, this evil is the necessary effect of that freedom."

Federalist attacks on Greenleaf backfired. The *New York Journal*'s circulation greatly increased, allowing Greenleaf to buy additional printing equipment and to improve the look of the paper. The first front page in the revised journal contained a quote from a British opposition leader: "To argue against any branch of liberty from the ill use that may be made of it, is to argue against liberty itself."

Open conflict between the two political parties further escalated over what the Republicans called Federalist elitism, and over Federalist foreign policy opposing the French Revolution. The Republicans favored the ideals of the ongoing French Revolution and suspected the Federalists of being too closely aligned with the British. The Federalists saw danger in the French Revolution, fearing mob rule that could lead to anarchy in the streets of America.

Greenleaf and other publishers leaked a text of the proposed Jay Treaty. That treaty sought to resolve issues that remained unsettled following the Revolutionary War. The Federalists hoped the treaty would avert war with Great Britain and lead to better business opportunities for American farmers and merchants. The Republicans saw the treaty as a threat to republicanism (a form of government whereby power is held by the people and their elected representatives) and as an attempt by the treaty's designer, Alexander Hamilton, to promote aristocracy (a form of government whereby power is held by the nobility). Republicans believed the treaty would bring about closer economic ties with Britain and would strengthen the Federalist Party.

A leaked draft of the proposed treaty resulted in massive opposition street rallies in large cities, which nearly defeated the treaty. Although the treaty was narrowly ratified by the United States Senate in 1794, the forceful opposition encouraged the further growth of the Republican Party. The treaty debate made it clear that the United States had two strong and contesting political parties. It also fostered a new journalistic trend of newspapers being devoted to a political party.

In 1795, Greenleaf renamed his newspaper *Argus*, after the all-seeing, hundred-eyed giant of Greek mythology. The mission of the *Argus*, for which Greenleaf made no apology, was to promote the Republican Party. He believed the only way to compete for political power was through political parties and a free press. He said, "Liberty, without parties, can never be maintained."

Greenleaf objected to the criticism against a partisan press and he decried what he considered a fallacy, the so called *bad tendency* doctrine. The bad tendency doctrine asserted that some statements were so radical, offensive, and inflammatory that they had a tendency to cause violence. This notion was based on the English common law (in which past legal precedents are used to decide current cases). It meant that those who made statements leading to violence had a legal responsibility for them.

By the time of the presidential election of 1796, Greenleaf had become the elder statesman of a movement to oust the Federalists. His paper claimed the election was a choice between two patriots, Thomas Jefferson and Aaron Burr versus John Adams, a "white-washed whig" (Whigs being a British political party) who was beholden to a foreign king. The hotly contested election was very close, with Adams elected as president by only three electoral votes: 71 for Adams and 68 for Thomas Jefferson.

With the second highest number of electoral votes, Jefferson was elected vice president. At the time, the Constitution called for each elector to cast votes for two different presidential candidates, which could result, as it did in this election, with a president and vice president from opposing political parties. (This startling event prompted the passage of the Twelfth Amendment, adopted in 1804, that changed the procedure by requiring the electors to cast one vote for president and a second vote for vice president.)

President Adams, hoping to improve relations with France, sent diplomats to Paris in 1797. When the American diplomats met their French counterparts, the French demanded a $10 million bribe (approximately $200 million in today's currency) before negotiations could begin. The three French diplomats involved were referred to as X, Y, and Z. When the U.S. diplomats refused to pay, Mr. X threatened the United States with war. The XYZ Affair damaged relations between the United States and France. Many Federalists called for war with France, while Republicans accused the Federalists of creating war fever.

In the end neither country declared war, but fears and tempers did flare. In July 1798, a French warship seized a U.S. merchant ship in international waters beginning a naval conflict between the two countries. France sank several U.S. naval vessels and U.S. merchant ships in the Atlantic Ocean and the Gulf of Mexico. The U.S. Navy also captured and sank French naval vessels and merchant ships. Hamilton claimed, without proof, that the French were assembling an army to invade America. One Federalist paper proclaimed, "He that is not for us, is against us." Jefferson and the Republicans were accused of being traitors.

In 1798, the Federalists, still in control of the executive and legislative branches of government, enacted the Alien and Sedition Acts. The Federalists said they were acting out of a concern for national security. They feared a French invasion of the United States. They also feared that pro-Republican French and Irish immigrants in the United States might serve as spies for the French. Many new arrivals were people sympathetic to the French Revolution who had been forced out of their European countries. Federalists feared that once they obtained citizenship, these immigrants would vote for Republicans, who were believed to be overly sympathetic to the ongoing French Revolution and scheming to undermine the federal government. President Adams declared that the foreign influence must be "exterminated."

The Alien Acts required an immigrant to have lived 14 years in the United States before becoming a citizen. (An "alien" is a foreign person, who is not a citizen, residing in a country.) Federal law had previously mandated a 5-year U.S. residency requirement for citizenship. The acts also permitted the arrest, detention, and deportation of all male citizens of an enemy nation if war were to break out.

A major goal of the Sedition Act was to shut down the opposition press until after the election of 1800 (sedition is conduct or speech inciting people to rebel against government authority). The act had three major provisions: (1) outlawing conspiracies to oppose any measure of the government; (2) making it a crime for anyone to express any false, scandalous, and malicious writing against Congress or the president; and (3) making it illegal to publish words that had "bad intent" to defame the government or cause hatred of the people toward it.

The Federalists attempted to justify the Alien and Sedition Acts by claiming they were necessary to protect national security from foreign enemies. The Sedition Act did allow for the "truth of the matter" defense and for a jury to determine whether the defendant had "bad intent." The act's penalties ranged from 6 months to 5 years in prison and a fine of up to $5,000 ($100,000 in today's currency). The law went into effect on July 14, 1798, and was set to expire on March 3, 1801, the last day of Adams's term in office.

Most of the indictments under the Sedition Act were against publishers and editors. Some papers shut down and some publishers became too intimidated to criticize the government. Other publishers continued to publish criticism of the government. The first person to be tried under the Sedition Act was Matthew Lyon, a Republican member of Congress from Vermont. Lyon, an opponent of war with France, wrote a letter criticizing President Adams that was published in a Republican newspaper.

Lyon was unable to find a defense attorney, so he defended himself. He was tried in a heavily Federalist town in Vermont. Under the law, the burden of proof was on him; the defense did not have to prove his words false. Lyon argued that expressing political opinions should not be subject to the truth test. He asked the jury to consider how it could be possible to prove that a political opinion was false.

The jury found him guilty of sedition with "bad intent." He was sentenced to 4 months in jail and fined $1,000 ($19,600 in today's currency). From his jail cell, he ran for and won reelection to the House of Representatives.

James Madison argued that the Alien and Sedition laws were unconstitutional in that they violated the First Amendment's protection of freedom of speech and press. The Federalists maintained that the law was necessary to defend against attacks by both foreign and domestic enemies. They claimed the First Amendment prevented the government from censoring before publication but did not protect false and malicious expression after publication.

This dispute over the meaning of the First Amendment could not be settled by the Supreme Court. At that time, the high court had not yet held that it had the power to find an act of Congress unconstitutional, and thus null and void.

That authority, called judicial review, was established in the case of *Marbury v. Madison* in 1803, when the Court for the first time declared a federal law to be unconstitutional.

Altogether, 25 prominent Republicans were arrested under the Sedition Act. Fifteen of the arrests resulted in charges being brought. Ten of those cases were brought to trial, with all 10 resulting in convictions. Thomas Greenleaf was not among them; before he could be charged and tried for seditious libel, he fell victim to yellow fever and died in the summer of 1798.

Greenleaf had married Ann Quackenbos in 1791. She cared for her family and home. She also provided meals and lodging for those who were employed in the printer's office. When Thomas died, Ann was left with a newspaper business, several small children, and no husband.

After suspending publication of the *Argus* for several months, Ann started it up again in November 1798. The newspaper continued to attack the Adams administration. Ann was charged with crimes under the Sedition Act, but her trial was delayed because she too contracted yellow fever.

Alexander Hamilton urged the state of New York to prosecute her newspaper. The *Argus* had reprinted a widely published article criticizing Hamilton for attempting to buy out and close a Republican newspaper in Philadelphia. The article also included Hamilton's admitted history of paying blackmail in the case of an affair he had with a married woman.

With Ann being too sick to stand trial in federal court, the attorney general of New York instead prosecuted the *Argus* editor, David Frothingham, in state court. Frothingham had recently been hired to manage the office and to edit the newspaper. He was tried and convicted under the common law doctrine of seditious libel, and not the Sedition Act. Frothingham was sentenced to 4 months in prison and fined $100. (His salary at the time was $8 a week, $156 in today's currency.) After being released from prison, he did not return to the printing business.

By the time Ann Greenleaf was well enough to stand trial in federal court, the federal attorney for New York had decided not to prosecute her case. Public opinion had turned against the Federalist Party, and there was concern among the Federalists that Sedition Act prosecutions would harm the party in the election of 1800.

In the presidential election of 1800, which had to be decided by the House of Representatives, Thomas Jefferson was elected president. Jefferson, a Republican, referred to his victory as "the revolution of 1800" because the two competing parties had such different visions on how America should be governed.

In one of his first actions in office, Jefferson issued a presidential pardon to all who had been convicted under the Sedition Act, and ordered any of those convicted under the act who were still in prison to be released. In Jefferson's Inaugural Address, he said,

Every difference of opinion is not a difference of Principle. We are all Republicans—we are all Federalists. If there be any among us who would wish to dissolve this Union or to change its republican form, let them stand undisturbed as monuments of the safety with which error of opinion may be tolerated where reason is left free to combat it.

The major sources for this chapter were:

The Alien and Sedition Acts: Defining American freedom. (n.d.) Los Angeles, CA: Constitutional Rights Foundation. Available at http://www.crf-usa.org/america-responds-to-terrorism/the-alien-and-sedition-acts.html

Evans, E. J. (1990). *Freedom of the press.* Minneapolis, MN: Lerner Publications Company.

Pasley, J. L. (2011). Thomas Greenleaf: Printers and the struggle for democratic politics and freedom of the press. In A. F. Young, G. B. Nash, & R. Raphael (Eds.), *Revolutionary founders, rebels, radicals, and reformers in the making of a nation* (pp. 668–704). New York, NY: Alfred A. Knopf.

Young, A. F. *The democratic republicans of New York: The origins, 1763–1797.* Chapel Hill, NC: University of North Carolina Press.

LEARNING ACTIVITIES FOR "CHILLING EFFECT"

Facts of the Case

1. What was the impact of Johannes Gutenberg's invention?
2. What is seditious libel?
3. What is meant by the term *chilling effect*?
4. What is meant by the term *bad tendency*?
5. What new trend in journalism was brought about by publishers such as Thomas Greenleaf?
6. What were the Alien and Sedition Acts?
7. Why did President Adams say that foreign influence must be "exterminated"?

Historical Understanding

1. Why were publishers, more than authors, charged with seditious libel?
2. How did the Federalist Party and the Republican Party differ on the meaning of the First Amendment's protection of freedom of the press?
3. What precedent was set by the case of John Peter Zenger?
4. How did Thomas Greenleaf and George Washington differ in their views of political parties?
5. How did the Federalist Party and Republican Party differ in their views on the role of the federal government?

Expressing Your Reasoning

Should the Greenleafs have been free to publish whatever they wanted about government officials? Why or why not?

Key Concepts from History

What do the following have in common?

1. *Near v. Minnesota* (1931): The U.S. Supreme Court struck down the Minnesota Gag Law of 1925. That law permitted state courts to issue orders that prevented publication of stories accusing public officials of criminal activity. The court held that a law that permitted intervention before publication violated the protection of freedom of the press guaranteed by the First Amendment to the Constitution. The court did indicate in its decision that such prepublication censorship might be justified in certain cases, such as those involving national security or control of obscenity.

2. In the case of *New York Times Company v. United States* (1971), the Supreme Court denied an injunction (a judicial order that restrains an action) sought by the administration of President Richard Nixon. The injunction would have prevented *The New York Times* and the *Washington Post* from continuing to publish a top secret document called the Pentagon Papers. Both papers began publishing a series of articles from the document in June 1971. The document, produced by the U.S. Department of Defense, was a history of the ongoing Vietnam War. The government argued that the document contained materials that would have a harmful effect on national security. Within 2 weeks of the stories first being published, the Supreme Court heard the case and denied the injunction. The high court declined to invoke the national security exception to pre-publication censorship that had been suggested in the *Near v. Minnesota* case.

3. *Nebraska Press Association v. Stuart* (1976): The U.S. Supreme Court overturned an order by a Nebraska judge that sought to restrict the parties in a criminal case from publicly discussing the case during the trial. The order not to discuss the case, known as a gag order, applied to reporting of the trial by the press. The court suggested there were other means of securing a fair trial without the issuance of a gag order.

Historical Inquiry

The Sedition Act expired during the first term of President Thomas Jefferson without the Supreme Court having ruled on whether the act was constitutional. Are newspapers now free of the threat of libel lawsuits if they write stories about public officials, and others in the public eye, even if the published information proves to be false?

Using online and other sources, test the hypothesis that newspapers are free of libel when publishing stories criticizing public officials, or those in the public eye, even if the published information proves to be false. Compose a short essay in which you accept or reject the hypothesis. Use evidence to support your decision. To begin your investigation, the following search terms will be helpful:

- *New York Times v. Sullivan* (1964)
- *Carol Burnett v. National Enquirer* (1981)
- Actual malice
- Freedom of the press
- Political defamation
- Public figures and libel
- Donald Trump and libel suits

CHAPTER 10

Back to Africa

The American Colonization Society and Daniel Coker's Mission to Settle West Africa

Artistic portrait of Daniel Coker, a Founder of the African Methodist Episcopal church. First African American Missionary to Sierra Leone. 1845, Artist unknown

Courtesy of the Library of Congress.

On February 6, 1820, the ship *Elizabeth* set sail from New York for West Africa. Daniel Coker, 85 other Black Americans, and three White agents from the American Colonization Society (ACS) were on board. The ACS was a group of unlikely allies: slave owners and abolitionists. They thought the relocation of free Blacks to Africa was the best solution for dealing with free Black people in the United States.

The U.S. government contributed $31,000 (nearly $650,000 in today's currency) toward the cost of the voyage and the settlement efforts. The Black emigrants on the *Elizabeth* were men, women, and children. Among them were skilled workers such as mechanics and nurses. The passengers also included a few White workers.

The Black emigrants planned to settle in Liberia in West Africa. The journey was reminiscent of the *Mayflower* voyage 200 years previously, when English Pilgrims sailed to the New World to establish a religious community. However, there was a key difference. The Black emigrants sought political and social freedom, not religious freedom.

Resettlement of free Blacks (former Africans and their descendants) in Africa was not a new idea in 1820. In 1787, Thomas Jefferson expressed interest in the idea. Nor was the idea a uniquely American one. In 1783, when it seemed clear the Americans would defeat the British, the British Army evacuated more than 2,000 Black Loyalists from their former colonies. These were inhabitants of British America of African descent who had fought for the British in the Revolutionary War. In exchange for their support of the British, the Black Loyalists were sent to the West Indies, England, Germany, Belgium, Quebec, or Nova Scotia.

In 1787, the British-owned Sierra Leone Company, supported by the British Crown, funded a settlement of 400 English Black Loyalists in Sierra Leone in West Africa. The settlement, called the Province of Freedom, struggled to survive politically and economically. When the Sierra Leone Company collapsed, another group, the African Institution, took over its mission and sponsored the migration of formerly enslaved people to Sierra Leone. In 1808, Sierra Leone was established as a British colony, leading to increased migration of free Blacks to Africa.

At this time, more than 40 years before President Lincoln signed the Emancipation Proclamation that gave enslaved people in the United States their legal freedom, the American people were sharply divided in their opinions on slavery and enslaved people. Although slavery was illegal in many states at the time of the *Elizabeth*'s voyage, and in several states, free Black males who owned property could vote, even many abolitionists thought Black people were inferior to White people. Many Americans were deeply worried about the problem of free Blacks in the United States.

When the Constitution was drafted, the country had about half a million enslaved people, most of whom lived in the South. The drafters of the Constitution disagreed on how to reconcile the country's commitment to liberty and human equality with the South's insistence on preserving the institution of slavery. As a result, the drafters made various compromises in the U.S. Constitution, which addresses slavery three times (although the words *slavery* and *slave* are not used).

After the ratification of the Constitution in 1788, the abolitionists made some political progress on the issue of slavery. On March 22, 1794, Congress passed the Slave Trade Act of 1794, which outlawed the production or preparation of any ship or vessel "for the purpose of carrying on any trade or traffic in slaves." However, despite some ship seizures and some fines, the slave trade continued between the United States and Africa. Between 1800 and 1808, for example, Georgia and South Carolina imported more than 100,000 enslaved people.

As the 1808 deadline approached, the U.S. Congress realized it had to deal with Article 1, Section 9, Clause 1 that allowed the states to import slaves only until 1808. The Act of 1807 stated that newly enslaved people could not be imported into the United States. On January 1, 1808, President Thomas Jefferson stated:

> I congratulate you, fellow-citizens, on the approach of the period at which you may interpose your authority constitutionally, to withdraw the citizens of the United States from all further participation in those violations of human rights which have been so long continued on the unoffending inhabitants of Africa, and which the morality, the reputation, and the best interests of our country, have long been eager to proscribe.

Despite this political progress toward limiting slavery, illegal importation of slaves continued in the United States, and slavery was still legal in the southern states. In the northern states, although slavery was mostly illegal, the question of how free Blacks and Whites could live together was not resolved. Many Americans, including Jefferson, believed that Whites would continue to be prejudiced toward Black people and that Blacks would be forever bitter and resentful toward Whites for enslavement and other mistreatment. Furthermore, many people, again including Jefferson and some free Blacks, were drawn to the idea of relocating free Blacks to Africa. Jefferson viewed relocation of Blacks not as expulsion, but as liberating, analogous to the British coming to America to escape oppression. He thought Blacks could start a new country for themselves in Africa.

Captain Paul Cuffee, an African American Quaker, abolitionist, and successful ship builder, was one of these people who supported the colonization of free Blacks in Sierra Leone. In 1807, he collaborated with John Kizell, a first generation African American from the Sherba people of Sierra Leone and a Black Loyalist.

Cuffee, Kizell, and others drafted a petition for the African Institution, explaining the need for the colonists to work in the areas of agriculture, commerce, and whaling, to survive in the African colony. The Institution, which agreed with this analysis, supported Cuffee and Kizell's efforts to found the Friendly Society of Sierra Leone as a mutual-aid merchant group based on emigration and trade. The mission of the group was to benefit both the Indigenous population and the newly arrived colonists. Cuffee planned to make annual voyages that would transport free Blacks from the United States to Africa and return with valuable African raw materials.

On December 10, 1815, Cuffee transported a group of 38 free Blacks to Sierra Leone on his ship at his own cost. These were the first African Americans to voluntarily relocate to Africa from the United States. A number of religious leaders, including Robert Finley, a Presbyterian minister from New Jersey, praised Cuffee's efforts. Finley thought the relocation of Blacks from the United States to Africa would improve their social and political condition, which could never be accomplished if they lived alongside Whites.

The voyage and settlement efforts, however, were more costly than Cuffee had anticipated—for example, the cargo sold at undervalued prices. Without financial support from either private donors or the U.S. Congress, his dream of mass emigration to Sierra Leone (as well as to Haiti) could not be realized. He did not live to see more successful colonization efforts in West Africa.

On December 28, 1816, Finley founded the American Colonization Society, also known as the Society for the Colonization of Free People of Color of America. Other founding members of this group were John Randolph, a slave owner and U.S. Representative from Virginia, and Henry Clay, a slave owner and U.S. Representative from Kentucky, and a future speaker of the House, U.S. senator, nominee for president, and U.S. secretary of state. The ACS formed a committee that prepared a request asking Congress for support of a colony for free Blacks. On February 11, 1817, Congress issued a joint resolution, "Report on Colonizing the Free People of Colour of the United States," that supported colonization. However, Congress, not wishing to define the United States as a colonizer, provided little other support.

Although the abolitionists and slave owners in the ACS had the same goal—the resettlement of free Blacks in Africa—their reasons differed. The slave owners thought the relocation of free Blacks to Africa would weaken, if not suppress, rebellion by enslaved people in the United States. The thought was that free Blacks, who were described as a "perpetual excitement" to enslaved people, posed a threat to slave societies in the South. The abolitionists thought that the free Blacks would have better lives in Africa.

Yet the ACS took no official position on emancipation or abolition in the United States. The reason may have been that the ACS comprised two groups that held differing views on emancipation. One group was evangelicals and Quakers who supported abolition of slavery and thought that free Blacks would have better opportunities for freedom in Africa than in the United States. The other group was slaveholders who believed that repatriation was a means of removing free Blacks from society and avoiding slave rebellions.

What was the response among free Blacks in the United States to the ACS and its efforts to colonize West Africa with free Blacks? Responses varied. Some African Americans agreed that emigrating from the United States to Africa gave free Blacks the opportunity for a better life. Others strongly opposed the colonization scheme.

In January 1817, James Forten, an African American abolitionist and successful Philadelphia businessman, along with Bishop Richard Allen of the African Methodist Episcopal (AME) Church and others, organized a meeting in Philadelphia to discuss the colonization efforts. The meeting drew 3,000 attendees. Forten had supported Cuffee's 1815 voyage to West Africa, but his views on colonization changed when he heard the anticolonization objections.

When Forten called for a vote, no one in the 3,000-person meeting voted in favor of colonization. The "nays" were deafening. The naysayers said the United States was a country their people had fought and died for. They owed it to the enslaved people to remain on American soil and fight for their legal rights. Furthermore, they identified too many problems in Liberia: disease, resistance by Indigenous peoples, and the constant threat of illegal slave traders.

In 1818, Samuel John Mills, a missionary and a founding member of the ACS, and Ebenezer Burgess, a professor of mathematics at Burlington University, traveled to the West Coast of Africa to survey possible sites for colonies. The ACS and a wealthy ship builder provided funds for the trip. They explored Sierra Leone and Sherbro Island, toured schools and churches, and assessed the quality of the land. They concluded that the land was arable and that the Indigenous population would welcome the colonists.

Mills died from fever on the return trip from Africa, but Burgess survived and later reported findings to the ACS and the U.S. Congress. Burgess recommended colonization in this region of Africa for the following reasons: the agricultural conditions were favorable and mutual trade would benefit both the United States and Africa.

The Act of 1819 gave President James Monroe, who supported colonization, the authority to seize slave ships and vessels that transported "any negro, mulatto, or person of color" and to deliver such persons into local government authority "residing upon the coast of Africa." The U.S. Congress also appropriated $100,000 to help with relocating enslaved people to Africa.

In 1820, the ACS sponsored the trip that was led by Daniel Coker. Coker was born enslaved in 1780 as Isaac Wright, the son of Susan Coker, a White indentured servant, and Edward Wright, an enslaved person. Coker was raised with his White half-siblings and allowed to attend school with them. While in school, he escaped from slavery in Maryland and fled to New York, where he changed his name to Daniel Coker and was ordained as a Methodist minister.

Coker secretly returned to Maryland where, with the help of friends, he purchased his freedom—a rare option known as self-purchase—and began speaking publicly against the institution of slavery. He encouraged African American Methodists to withdraw from the White-dominated church and to form their own church. When these efforts were unsuccessful, he formed the African Bethel Church, later named the Bethel AME Church in Baltimore. However, there were problems when Coker criticized the preaching style of his colleague, Bishop Allen. As a result, Coker was dismissed from the AME Church. He was readmitted in 1819, but was not permitted to preach.

Coker did not at first support the ACS's colonization plans. Yet, given his experience with the AME Church and his own financial difficulties, he apparently saw the ACS's invitation to lead the Black emigrants to Africa as a new opportunity. Based on his comments in his ship's diary, it is clear the missionary aspect of the venture also appealed to him. On the voyage he founded the first foreign branch of the AME Church. On March 17, 1820, more than 40 days after leaving

New York, Coker and the other passengers on the ship *Elizabeth* anchored at Sherbro Island off the coast of Sierra Leone.

Immediately, problems arose. There was no clean water and no fresh food. Worse, a number of the colonists and all three ACS agents died from disease and fever. The ACS relocated the colonists, now called Americo-Liberians, to Providence Island at Cape Mesurado in present-day Liberia. Coker, who had been asked to take charge of the venture, remained in Sierra Leone.

However, the new location presented many difficulties as well. Besides the same environmental challenges, social and political conflicts, including raids by the Kru and Grevo people, erupted. The Americo-Liberians, who were better educated and thought they were superior to the Indigenous population, seized political leadership. Political control even meant excluding the Indigenous population from birthright citizenship until 1904. However, the Americo-Liberians established missions and schools for the local peoples.

A number of motives inspired the colonization of West Africa by free Blacks from the United States. Some religious leaders saw colonization as an opportunity to introduce Christianity to West Africa. Leaders such as Finley thought that African Americans could "civilize" Africa. He explained the benefits of the movement: "We should be cleared of them and Africa would receive partially civilized and Christianized settlers, and the Negroes could enjoy a better situation."

Other supporters of colonization in West Africa saw opportunities for trade that could be economically profitable for the United States. Although the United States was never remotely an African colonizer on the scale of, for example, Belgium, Portugal, France, and Germany, Americans recognized that a settlement in West Africa with English-speaking American colonists would facilitate access to the African continent's valuable raw resources.

Most Black Americans eventually opposed the colonization scheme. Frederick Douglass, the African American social reformer, writer, and abolitionist, was a strong opponent. He said no state or national funds should be appropriated to support such schemes.

In 1850, there were 434,495 free Blacks in the United States. Only a small fraction emigrated to Africa—around 15,000 by 1867. Besides the environmental challenges and both internal and external conflicts, the Americo-Liberians had received no support from the U.S. government beyond the $100,000 appropriated by Congress. By the 1830s, even support from the ACS declined. However, the ACS's work led to the founding of Liberia, Africa's first and oldest republic.

Liberia, which is Latin for "land of the free," became an independent country in 1847. It is the only African republic to have self-proclaimed independence without revolt. Its capital, Monrovia, is named for President James Monroe. The Liberian flag, with its single star and red and white stripes, is modeled after the U.S. flag. Liberia today has a representative democracy patterned on the democratic institutions of the United States.

Other African American leaders have, from time to time, promoted Black emigration. Perhaps the best known is Jamaican-born Marcus Garvey, who founded the Universal Negro Improvement Association in 1914 with a "Back to Africa" goal. He thought that only in Africa would Blacks achieve self-emancipation.

What happened to Daniel Coker? In 1821, his wife and two children joined him in settling in Hastings, Sierra Leone. Coker wrote in his diary, at sea, on February 24, 1820: "May He that was with Moses in the wilderness, be with us; then all will be well." For Coker's descendants, who still live and thrive in Freetown, Sierra Leone, his prophecy seems fulfilled.

The major sources for this chapter were:

Brooks, Jr., G. E. (1974). The Providence African Society's Sierra Leone emigration scheme, 1794–1795: Prologue to the African Colonization Movement. *The International Journal of African Historical Studies, 7*(2), 183–202.

Burin, E. (2005). *Slavery and the peculiar solution: A history of the American Colonization Society.* Gainesville, FL: University Press of Florida.

Ciment, J. (2013). *Another America: The story of Liberia and the former slaves who ruled it.* New York, NY: Hill and Wang.

Mehlinger, L. R. (1916). The attitude of the free Negro toward African colonization. *Journal of Negro History, 1*(3), 276–301.

Nash, G. B. (2006). *The forgotten fifth: African Americans in the revolutionary era.* Cambridge, MA: Harvard University Press.

Walker, G. S. (2014). *A conspiracy to colonize 19th century United States free Blacks in Africa by the American Colonization Society.* Bloomington, IN: Trafford Publishing.

LEARNING ACTIVITIES FOR "BACK TO AFRICA"

Facts of the Case

1. How did the U.S. Constitution address slavery?
2. What problems did the colonists face in West Africa?
3. Why did Daniel Coker change his mind about the colonization of Africa?
4. How did Liberia differ from other African countries regarding how it achieved its independence?

Historical Understanding

1. Why did some slave owners and, initially, some abolitionists support the American Colonization Society (ACS)?
2. Why did most free Blacks oppose the mission of the ACS?
3. Explain whether the ACS was successful in its mission to colonize Africa with free Blacks.

Expressing Your Reasoning

Should Daniel Coker have led a group of emigrants to settle in Africa in 1820? Why or why not?

Key Concepts from History

What do the following have in common?

1. Martin Delaney was a 19th-century African American abolitionist, physician, journalist, and writer. He was among the first Black people accepted to Harvard Medical School. Soon after he was admitted, he and the other two Black classmates were dismissed, despite objections from other students and staff. He was furious. In 1859, he traveled to Liberia to explore the possibility of a new Black nation there, even signing an agreement with chiefs in the Abeokuta region that would allow settlers to live on "unused land" in exchange for working for the good of the community. These plans never materialized, however, and his dreams of a Black nation were not realized.

2. Alexander Crummell was a 19th-century African American Episcopal priest. He developed the concept of pan-Africanism. Crummell believed that African peoples (from the Americas, West Indies, and Africa) should unify. In 1853, he moved to Liberia where he took a faculty position at Liberia College in Monrovia and where he worked to convert native Africans to Christianity. His attempts to persuade other Black Americans to move to Liberia were not successful, given that most Black Americans were more interested in achieving equality at home than in converting Africans to Christianity. He was an important influence on Marcus Garvey and W. E. B. DuBois, 20th-century African American leaders.

3. Marcus Garvey was an early 20th-century political leader, journalist, and entrepreneur from Jamaica. In 1919, he founded the Negro Improvement Association and African Communities League to promote the general uplift of people of African ancestry. He advanced an enormously popular and influential vision, known as Garveyism—the belief in the economic, social, and political empowerment of persons of African ancestry across the globe. He believed Black people should have a permanent homeland in Africa. In 1920, he launched the Liberia program, which was aimed at building colleges and industries in Liberia, but his efforts were stymied because of European opposition. His ideas influenced the Rastafarian Back to Africa movement in Jamaica.

Historical Inquiry

Did the founding of Liberia by the ACS lead to different political and social circumstances for Liberia compared to other African countries?

Using online and other sources, test the hypothesis that the founding of Liberia by the ACS led to different political and social circumstances for Liberia compared to other African countries. Compose a short essay in which you accept or reject the hypothesis. Use evidence to support your decision. To begin your investigation, the following search terms will be helpful:

- Liberia
- U.S.–Liberia relations
- William V. S. Tubman
- Charles Taylor
- Helene Cooper

CHAPTER 11

Gerry's Salamander

Governor Elbridge Gerry's 1812 Redistricting of Massachusetts

"The Gerry-Mander" by Elkanah Tisdale

Originally published in the *Boston Gazette*, 1812.

On February 11, 1812, Massachusetts Governor Elbridge Gerry signed a bill into law that redrew the Massachusetts state senate electoral districts. This law, which changed the boundaries of the state's senate electoral districts, was intended to benefit Gerry's political party, the Democratic-Republican Party, in that year's election. (The Democratic-Republican Party became known as the Republican Party, but not the same Republican Party that was founded in 1856.)

After the election of 1812, redistricting became known as *gerrymandering*, when boundaries are drawn to gain advantage for a political party or other group. Gerry's Republican Party retained control of the state Senate after the 1812 election. However, the Federalists won control of the state House of Representatives, and Governor Gerry lost his office to his Federalist opponent.

According to legend, after Governor Gerry signed the redistricting bill, the editor of the *Boston Gazette,* Benjamin Russell, who was a Federalist, hung a map of the redrawn districts in his office. When Gilbert Stuart, the famous portrait painter of the era, visited Russell's office, he observed that the redrawn Essex South District had the shape of a lizard-like amphibian, the salamander. After drawing a dragon's head, wing, and claws on the district, Stuart exclaimed: "That will do for a salamander!" Russell responded: "Better say a Gerry-mander!" (The word *gerrymander* as it is written today, without the hyphen, is a portmanteau word, a blend of two words or parts of words. Thus, *gerrymander* blends Governor Gerry's last name and the second part of *salamander.*)

Whether the origin story is true or a legend, on March 26, 1812, the *Boston Gazette* printed a cartoon-map of the redrawn districts (shown above) titled "The Gerry-Mander." Elkanah Tisdale, a well-known early 19th-century painter, engraver, and cartoonist, had drawn the cartoon-map with the description: "A new species of monster, which appeared in Essex South District in January last." Some 80 newspapers in the country reprinted the cartoon with its "Gerry-Mander" title and the description.

Redistricting of the U.S. congressional districts (not the states' legislative districts) is mandated by the U.S. Constitution to occur every 10 years, following the most recent census of the U.S. population. According to the U.S. Constitution, every representative in the U.S. House of Representatives should represent an equal number of citizens. The decennial census in the United States, which counts the citizens, is used to apportion the number of U.S. House of Representative seats to each state.

Because the Constitution is silent on the redistricting process, the states may conduct the process as they choose. Districting guidelines have evolved over time: *compactness* (a district's geographical shape and how the interior is dispersed within its boundaries); *contiguity* (all parts of a district are physically connected); and *respect for political subdivisions* (minimizing the crossing of city, county, town, and other municipal boundaries). When district boundaries require change, however, the opportunity to draw them for political gain arises. Gerrymandering can violate the guidelines of compactness, contiguity, and respect for political subdivisions.

At the present time, in over half of the states, state legislatures control the redistricting process (for state legislative districts as well as congressional districts). The incumbent majority party has the most influence on how the district boundaries are drawn. Twenty-one states use bipartisan or nonpartisan commissions to oversee the process, but it is not clear how independent such commissions are when governors and majority parties appoint the commission members.

Gerrymandering did not originate with Governor Gerry. It is a practice that was a long tradition in American politics, dating from the Colonial Era. In 1788, after Virginia ratified the U.S. Constitution and became the tenth state subject to the laws of the central government, the former governor of Virginia, Patrick Henry, persuaded the Virginia state legislature to redraw the state's fifth congressional district in an attempt to defeat James Madison, Henry's political rival. However, Madison defeated James Monroe in the congressional race. Historians have observed that this was the first case of redistricting in the United States that was intended to achieve political gain, as well as the only congressional race in which two future presidents ran for office against each other.

Elbridge Thomas Gerry was born on July 17, 1744, in Marblehead, Massachusetts. His father was a wealthy merchant, and his mother was the daughter of a successful Boston merchant. As a child Gerry had private tutors. He enrolled at Harvard College at age 14. After his college studies, he joined his father's business and soon became one of the wealthiest merchants in Massachusetts.

Gerry was generally regarded as a man of high moral character and sound judgment, as well as a tireless advocate for colonists' rights. However, some people found Gerry difficult because of his independent streak and strongly held opinions. One of Gerry's colleagues, referring to their work at the Constitutional Convention, said Gerry "objected to everything he did not propose."

In 1772, Gerry was elected to the General Court of the Province of Massachusetts Bay. Two years later, he was elected to the First Continental Congress and then to the Second Continental Congress. He was a delegate to the Constitutional Convention in 1787 in Philadelphia. He signed both the Declaration of Independence and the Articles of Confederation. He refused, however, to vote for the U.S. Constitution in 1787.

Gerry was concerned about the well-being of U.S. citizens under a federal government with new and expanded powers. He thought a central government should be active and possess authority but should also protect the individual rights of its citizens. This was a strongly expressed opinion that was not without political risk.

As a delegate to the 1787 Constitutional Convention, Gerry had several objections to the proposed U.S. Constitution and advocated for passage of various amendments. For example, he supported indirect elections for both the U.S. Senate and the U.S. House of Representatives. In a system of indirect elections (such as the election of the U.S. president and vice president), citizens elect people (the Electoral College) who choose among the candidates, rather than directly electing the officeholders. In its final form, the U.S. Constitution adopted indirect elections only for the U.S. Senate (later changed to direct elections by the Seventeenth Amendment).

In the ratification process for the U.S. Constitution, two opposing groups emerged. Supporters of the Constitution called themselves Federalists and favored a centralized, national government; opponents of the Constitution called themselves Anti-Federalists and favored states' rights and local government. When the ratification process ended after Rhode Island (the 13th and final state) ratified the Constitution, the two groups formed political parties: the Federalists and the Democratic-Republicans (called Republicans). At this time Gerry belonged to neither party.

As an elected representative to the U.S. House of Representatives, Gerry worked to draft and pass the Bill of Rights (the first 10 amendments to the U.S. Constitution), which was ratified in 1791. Like the Constitution, the Bill of Rights inspired debates and disagreements. Gerry was again vocal in these discussions, but some of his proposals were not adopted.

Somewhat disillusioned with politics, Gerry withdrew from political life in 1792. He declined to run for re-election to the U.S. House of Representatives and returned to Massachusetts to work on his farm and to care for his nine children and his wife, who was often ill. However, it was not long before he returned to political life. Encouraged by President John Adams, Gerry agreed to be a representative for Massachusetts in the 1796 Electoral College.

In 1797, President Adams appointed Gerry to the U.S. diplomatic commission to France to participate in negotiations over France's seizure of U.S. ships in the Atlantic Ocean. These negotiations resulted in the infamous XYZ Affair. (The Americans were unable to meet formally with the foreign minister and instead had to meet with three intermediaries, who later became known as X, Y, and Z). The affair led to an undeclared war called the Quasi-War. Although Gerry was accused of siding with the French in the affair, he was later vindicated. By that time, however, his reputation had suffered owing to hostile press reports.

After the Federalists accused Gerry of contributing to the breakdown in these negotiations, he reluctantly became a member of the Republican Party. Following several unsuccessful runs for governor of Massachusetts against Federalist opponents, Gerry was elected governor in 1810. Massachusetts Federalists and Republicans opposed one another on most issues. Because he favored nonpartisan politics, Gerry continued to oppose the idea of political parties. At his first inaugural address as governor, he supported reconciliation of the two political parties and called on the United States to form a strong bond against "two gigantic combatants" (Britain and France). His first term as governor was relatively calm owing to his appointment of moderate members to his administration and to a decrease in conflicts between the Republicans and the Federalists.

Gerry's second term as governor was much stormier. He suspected the Federalists were trying to restore the British monarchy in the former colonies. Gerry also feared a group of Federalists might try to start a civil war in order to separate New England from the national government. To head off such a secessionist movement, Gerry replaced many appointed Federalist officeholders with Republicans.

By this point the Republicans had control of both houses of the Massachusetts legislature. To ensure continuance of their control, in February 1812, in advance of the 1812 elections, Governor Gerry signed into law a bill that the Republicans in the Massachusetts House of Representatives had passed. The bill divided Massachusetts into state senate districts along highly partisan lines. Previously, the county lines established the district boundaries. The redistricting favored the Republican Party because the Federalist Party supporters were concentrated in only a few districts, whereas the Republican supporters were spread among many districts. (The law applied to elections of Massachusetts state senators and not to congressional elections.)

As expected, the Federalists angrily objected to the redistricting bill for both pragmatic and principled reasons. They argued that the redistricting was a scheme to help the Republicans maintain control of the Massachusetts Senate. The Federalists also argued that the redistricting would undermine governmental institutions by allowing a minority party to govern and thereby obstruct the will of the people. The Federalists believed the new districts were intentionally arranged to give a party with fewer members (Republicans) control of the Senate by a large majority.

Members of the Republican Party strongly supported the redistricting bill. Using tit-for-tat reasoning, they claimed the Federalists had unfairly redistricted Massachusetts in both 1784 and 1794. According to the Republicans, the Federalists had redistricted in their favor before and, given the opportunity, would do it again.

After Governor Gerry signed the 1812 redistricting bill, the state senate district boundaries were indeed redrawn. Twenty-nine Republicans and 11 Federalists were then elected to the Massachusetts state senate in the 1812 election, even though the Federalists had 1,602 more votes statewide than the Republicans (51,766 versus 50,164). However, in the same election Governor Gerry lost his bid for re-election to Caleb Strong (a Federalist) by 1,370 votes (52,696 versus 51,326). In addition, the Republicans lost the Massachusetts House of Representatives to the Federalists.

The 1812 election provided clear evidence that there were more Federalist than Republican voters in Massachusetts. It was also clear that the "Gerrymander" explained the Republicans' success in the state senate race.

Despite Gerry's defeat and the harsh criticism directed at him for signing the redistricting law, his political career was not over. President Madison selected him as his vice-presidential running mate in the 1812 election. The general expectation (then as now) is that a vice-presidential candidate will, at the very least, carry his or her state. Although Madison and Gerry were easily elected, only two of the 22 electors from Massachusetts voted for their ticket. Gerry served briefly as vice president until his death in 1814.

On June 16, 1813, the Federalists, who had regained control of the Massachusetts Senate, repealed the 1812 redistricting law. That, however, was not the end of gerrymandering. In the United States the practice has been used again and again. Many other democracies in the world also use some form of gerrymandering.

There are four general gerrymandering practices:

Cracking is the process in which voters of a similar type or with similar interests (typically based on race or economic status) are spread across many districts to prevent them from forming a sufficiently large voting bloc.

Packing is the process in which voters of a similar type or with similar interests are concentrated in a single electoral district to minimize their influence in other districts.

Hijacking is the process in which two districts are redrawn so as to force two incumbent officeholders of the same political party to run against each other in the redrawn district. The intention of this strategy is that one incumbent officeholder will lose, creating the possibility that the opposing political party can win in the other district.

Kidnapping is the process in which areas where an incumbent officeholder has significant support are moved to another district, making future wins less likely.

These gerrymandering practices may create some very oddly shaped districts, some of which seem to resemble, for example, frying pans, dumbbells, turkey feet, or, as we have seen, salamanders!

Not all redistricting practices are designed for partisan gain. For example, Arizona used affirmative gerrymandering to better represent the interests of Native Americans by separating the single district that included both the Hopi and Navajo nations. California used affirmative gerrymandering to create a coastal district separate from inland districts. More often, affirmative gerrymandering is intended to correct historic, antidemocratic injustices created by previous racial gerrymandering in which the intent was to disenfranchise African Americans by diluting their power through redistricting.

Despite the many objections to gerrymandering, the practice continues. Both major political parties in the United States have engaged in the practice. After the U.S. Census in 2010, many legislative districts were again redrawn. In this process, some legislatures employed consultants who, using sophisticated computer software, offered advice on how to redraw the districts to have maximum effect on elections. Typically, the goal was to ensure the re-election of incumbents who represent powerful electoral groups. One such consultant, David Winston, commented on the redistricting after the 1990 U.S. Census: "When I, as a mapmaker, have more of an impact on an election than the voters, the system is out of whack."

When these redistricting practices continue over time, they often make legislative districts politically noncompetitive. These districts so heavily favor one party that it is difficult to unseat incumbents. When incumbents (at both the state and federal levels) do not feel politically vulnerable, they can often become more extreme in their legislative actions because they have little fear of losing the next election. Recently, opponents of gerrymandering have been successful in the courts. In cases from Texas, North Carolina, and Wisconsin, federal courts have struck down redistricting that was influenced by politics or intentional discrimination. The 2017–2018 Supreme Court term includes two cases related to legislative redistricting: one from Wisconsin and the other from Maryland. In these cases, the justices will rule on whether partisan gerrymandering is constitutional.

Elbridge Gerry, who supported the rights and duties of democratic citizenship, once stated: "It is the duty of every man, though he may have but one day to live, to devote that day to the good of his country." However, history rarely remembers Gerry as this principled politician. Instead, he takes his place in history as the man who gave his name to the practice of partisan gerrymandering.

The major sources for this chapter were:

Azavea. (2009). Redistricting the nation. Available at http://www.redistrictingthenation.com

Barasch, E. (September 19, 2012). The twisted history of gerrymandering in American politics. *The Atlantic.* Available at https://www.theatlantic.com/politics/archive/2012/09/the-twisted-history-of-gerrymandering-in-american-politics/262369/

Barnes, R. (February 4, 2018). Opponents of gerrymandering keep winning, but it might not affect 2018. *The Washington Post.* Available at https://www.washingtonpost.com/politics/courts_law/opponents-of-gerrymandering-keep-winning-but-it-might-not-affect-2018/2018/02/04/83e5785c-078f-11e8-b48c-b07fea957bd5_story.html?utm_term=.6bf5d0783de1

Billias, G. A. (1976). *Elbridge Gerry: Founding father and Republican statesman.* New York, NY: McGraw-Hill.

Gerry, E. (October 18, 1787). Elbridge Gerry's objections (Letter to Massachusetts legislature). Available at http://teachingamericanhistory.org/library/document/elbridge-gerrys-objections-letter-to-massachusetts-legislature/

Griffith, E. C. (1907). *The rise and development of the gerrymander.* Chicago, IL: Scott, Foresman and Company.

Hatfield, M. O. (1997). Elbridge Gerry. In M. O. Hatfield with the Senate Historical Office (Eds.), *Vice presidents of the United States, 1789–1993* (pp. 63–68). Washington, D.C.: U.S. Government Printing Office, 1997. Available at http://www.senate.gov/artandhistory/history/resources/pdf/elbridge_gerry.pdf

Martis, K. C. (2008). The original gerrymander. *Political Geography, 27*(8), 833–839.

Williams, L. (August 16, 2013). 5 terrible acts of voter discrimination the Voting Rights Act prevented—but won't anymore. *Mother Jones.* Available at http://www.motherjones.com/mojo/2013/08/voting-rights-act-anniversary-discrimination-laws

LEARNING ACTIVITIES FOR "GERRY'S SALAMANDER"

Facts of the Case

1. How does the U.S. Constitution address political representation for the legislative branch?

2. Which political offices did Elbridge Gerry hold in his career?
3. Why did Gerry refuse to vote for the U.S. Constitution?
4. What were the results of the 1812 election in Massachusetts?

Historical Understanding

1. Why have commissions and legislatures used the practice of gerrymandering?
2. What were Gerry's core political beliefs about the role of government?
3. How did the Federalists' political views differ from those of the Republicans?

Expressing Your Reasoning

Should Massachusetts Governor Elbridge Gerry have signed the 1812 redistricting bill that redrew the Massachusetts Senate districts to the advantage of his Republican Party? Why or why not?

Key Concepts from History

What do the following have in common?

1. Until the enactment of the Voting Rights Act of 1965, many states had laws that required would-be voters to take a reading test, interpret a passage from the Constitution, or bring a registered voter with them to vouch for their "good character" in order to vote. These laws were designed to disenfranchise African Americans.
2. In 2001, the board of aldermen in the town of Kilmichael, Mississippi, all of whom were White, canceled town elections because of the large number of Black candidates on the ballot.
3. In 2014, a series of court rulings struck down new voting restrictions (for example, stricter voter identification laws, cutting back early voting, and new restrictions on voter registration drives) in states. The courts ruled that these restrictions were aimed to restrict minority voters, although supporters of the restrictions have claimed they were meant to prevent voter fraud.

Historical Inquiry

The 1812 redistricting plan under Governor Gerry was not the first case of gerrymandering in the United States. Did Supreme Court rulings on political gerrymandering end the practice's influence on the American political system?

Using online and other sources, test the hypothesis that Supreme Court rulings on political gerrymandering ended the practice's influence on the American political system. Compose a short essay in which you accept or reject the hypothesis. Use evidence to support your decision. To begin your investigation, the following search terms will be helpful:

- Political gerrymandering
- Affirmative gerrymandering
- Redistricting
- *Davis v. Bandemer* (U.S. Supreme Court case)
- *Vieth. v. Jubelirer* (U.S. Supreme Court case)

CHAPTER 12

A Bowl with One Spoon

Chief Tecumseh and the War of 1812

Fictionalized Portrait of Chief Tecumseh

Courtesy of the Ohio History Connection.

Tecumseh (born 1768) was one of the most notable Native American leaders in American history. He formed the largest and most powerful confederation (an organization of united groups) of Indian tribes in the history of North America. In Shawnee, his name means "Shooting Star" or "Panther Across the Sky." Friends and foes alike described him as noble, honorable, intelligent, charismatic, handsome, and extremely well spoken. But for his death at a young age, he might have become a leader of a great Indian nation on the North American continent.

Tecumseh's goal was to unite Native people of different tribes into a confederation to defend their land from the rapid westward expansion of settlements by European Americans. He argued that land was held in common by all Native people and should not be divided, sold, or given away by tribal chiefs in treaties. Indian hunting territories were to be shared among Indians. Tecumseh's idea was represented among Native Americans as "a bowl with one spoon."

In 1768, Tecumseh was born as a member of the Shawnee tribe along the Mad River in western Ohio. His father, who may have been either Shawnee or Creek, died in 1774 in a Shawnee battle with the Virginia militia. Tecumseh's mother is believed to have been Shawnee through both her father and mother.

In 1779, along with other Shawnee, his mother migrated to Missouri. Tecumseh and an older sister, who raised him, did not follow their mother to Missouri, but continued to live in what is now Ohio. As an adult, Tecumseh was married twice and had one son each by his two wives. He sent his first wife back to the village she came from, because he thought that she did not take proper care of their infant son. After his second wife died, Tecumseh's sister raised his sons.

The Shawnee were known to be a people on the move, traveling from place to place in search of better locations for hunting, building temporary villages for protection. For the most part, these travels were in what is known as the Old Northwest, principally in what would become the states of Ohio, Indiana, and Kentucky.

The Shawnee's nomadic way of life brought them in contact with many other Indian tribes. Other prominent tribes in the lower Great Lakes region who were also concerned about the White invasion of tribal lands were the Potawatomi, Ojibwa and, farther to the south, the Muscogee Creek, Seminole, Choctaw, Cherokee, and Chickasaw.

The livelihood of Shawnee men came mostly from hunting and trapping. Shawnee women did the farming, cooking, and caring for children. The Shawnee erected dome-shaped temporary homes called wigwams made from tree bark, brush, and animal hides. Over time, treaties and westward expansion by White settlers forced the Shawnee to relocate from their traditional hunting grounds. These new areas were often less productive for hunting and trapping. As a result, the Shawnee became more dependent on European traders for food, clothing, and guns.

The U.S. government made efforts to have Native Americans adopt the American settlers' way of life. That meant farming more, raising animals, and relying less on hunting. Accordingly, Indian men were induced to join the women working the fields to grow crops. American officials believed changing the Indian way of life would enable them to assimilate better into American culture. At the same time, they would rely less on hunting over their tribal lands, which would open up additional land for American settlers.

Some older tribal chiefs considered treaties the best response to relentless expansion by White settlers. In the treaties, Indians traded land for European supplies and ongoing payments of money called annuities. The older chiefs thought these treaties were necessary to prevent the destruction and eventual elimination of their tribes. Younger, more assertive leaders, like Tecumseh, however, wished to challenge American expansion, even if it meant war. There was tension among Indian leaders, and conflict increased between Indians and American settlers.

At the same time (1754–1763), there was war in Europe between Great Britain and France that extended to North America. Both nations had extensive fur-trading interests and settlements in North America. Explorers from both countries never found the gold or silver they had been seeking in North America, or a faster waterway to Asia to obtain silk and spices. Fur trading, however, became a very profitable business. There was high demand for furs in Europe. Native people traded furs for the Europeans' guns, metal cooking utensils, and cloth.

It is estimated that by 1775 the Indians' trade with Europeans resulted in almost every Indian man owning a musket or rifle and every Indian woman owning metal kettles and other cooking utensils. Trade often included whiskey, and alcohol abuse became a problem for many tribes. Drunkenness disrupted family life and relationships among tribes.

Excessive hunting and trapping of animals for fur resulted in the near depletion of some animals in the eastern portion of North America. To secure more animal pelts for their European trading partners, hunters pushed westward into hunting grounds that were being used by other tribes. War between tribes resulted.

Competition and conflict between Great Britain and France intensified. Between 1698 and 1763, France and Great Britain fought four wars for control of North America. Both sides were dependent on military support from Native people, the French more than the British. The British had a population advantage (two million English settlers compared to 60,000 French settlers).

In the mid-18th century, the great European powers were engaged in what is called the Seven Years' War (1756–1763). France, Austria, and Russia were on one side, Great Britain and Prussia on the other. In North America, the war was carried on by the French with their Native allies against the British with theirs, and is known as the French and Indian War. The focus was on the Ohio Valley, which included traditional Shawnee lands.

At first, believing that the British posed a greater threat of settlement on Indian lands, the Shawnee allied with the French. In 1758, however, halfway through the war, the Shawnee changed sides. They signed an agreement with the British that required Great Britain to protect Indian tribal lands from encroachment by settlers. (The agreement was not honored by the British.)

After suffering setbacks early in the war, the British were victorious. In the 1763 Treaty of Paris that concluded the conflict, France was forced to cede the land it had claimed east of the Mississippi to Great Britain. The absence of French control over their mostly rural settlements in the region meant that France could not check the westward expansion of British settlements into tribal lands.

The American Revolutionary War ended 2 decades later, in 1783, with another Treaty of Paris. That treaty provided for United States' sovereignty over all lands east of the Mississippi and south of the Great Lakes, except for Spanish Florida.

Native American tribes were not party to the treaty and did not recognize its legitimacy. Increased American settlement into what had been tribal lands provoked Indian attacks on American settlers. These in turn sparked revenge attacks by American settlers on Native Americans. Further, following the adoption of the U.S. Constitution in 1789, the American government hoped to raise money by selling large tracts of what were formerly tribal lands to American settlers. Land was acquired through treaties made with tribes, who were then moved to new locations farther west. Many Indian people resented these policies. Between 1785 and 1795, battles were fought between the Big Knives (the Americans) and Indians in what is known as the Northwest Indian War.

During this period Tecumseh took part in attacks against White settlers and settlements in Ohio, Kentucky, and Tennessee. It is not certain whether Tecumseh took part in the Battle of Fallen Timbers in Ohio in 1794, the last battle of the Northwest Indian War. General "Mad" Anthony Wayne led a sizeable American force of professional soldiers. The force quickly defeated a much smaller force of Indians from several tribes joined by a British militia.

The defeat at the Battle of Fallen Timbers prompted the British to settle differences remaining from the end of the American Revolutionary War. In 1794, the Jay Treaty between Britain and the United States settled several lingering differences between the two countries.

Among the provisions of the Jay Treaty was the requirement that the British withdraw their military forces from American territory. They had been very slow to withdraw since the end of the Revolutionary War. In exchange, British and French traders were permitted to continue their fur-trading businesses. This withdrawal did not serve Indian interests: Even though the British were a somewhat unreliable ally to the Indians, the presence of British forces was a check against American expansion.

The defeat of the Indians led also to the Treaty of Greenville in 1795 between the United States and several tribes. That treaty redrew boundaries to the disadvantage of Indians. It also provided for annuities and supplies by the United States to tribes that signed the treaty. The result was more Indian dependence on the American government.

Tecumseh was upset by the outcome of the Battle of Fallen Timbers. He became even angrier at the signing of the Treaty of Greenville. As one of many chiefs, he refused to sign it or honor its provisions. Tecumseh was convinced that the only way to stop American expansion was to form a strong and united confederation of Indian tribes that could demand the return of Indian lands and deter further White encroachment. He hoped for support from the Indians' unreliable ally, the British.

The British saw the value of a powerful Indian confederacy as a buffer between American territory and what remained of British territory in North America. At the same time, they did not want to push the Americans into war or move them closer to the French, with whom the English continued to be at war in Europe.

Forming a confederation among Indian tribes was difficult. Tribes had different languages and cultures. Jealousies and competition among tribes was also an obstacle. Many tribes had weak leadership. Some tribes—for example, the Shawnee—had village civil chiefs who clashed with village war chiefs. With tribes spread geographically over hundreds of miles, communication and organization were problematic. In addition, there were some tribes and tribal leaders who came to believe that adjusting to a sedentary farming way of life was better than going to war with an ever more powerful American army.

By 1800, Tecumseh had become a more prominent leader and was leading his own band of warriors. They established their own village on the White River in eastern Indiana. Joining Tecumseh in the new village was his younger brother Lalawethika, who had a reputation for laziness and drunkenness. Lalawethika claimed to have had a series of visions with the Great Spirit. His visions instructed him to preach a return to Native traditions and ways of living. He called for rejecting the ways of the White man, including their clothing, utensils, and whiskey. Lalawethika personally reformed his ways, including drunkenness. He preached that Indians would have deliverance from their problems.

Lalawethika changed his name to Tenskwatawa ("The Open Door"). He became known as The Prophet. He supported his visions with a claim that he had predicted an eclipse of the sun. In addition to Shawnee, members of other tribes flocked to his teachings when word spread of his visions and his eclipse prediction. Tecumseh was at first skeptical of his brother's religious teachings but became more of a believer, and he realized how religious enthusiasm could help in rallying Indians to a common cause. Over time, he was able to convert The Prophet's religious movement into a political one.

The two brothers, buoyed by their newfound success in attracting a following, moved their village eastward to Ohio at the juncture of the Wabash and Tippecanoe rivers. They named the village Prophetstown. Tecumseh and The Prophet traveled to other tribes and were encouraged by the positive responses that the Prophet's leadership and religious teachings received.

In 1803, William Henry Harrison, the governor of the Indiana Territory (later to become the ninth president of the United States), signed the Treaty of Fort Wayne with Miami chief Little Turtle and several other prominent chiefs of various tribes. The Shawnee were included in the negotiations and the treaty signing, but Tecumseh played no role. The treaty ceded three million acres to the United States. Tecumseh disavowed the treaty and its signers, claiming the chiefs had no authority to make the treaty. He warned White settlers against settling in the land and began organizing Indians to fight settlers who did not heed the warnings.

Tecumseh and his message of resistance appealed to many tribes. He surpassed his brother as leader of the movement. He traveled to areas of the Midwest with his message of preventing loss of more tribal lands to the Big Knives. In 1811, he traveled south in search of more recruits. His travels took him as far south as Florida, but his success in recruiting warriors to his cause was greater in the Midwest than in the South. Tecumseh was able to put together a united force of several thousand warriors.

In his orations to other tribes, Tecumseh emphasized three themes: (1) Indians must be united to stop White expansion westward; (2) no one Indian nation could sell land also claimed by other nations; and (3) Native people and lands were "a bowl with one spoon" (meaning that all Indian nations had a collective right to the land and therefore all previous treaties should be invalidated).

As Tecumseh traveled to other tribes with his message, he made a powerful and frequently repeated speech. White observers credit these words to it:

> Where today are the Pequot? Where are the Narragansett, the Mohican, the Pocanet, and other powerful tribes of our people? They have vanished before the avarice and oppression of the white man, as snow before the summer sun. Will we let ourselves be destroyed in our turn, without making an effort worthy of our race? Shall we, without a struggle, give up our homes, our lands bequeathed to us by the Great Spirit? I know you will say with me, Never! Never!

This speech inspired many Indians. It also worried White settlers who feared violence. Tecumseh's confederation extended as far south as Florida, west to Nebraska, east to New York, and north into Canada.

The confederation worried Indiana Governor Harrison, who recognized the power of Tecumseh as a leader. The governor was the principal American official assigned to the task of settling the Indian problem in the Northwest Territory (established in 1787 by the Northwest Ordinance, it included what are now the Great Lakes states of Ohio, Indiana, Illinois, Michigan, Wisconsin, and a portion of Minnesota). On several occasions, at least one where violence was threatening, Harrison met with Tecumseh to try to convince him to be cooperative. Tecumseh responded with his message of resistance. The two were never able to reach an agreement. Harrison told Tecumseh that if God had wanted the Indians to be united, he would not have given them all different languages. Tecumseh was incensed by the remark.

Not all Native people were persuaded by Tecumseh's appeal. Some tribes benefited from adopting a farming lifestyle. Some chiefs controlled the annuities awarded by the United States as part of treaties, which made them protective of the annual cash payments by the federal government and disinclined to give them up to go to war with the Americans. Some tribes had become dependent on European goods, especially guns.

Wapakoneta was an example of a village that wanted nothing to do with Tecumseh's confederation. In 1798, Shawnee Chief Black Hoof had led his followers to Ohio and took over Wapakoneta from the Ottawas. Although Black Hoof was a powerful warrior leader, the Indian defeat at the Battle of Fallen Timbers had changed his thinking. His Shawnee village adopted agricultural methods that were introduced to them by White missionaries. They worked to prove they had adopted the ways of White settlers. By 1808, the village had over 500 Shawnee. Black Hoof was credited with preventing the majority of the Shawnee nation from joining Tecumseh's movement.

Tecumseh was not deterred by his failure to convince all Indian leaders or warriors to be part of his confederation. In 1810 and 1811, he continued to recruit warriors who were eager to fight the White settlers and the Big Knives. During this time, he became concerned that some warriors would not wait for the confederation to be fully formed before striking against White settlers, which did in fact happen. Governor Harrison became alarmed by Tecumseh's growing power and by Indian attacks against American settlements. Tecumseh had been able to assemble a multination confederation that crossed linguistic, cultural, and geographical boundaries. Harrison decided to act before it was too late. Later in 1811, he assembled a large military force and marched to Prophetstown while Tecumseh was traveling in the South.

The Prophet had been left in charge of the village. Word came of Harrison's force and its encampment not far from the village. The Prophet believed Harrison was poised to attack and that the Shawnee warriors' best chance of success was to strike first. Their attack was initially successful, but in the end the Shawnee were forced to retreat from the village. Although what became known as the Battle of Tippecanoe ended in a near draw, Harrison declared victory and shortly thereafter burned the village, its supplies, and nearby crops.

It was now left to Tecumseh to rally the various tribal warriors, but his efforts were derailed as the War of 1812 broke out between the United States and Great Britain. Tecumseh was faced with the choice of remaining neutral or joining with the British against the Americans. Although he did not fully trust the British, he decided to oppose the Americans. He believed the Native American way of life would be destroyed if the Americans were able to defeat the British. The British promised to respect and protect Indian tribal lands.

The British were at a great disadvantage. Their supplies were limited, and their lines of supply and communication to their headquarters in Quebec were long and difficult to maintain. In addition, they were vastly outnumbered by American settlers and American troops. Another problem was that not all Indian tribes supported Tecumseh's decision to join the British. During the War of 1812, 14 years after establishing the village at Wapakoneta, Black Hoof joined with Little Turtle as allies of the Americans against the British and Tecumseh's warriors. Chief Black Hoof was convinced that the fortunes of his people were better served by aligning with the United States.

Early British and Indian successes around Detroit gave way to the strength of American troops. The British were quick to retreat into Canada, and Tecumseh's forces reluctantly followed them. Tecumseh regarded the British as cowards, afraid to stand their ground and fight.

The British retreat continued northward in Canada. With the British still unwilling to fight, Tecumseh had his warriors take on the Big Knives without the British at the Battle of the Thames, in Ontario, Canada. On October 5, 1813, he was shot and killed. His body was never recovered. With his death his confederation ended. There was no chief equal to Tecumseh who could sustain the confederation.

The war officially ended in 1815 when the U.S. Senate ratified the Treaty of Ghent. The Americans felt victorious in the War of 1812. They had stopped the British and had won several key battles, including the legendary Battle of New Orleans—a battle fought without either side knowing that a peace treaty had already been signed. English and French fur traders were prohibited by the treaty from engaging in fur trading unless they became U.S. citizens, which most did.

The British believed they had won the war because they kept possession of Canada and continued the maritime policies that had in large part prompted the war. Most Canadians were pleased to remain part of the British Empire.

Tecumseh helped shape the history of Canada. The power of his confederation forced the American military to send troops westward to protect their settlements and outposts. Without the threat of Tecumseh, American forces might have marched north from New England and split the British colony in half, possibly severing Canada from the British Empire.

At its height, the Shawnee population in North America was about 10,000 people. It was reduced over the years by war and disease to fewer than 4,000. Presently, there are about 15,000 Shawnee living mostly in Oklahoma.

The major sources for this chapter were:

Calloway, C. G. (2007). *The Shawnees and the war for America*. New York, NY: Viking/ Penguin.

Hurt, D. R. (1996). *The Ohio frontier, Crucible of the old Northwest, 1720–1830*. Bloomington, IN: Indiana University Press.

Sugden, J. (2013). *Tecumseh: A life*. New York, NY: Macmillan.

LEARNING ACTIVITIES FOR "A BOWL WITH ONE SPOON"

Facts of the Case

1. Why was it difficult for Indians to unite into confederations?
2. Why did Indians oppose westward expansion of White settlers?
3. Why did the British support Tecumseh's confederation?
4. What was the outcome of the Battle of Fallen Timbers? Of the Battle of Tippecanoe? Of the Battle of the Thames?
5. What did Tecumseh hope to achieve with his confederation?
6. How did the fur trade affect the settlement of America?

Historical Understanding

1. Why did the American government encourage Indians to adopt an agricultural way of life?
2. Why did some Native Amerian leaders oppose Tecumseh's attempt to form a confederation?
3. Who was William Henry Harrison?
4. What was the significance to Indians of the French and Indian War?
5. What was the significance to Indians of the War of 1812?

Expressing Your Reasoning

Should Chief Tecumseh have joined forces with the British in the War of 1812? Why or why not?

Key Concepts from History

What do the following have in common?

1. The Triple Entente was a mutually supportive association among Russia, France, and Great Britain. It was an outgrowth of a secret agreement made between Russia and France in 1895. Both countries felt threatened by a powerful Germany. Great Britain, also feeling threatened by Germany, especially by its powerful navy, joined the informal association in 1907. The Triple Entente did not require the three nations to go to war if one of them were attacked, but asserted that each had a "moral obligation" to support the others. At the time, the participating nations believed they benefited from the agreement because adversaries would be less likely to attack if they feared involving other nations. Opposing this association were the Central Powers of Germany and Austria-Hungary. The two nations pledged support to each other if either was attacked by Russia. These opposing, tangled relationships drew all the nations of the Entente and Central Powers into World War I. It was one of the most deadly and costly wars in world history, eventually involving many other countries, including the United States in 1917.
2. In 1994, an agreement signed by Canada, Mexico, and the United States went into effect. Called the North American Free Trade Agreement (NAFTA), it created a trade bloc among the three nations. After much debate in the U.S. Congress, both the House of Representatives and the Senate approved the agreement. Although it received votes from both Democrats and Republicans, Republicans were more supportive. The treaty was negotiated during the presidency of George H. Bush and ratified while Bill Clinton was president. A major purpose of the treaty was gradually to remove most tariffs (duties paid on imported and exported goods) among the three nations. Other provisions

of the treaty reduced barriers on investment by the three countries. The treaty provisions were intended to stimulate job growth and economic development in all three countries. Supporters of the agreement in the United States claim the treaty has resulted in substantial economic growth. Opponents argue that it has resulted in the loss of hundreds of thousands of manufacturing jobs to Mexico where workers are paid much lower wages.

3. The North Atlantic Treaty Organization (NATO) was based on the North Atlantic Treaty signed in 1949. It is an organization of nations who have agreed to a collective defense arrangement. Its members agree to a mutual defense if one of its countries is attacked by a nation outside the organization. The organization currently consists of 28 nations from Europe and North America, including the United States. The treaty was a response to expansionistic threats from the Soviet Union after World War II; a means to avoid military dictatorships in Europe, like those previously in Germany and Italy; and a vehicle to promote integration and cooperation among European nations.

Historical Inquiry

Tecumseh's death at the Battle of the Thames meant the end of the most powerful Indian confederation ever assembled in North America. Did the end of the Tecumseh confederation in 1813 mean the end of Indian resistance to westward expansion by American settlers into Indian tribal lands?

Using online and other sources, test the hypothesis that the defeat of the Tecumseh confederation meant the end of Indian resistance to the westward expansion by American settlers into Indian tribal lands. Compose a short essay in which you accept or reject the hypothesis. Use evidence to support your decision. To begin your investigation, the following search terms will be helpful:

- Indian resistance
- Sitting Bull
- Geronimo
- Indian removal
- Wounded Knee
- Chief Joseph
- Standing Rock Sioux

Part IV

MANIFEST DESTINY
1829–1849

CHAPTER 13

A Woman's Place Is in the Factory

The Lowell Mill Strikes and Labor Reforms

Winslow Homer, "The Bobbin Girl" (1871)

In the early 1800s, the United States was rapidly expanding, both in geographic size and in population. In 1803, the country acquired the Louisiana Territory from France (approximately 827,000 square miles west of the Mississippi River) in a $15 million deal known as the Louisiana Purchase. This territory, which doubled the size of the United States, extended from the border with Canada to New Orleans, and eventually added 13 new states to the Union. With this "opening of the West," the country's population increased from 10 million in 1820 to more than 20 million by 1850 while land-hungry citizens, including new immigrants, moved westward.

These were also the years of rapid manufacturing growth and the development of market economies, particularly in the northeastern corner of the United States. When farmers could grow more food than their families or their local markets need-ed, they began to look for places where they could sell their surplus products. As the country's network of canals and railroads increased, new markets opened up. Villages became factory towns when automation and mechanization revolutionized manufacturing. Businesspeople in New England, who used the ample supply of water from streams and rivers to power their machinery, built textile mills and em-ployed large numbers of workers.

The factory owners needed a skilled and dependable workforce if their textile mills were to be successful. Some factory owners hired women, children, and even entire families to work in the mills. A group of businessmen known as the Boston Associates recruited thousands of New England farm girls as mill workers.

In 1810, Francis Cabot Lowell, an American businessman, visited textile mills in England to learn how the British used water-powered looms. After making im-provements to the British water-powered spinning and weaving machines, Low-ell and his shareholder partners founded the Boston Manufacturing Company in 1814. They built a textile mill in Waltham, Massachusetts, along the Charles River. The Waltham Mill, in which all steps in converting raw cotton to cloth took place in a single factory building, was the first "integrated" textile mill in the United States. This was the beginning of what would become the American factory system.

The Waltham Mill manufactured inexpensive cotton cloth for New England farmers, for settlers in the West, and for foreign export. The mill hired young girls and women, many of them immigrants, to work in the factory. They lived in factory-owned boardinghouses, on average six to a room, and were supervised by "keep-ers" (older women) who were responsible for reporting any "improper conduct."

After Lowell's death from pneumonia in 1817, his partners continued in the textile industry with the founding of the Merrimack Manufacturing Company. They bought land near the rapids of the Merrimack River, a more powerful river than the Charles, and built more factories and more boardinghouses.

The first run of cotton calico cloth, priced at 37 and a half cents a yard, was produced in 1823 in the factory located at the waterfall on the Merrimack River called the Pawtucket Falls. This was the site where the town of Lowell, America's first planned factory town, was founded in 1826. Lowell, the country's largest tex-tile center, was later known as the "Cradle of the American Industrial Revolution." Churches were built, a fire company was founded, and bookstores had lending li-braries with a 25-cent-per-month membership fee. Children attended free schools. By 1833, about 3,800 of the 5,000 mill workers were girls and young women. In 1836, when its population reached 18,000, Lowell was chartered as a city. Lowell became known as the "City of Spindles."

Women in mid-19th-century America had few legal rights. They could not vote, had no right of inheritance, and no claim to their earnings. For Black women in the North, who faced great prejudice, the situation was even worse than for White women. As a general rule, a woman's place was in the home. She cooked, sewed, raised the children, and managed various family matters. Above all else, she had to behave in a religious, decent, and proper way. Working outside the home was frowned on. Society shunned women who broke these rules of behavior.

Yet often women had to support, or help support, their families, especially when abandoned by husbands or widowed. No government welfare or support was available. For the few jobs open to women, the pay was low. Female household workers might earn 50 cents to a dollar a week (the equivalent of $13 to $26 in today's currency). Women who went from house to house offering their services as weavers or seamstresses might earn 75 cents a week. Female teachers earned even less than servants and seamstresses.

Economic recessions (periods of economic decline) and bank failures in early to mid-19th-century America made money scarce for many farming families. Because they had debts to pay and sons to educate, farm families looked for other sources of income. Cash wages paid to factory workers were hugely attractive.

The first "Lowell Mill Girls" were the daughters of New England farmers. Most were between the ages of 15 and 30, although some were as young as 10. Eventually, they made up three-fourths of the entire workforce at the Lowell textile mills. They went to work in the mills primarily to earn money for the family and sometimes to help pay for a brother's college education, but also to be near the educational and social opportunities that city life offered.

Although the Lowell Mill Girls were paid only half as much as men working in the mills, their wages were still six to seven times more than teachers' wages. Newly hired women in the mills might earn 55 cents ($14 today) a week, while more skilled workers could earn $4 ($104 today) or more a week. On average, women's wages, paid in cash daily, were about $2 a week ($52 today).

Life on a farm for young women was often hard, lonely, and boring. The City of Lowell offered the excitement of new people, shops, lectures, and concerts. Despite the monotonous labor, long hours, and often-harsh living conditions typical of the early factory system, to some extent these young women experienced more independence and greater self-esteem as wage earners.

The textile factory owners believed it was essential that the women mill workers maintained their good character—as, they argued, good morals led to higher productivity and thus more earnings. The factories paid the keepers, who were company employees, a set amount of money for each woman resident. Charges for food and miscellaneous items were deducted from each woman's wages. The boardinghouse doors were locked at ten o'clock, and no visitors were allowed in without proper permission. The women were also required to attend public worship. These were requirements of the contract the textile workers signed with the company.

The contract also required the workers to work for 12 months and to give 2-weeks' notice if they were going to leave. Women typically worked 13 hours a day in the summer and from daylight to dark in the winter. The women attended an average of three looms a day, and some attended four. The noise from the machines was so loud that the women stuffed cotton in their ears and communicated using hand signals. One half hour was allowed for each meal, and factory bells rang out the work and meal times. This was the pattern of work in the mills—6 days a week.

An 1846 report on factory life in the cities of Lowell and Manchester described a textile factory floor:

> The atmosphere of such a room cannot of course be pure; on the contrary it is charged with cotton filaments and dust, which, we are told, are very injurious to the lungs. On entering the room, although the day was warm, we remarked that the windows were down; we asked the reason, and a young woman answered naively: "When the wind blew, the threads did not work so well."

However, some descriptions of the Lowell factories were less negative. Among the well-known people who were favorably impressed by Lowell and its textile factories were President Andrew Jackson, General William Henry Harrison (later the ninth U.S. president), and Charles Dickens, the English novelist. Dickens, who knew a great deal about the miserable conditions of factory workers in England, was especially impressed by the piano in the boardinghouse and by the fact that the "young ladies subscribe to circulating libraries." He praised their *Lowell Offering*, which he described as a periodical with "original articles, written exclusively by females actively employed in the mills." Davy Crockett, legendary frontiersman and member of the Whig Party in Congress, visited Lowell in 1834, and praised the working conditions:

> I could not help reflecting on the difference of condition between these females, thus employed, and those of other populous countries, where female character is degraded to abject slavery. Here were thousands, useful to others, and enjoying all the blessings of freedom, with the prospect before them of future comfort and respectability. . . .

Some young women who were members of families that had been wealthy in previous generations found factory work exhausting and dangerous. Boardinghouse life was unhealthy and crowded. One woman said her life was worse than "the poor peasant of Ireland or the Russian serf who labors from sun to sun." Another woman, Lucy Larcom, who began as a doffer (remover) of bobbins (spinners) when she was 12, according to a historian, expressed that she "hated the confinement, noise, and lint-filled air, and regretted the time lost to education."

By the mid-1830s, with overproduction in the textile industry, a surplus of raw cotton, and a fall in the price of cloth, the textile mills were less and less profitable.

In these same years, the national economy worsened. The textile mill owners' response to hard times was to reduce workers' wages. In 1834, they cut wages by as much as 15 to 20%. When the women mill workers protested, claiming "Union is Power," the Lowell mill owners fired the women who organized the protests. In 1836, the mill owners cut wages again—this time by another 5%.

The women then began to talk of striking. In October 1836, Harriet Hanson, an 11-year-old girl, and 2,000 others walked out of the Lowell mills in one of the first textile factory strikes in the country's history. They had no banners, no signs, no flags, but they gave speeches. It was the first time women in the United States spoke publicly in favor of labor reform. They also sang as they marched. One song began: "Oh! Isn't it a pity, such a pretty girl as I / should be sent to the factory to pine away and die."

However, the strike was unsuccessful: The mill owners could afford to operate without the striking workers because there was an oversupply of workers. The strike lasted only a few days. When the mill owners did not agree to the women's demands, most of the women returned to work.

The names of the women thought to be the troublemakers and fired were placed on a blacklist, which was shared with other factory owners. Charges against these women included "mutiny," "disobedience to orders," and "dissatisfaction with wages." No woman on the blacklist was likely to find employment at another mill.

The national economic situation continued to worsen. The Panic of 1837 sparked a major recession that lasted until the 1840s and weakened the textile workers' bargaining power. The crisis was caused by speculative lending practices in western states, the decline in cotton prices, and the banks' sharp increase in interest rates on loans. Banks collapsed, bankruptcies increased, the price of goods declined, and unemployment rose dramatically—as high as 25% in some places.

As labor unrest spread among the women textile workers, they began to resist in a more organized way. In 1844, Sarah Bagley and other women founded the Lowell Female Labor Reform Association with Bagley as its first president. They charged the factory owners with making excess profits and failing to provide safe and healthy working conditions. After petitioning the Massachusetts legislature for reform of their working conditions, the association convinced the state to increase meal times at the factory from 30 to 45 minutes.

The association was not a strong supporter of worker strikes. Instead, it held conventions where it promoted labor reforms by preparing resolutions and petitions that were sent to legislators. The women who attended the conventions (held on workdays) were told to report illness as the reason for their absence from the factories. Any woman with an unexcused absence would probably have been blacklisted.

Sarah Bagley also wrote for the *Voice of Industry*, a labor publication dedicated to improving working conditions. In 1846, when one factory tried to make the women tend four looms instead of three, a group of women signed a pledge in which they refused the additional work without an increase in their wages. If a woman refused to sign the pledge, she was named in the *Voice of Industry* and listed as a "traitor" to the reform movement. Given this rather strong-armed threat, all the women signed the pledge, and the factory dropped the plan.

Previously, in 1845, Bagley and others collected more than 10,000 signatures from Massachusetts (2,000 of which were from working men and women of Lowell) on a petition requesting that the workday be reduced from 13 to 10 hours. When they presented their petition to the Massachusetts legislature, it was an extraordinary moment in the history of labor in the United States. It was the first time any state legislature held hearings on the harsh working conditions in factories. Bagley and her coworkers testified to the long hours, the hot and poorly ventilated work rooms, the short time allowed for meals, and the unhealthy and exhausting nature of the work.

After a legislative committee visited the Lowell and Manchester factories, the members published a report: *Massachusetts Investigation into Labor Conditions*. In the report, the committee admitted it had previously "distrusted the accounts" from the labor reform movement, but the visit convinced them that the noise in the factories was "frightful and infernal," and attention to two looms (not the four the mill owners wanted) "is as much as should be demanded."

However, the committee also concluded that a 10-hour workday was not needed. The committee chairman, William Schouler (a representative from the City of Lowell), said the legislature did not have the authority to set the "hours of work" and that the length of the workday was an issue between the factories and the workers. The committee's report stated: "Labor is intelligent enough to make its own bargains, and look out for its own interests without any interference from us."

Many other Massachusetts politicians agreed with Schouler. A state senate committee concluded that employer–employee relationships were not government issues. This committee reported that governments should not "deprive the citizen of his freedom of contract." Their explanation was that workers freely agree to work in the factories; therefore, they have no right to object to an employer's conditions and rules. Factory work was not slave labor, and workers could always leave. One committee member described factory work: "It is a most perfect democracy. Any of its subjects can be depart from it at pleasure without the least restraint."

Although they lost the war over the 10-hour workday, Bagley and the others won one battle, which must have pleased them. The women could not vote, but they could participate in political campaigns. And they did. Their protests against Schouler's position on the shortened workday led to his defeat in the next election.

Gradually, the favorable reputation of the factory system in the Massachusetts mill towns faded. The mills began to hire more immigrants, who would work for very low wages and would not complain about the working conditions.

By 1850, about 50% of the women mill workers were immigrants, most of whom were Irish. Labor reformers continued to work for improvements in wages and working conditions; in 1853, the Lowell corporations reduced the workday to 11 hours (from 13 or even 16 hours) per day, which essentially ended the 10-Hour Movement. In 1874, long after Bagley's days as a labor activist were over, and after a 30-year struggle, Massachusetts finally legislated the 10-hour workday.

In the early and mid-20th century, the 8-Hour Movement (or the 40-Hour Week Movement) succeeded in the United States as the result of various federal and state laws. One of the first adopters was the Ford Motor Company, which in 1915 reduced its shifts from 9 hours to 8 hours. The company's founder, Henry Ford, believed too many working hours were bad for workers' productivity, and indeed, the result was an increase in Ford's productivity.

Although the 40-hour workweek is standard today in the United States, other countries have reduced the workweek still further. France, for example, adopted the 35-hour workweek in the year 2000. In the early 21st century, some companies and organizations in Sweden are experimenting with the 6-hour workday in the expectation that savings on sick leave and health-related expenses can offset productivity losses.

The major sources for this chapter were:

Cott, N. F. (1997). *The bonds of womanhood: Women's sphere in New England, 1780–1835*. New Haven, CT: Yale University Press.

Flanagan, A. K. (2006). *The Lowell mill girls*. Minneapolis, MN: Compass Point Books.

Howe, D. W. (2007) *What hath God wrought: The transformation of America, 1815–1848*. Oxford, UK: Oxford University Press.

Josephson, H. (1949). *The golden threads*. New York, NY: Duell, Sloan and Pearce.

Robinson, H. (1976). *Loom and spindle*. Kailua, HI: Press Pacifica.

Ware, C. F. (1966) *The early New England cotton manufacture*. New York, NY: Russell and Russell.

LEARNING ACTIVITIES FOR "A WOMAN'S PLACE IS IN THE FACTORY"

Facts of the Case

1. Why were young women attracted to the Lowell factories?
2. Who were some prominent visitors to the Lowell factories and what did they report?
3. Describe working conditions in the Lowell factories.
4. What was the purpose of the Female Labor Reform Association?
5. Why did the Massachusetts legislature refuse to pass the 10-hour workday law?

Historical Understanding

1. What legal rights did men have that were denied to women in the early and mid-1800s?
2. In what ways was the Lowell factory system innovative for its time?
3. Why did the manufacturers' profits decrease in the 1830s and 1840s? How did they try to increase their profits?
4. Describe the Panic of 1837.
5. What is a *blacklist*?
6. What was the importance of the Female Labor Reform Association in the history of the American labor movement?

Expressing Your Reasoning

1. Should the Massachusetts legislature have passed a 10-hour workday law in 1845? Why or why not?
2. Were employers justified in firing workers who violated their employment agreements? Why or why not?

Key Concepts from History

What do the following have in common?

1. During the Industrial Revolution, the U.S. government took a hands-off approach to the relationship among workers, employers, and unions. This meant that businesses were largely left alone by the government regarding the regulation of wages and working conditions.
2. In the 1950s, President Dwight D. Eisenhower led the charge to build a state-of-the-art interstate highway system. Throughout this massive public works project that provided jobs for tens of thousands of Americans, the Eisenhower administration established and maintained distance between the federal government and the setting of wages, hours, and working conditions for the civil engineers, contractors and specialized workers who constructed the highways.
3. Alan Greenspan, chairman of the Federal Reserve of the United States from 1987 to 2006, removed many government controls on the banking industry. It is claimed that this practice was in part responsible for the subprime mortgage and credit crisis that began in 2007 and led to the Recession of 2008.

Historical Inquiry

The efforts of Sarah Bagley and other female workers helped the 10-hour work-day law to be eventually passed in 1874. Using online and other sources, test the hypothesis that after the Lowell Mill strikes, women have taken leadership roles in the labor movement. Compose a short essay in which you accept or reject the hypothesis. Use evidence to support your decision. To begin your investigation, the following search terms will be helpful:

- Women in labor history
- Working women in union history
- Mary Harris Jones
- Industrial Workers of the World
- Women's Trade Union League
- Leonora O'Reilly
- Lucy Parsons
- "Rosie the Riveter"
- Linda Chavez-Thompson

CHAPTER 14

The Will of the People

Cherokee Removal

Robert Lindneux, *The Trail of Tears* (1942)

Many hundreds of years before White people arrived, the Cherokee people inhabited parts of what are today the states of Georgia, North Carolina, Tennessee, Alabama, and South Carolina. They had migrated there from the Great Lakes region before the history of that region was recorded.

The Cherokees associated farming with women and hunting with men. For food and clothing, they depended on the deer, turkeys, bears, rabbits, and other game that the men hunted, and on the corn, beans, squash, and other crops that the women raised.

Cherokee homesteads were usually along a river valley or tightly clustered in more open terrain. Together, their homesteads comprised permanent villages. Although Cherokee men might travel great distances for the winter hunt, the villages did not relocate.

The first White people the Cherokee encountered were Spanish explorers during the 16th century in the present-day Southeast of the United States. Around 1700, Cherokees made contact with British traders who sought deerskins. There was a great demand for the skins in Europe, where they were used to make clothing and other goods.

Pushing westward before the American Revolution, White settlers began to encroach on Cherokee hunting grounds. In 1763, after the French and Indian War, the British Crown issued a proclamation prohibiting settlement west of the Appalachians. The Cherokees welcomed the proclamation, but settlers ignored it. Cherokees began to regard the colonists, not the Crown, as their enemy. Most sided with Britain when the American Revolution erupted.

During the Revolutionary War, Cherokees gave refuge to fleeing Loyalists. Cherokee warriors raided the frontiers of Georgia, South Carolina, North Carolina, and Virginia. Settlers from these four colonies invaded Cherokee lands in return, destroying houses, fields, and granaries. By the end of the war, American colonists had attacked more than 50 Cherokee villages, destroying fields and killing livestock. The Cherokees were compelled to give up more than 20,000 square miles of their domain, jeopardizing the Cherokee economy, so heavily dependent upon the deerskin trade.

In 1783, Britain and the United States signed the Treaty of Paris, ending the Revolutionary War. The treaty conveyed to the new nation all of England's rights and claims to the lands within its boundaries. The territory of the Cherokee Nation fell within those borders.

The new American Congress assumed that the new nation had a "right of conquest" over Native American tribes. The assumption was that if Britain lost its lands in America, then Britain's Native allies, enemies of the United States, also lost theirs. North of the Ohio River, Congress pursued what was called the "conquered nations" Indian policy, while south of the river, where the Cherokees lived, Indian policy was decided by the states. At the time, the boundaries of the eastern states extended west to the Mississippi River. Those states argued that England's authority had passed to them, and they acted on their claim. For example, the North Carolina legislature granted a large block of Cherokee lands to any residents who would move onto them, and Georgia forced the Cherokees to cede a large tract of land for its citizens.

Indian tribes resisted the takeover of their lands under these policies and violence ensued. To end the fighting, Congress changed policy. Making no right-of-conquest claims, Congress sought to negotiate peace treaties that would end the fighting and restrain the states.

The Treaty of Hopewell was signed by the U.S. and the Cherokees in 1785. It was a treaty between two nations that defined the Cherokees' boundaries and recognized the right of the Cherokee Nation to expel intruders from its lands. The treaty was a failure. Neither North Carolina nor Georgia respected it. Both states continued to expand into Cherokee country. Cherokee leaders protested to the Georgia governor, the state legislature, and the Congress, but their protests went unheeded.

The new Constitution of the United States, ratified in 1789, placed sole authority over Indian affairs with Congress and the president. George Washington's first secretary of war, Henry Knox, believed that the Indian tribes were sovereign, independent nations with rights to self-government within their borders. Knox was convinced that the major cause of warfare on the frontier was settlers' encroachment on Indian lands. The only way to stop it, he believed, was to exert legal control over the intruding settlers. Furthermore, he thought that the United States had an obligation to preserve and protect Native Americans. President Washington was in full agreement with Knox.

Congress endorsed this new approach to Indian policy. In 1790, it approved the Indian Trade and Intercourse Act. That act recognized the concept that the tribes were sovereign nations and that the United States should deal with them through negotiation of treaties subject to approval by two-thirds of the Senate. By the act, Knox accomplished his goal of excluding the states from conducting relations with the Indians.

With peace on the frontier, Knox addressed the longer-term matter of ensuring the Indians' survival. He and Washington, along with many Whites at the time, believed that the "uncivilized" characteristics of Indian culture existed because Native people knew no better. They were convinced that Indians were fully capable of becoming citizens and assimilating into American society.

The United States helped fund missionary organizations to go into the Indian nations. There, they would teach Indians how to grow wheat instead of corn; how to eat meals at regular times instead of when they were hungry; how to dress in European clothing; how to speak the English language; how to pray in church at designated times; and how to live the kind of life that Anglo Americans believed was a civilized life.

The "civilizing agenda" of Washington and Knox became a central feature of U.S. relations with the Cherokees. It encouraged the Cherokees to form compact communities where they would take up settled farming and abandon communal land holding. In the words of Thomas Jefferson, the ultimate aim was that Whites and Indians would "become one people."

Many Cherokees embraced the government's program. Although they had little enthusiasm for Christianity, many welcomed schools for Cherokee children established on Cherokee lands by Protestant missionaries. Students were taught to read the Bible, pray, cook, eat, keep house, and farm like White people. The division of labor of the "civilization" program was Euro-American, not Cherokee.

For example, boys rather than girls farmed.

Not all Cherokee parents wanted their children to attend the mission schools. Those students who enrolled tended to come from two types of families. Many were children of male British traders or Loyalists and Cherokee women. (The Cherokee considered these children to be wholly Cherokee, because their mothers were Cherokee.) Other Cherokee families sent their children to mission schools because they foresaw the end of Cherokee life based on hunting and subsistence farming. They looked to the "civilization" program and mission schools to prepare their children for a new Cherokee world.

For an economic elite of wealthy Cherokees, most of whom had mission educations, "civilization" brought even greater transformation. Guided by missionaries and U.S. Indian agents, and with southern planters as their models, these Cherokees began to imitate an Anglo-American way of life. Like their White southern counterparts, Cherokee planters bought slaves, raised cotton and other crops, tended herds of cattle and other livestock, and accumulated capital. They traded profitably with adjoining states. They also exported cotton and woolen goods to New Orleans.

Some of the wealthier Cherokees invested in taverns along the newly built roads, opened stores, and operated ferries and toll roads. The women of these households did not toil in the fields. African American slaves or White workers performed the agricultural labor. Some Cherokee planters became an economic elite who dominated political affairs in the Cherokee Nation.

Before contact with Whites, Cherokee law had been informal and clan-based. The emergence of disparities in wealth, and concerns about protection of property, led to creation of a written law code. Laws establishing a national police force and regulation of property through contracts, interest rates, and licensing were enacted. In 1817, a law was enacted giving the national Cherokee government exclusive authority to cede lands. In 1827, the Cherokees adopted a constitution modeled on the U.S. Constitution. It provided for a bicameral legislature (National Committee and National Council), a chief executive, and a judicial system.

The centralization of power came about in part because wealthy Cherokees wanted to protect their property. Primarily, however, it was intended to protect the homeland. Cherokees held their land in common, so individuals could not sell property on which they lived. The new constitution made clear that only the Nation had the authority to sell land. Further, in 1829, the National Council passed a law imposing the death penalty upon anyone who sold land without authority.

Another expression of Cherokee national identity was the invention and adoption of a Cherokee language. In the 1820s, a Cherokee named Sequoyah devised a syllabary (a set of written characters representing syllables) for writing Cherokee. Many Cherokees learned to read and write, in both Cherokee and English. Mastery of the Sequoyah syllabary was a source of pride for individual Cherokees.

Not all White people agreed that Native people could be "civilized." Some believed that Indians were inferior to Whites and that differences between the two were caused by unchangeable racial, rather than mutable cultural characteristics. This racist thinking influenced a call for removal of the eastern Indians to lands west of the Mississippi.

Demand for Cherokee lands from a mushrooming population of White settlers intensified. The Cherokees increasingly resisted sale of their lands and rebuffed proposals by federal Indian agents to negotiate treaties for cession of land. To resolve increasing tension over land on the Indian frontier, a growing number of Americans favored removal.

Andrew Jackson was commander of the army's southern district at the time. He had achieved much of his early fame as an Indian fighter. He said that if Indians would not sell their lands, they should be taken from them. Negotiating with Indians, he argued, was "absurd." Jackson believed that Congress should treat the Indians as subjects and "legislate their boundaries." Jackson was elected president in 1828. He had the support of southern voters who wanted him to expel the Cherokees from the southern states. Soon after his election in 1828, President Jackson pursued removal as a priority. He claimed that it was the only way to safeguard the Cherokees from the harmful effects of exposure to frontier settlers. Such contact, Jackson argued, would lead to the demise of the Cherokees. He explained that only their isolation in a safe and distant haven could save them from extinction as a people.

There were outspoken opponents of removal among American citizens, most from the Northeast. Missionaries who served among the Cherokees, and groups that supported the missionaries, offered evidence of Cherokee "civilization" and protested removal. Leading members of Congress, mostly members of the Whig Party that opposed Jackson and his Democratic Party, including Daniel Webster and Henry Clay, also protested. Skepticism about "civilizing" the Indians, fever for land, and party loyalty, however, won the day. The Indian Removal Act was signed into law by President Jackson in May 1830.

The new president had foreshadowed the act a year earlier in his First Inaugural Address. In that speech he said that the Native people of the East would have to make room for the waves of White population and "civilization." He added, "We now propose to acquire the countries occupied by the red men . . . by a fair exchange, and, at the expense of the United States to send them to a land where their existence may be prolonged and perhaps made perpetual. . . ." In the speech, Jackson acknowledged that removal would be painful for the Indians, but he went on to compare Indian removal to earlier migrations and settlement by Whites:

> . . . Doubtless it will be painful to leave the graves of their fathers; but what do they more than our ancestors did or than our children are now doing?

To better their condition in an unknown land our forefathers left all that was dear in earthly objects. Our children by thousands yearly leave the land of their birth to seek new homes in distant regions. . . . If the offers made to the Indians were extended to them, they would be hailed with gratitude and joy. . . . The policy of the General Government toward the red man is not only liberal but generous . . . the General Government kindly offers him a new home, and proposes to pay the whole expense of his removal and settlement. . . .

The act was bitterly debated in both houses of Congress. The final vote in the House of Representatives was 102 to 97; in the Senate, it was 28 to 19.

The Indian Removal Act provided:

- authorization of the president to acquire lands west of the Mississippi to move the Cherokees (and other Indian nations) in exchange for the lands where they then resided;
- a guarantee to the Cherokees of permanent possession of the exchanged lands west of the Mississippi (located in present-day Oklahoma);
- a requirement that the federal government pay the Cherokees for any improvements they had made to their lands in the East;
- payment to the Cherokees for the costs of travel to, and settlement of, the lands to which they were being removed;
- protection of the Cherokees from attacks at their new residence;
- affirmation of existing treaties between the United States and the Cherokee Nation; and
- a payment of $500,000 (approximately $13 million today) to the Cherokee Nation.

If they gave up all claims to tribal land, Cherokees would be allowed to remain in the East. They would then be residents of the state, subject to state laws. Very few made this choice.

The Cherokee National Council had announced that it would cede no more land. Its members had been united in opposing removal, but the situation had come to seem hopeless to some of them. Three Cherokee statesmen, all members of the Council, took the lead in support of a removal treaty: Major Ridge, a successful planter and highly respected veteran of the Creek War during which he had served as a major under then General Andrew Jackson; his New England–educated son, John Ridge; and mission school–educated Elias Boudinot, nephew of Major Ridge and editor of the widely read Cherokee newspaper, the *Cherokee Phoenix*. The *Cherokee Phoenix* was the first newspaper published by and for Native Americans or written (in part) in an Indian language.

These three elite dissenters led what came to be called the Treaty Party. They had concluded that relocation was the only path for saving the Cherokee people.

In their minds, there was no alternative but to negotiate with the United States to exchange their land in the East for a new homeland west of the Mississippi.

The defection of the Treaty Party horrified another member of the Cherokee elite, principal chief of the Cherokee Nation John Ross. Ross was the most prominent advocate of the Cherokees' cause in Washington, D.C. He led an effort to remove the three Treaty Party leaders from the National Council and forced Boudinot to resign as editor of the *Cherokee Phoenix*. Chief Ross wanted the Cherokees to speak in one voice against removal and he moved to silence the minority.

John Ross was born in 1790 to a Scots father and Cherokee mother. By ancestry, he was one-eighth Cherokee and seven-eighths Scottish. Under the Cherokee matrilineal (traced from mothers) system of ancestry, he was considered Cherokee. Because his mother was part Cherokee and belonged to the nation, her son belonged to her Bird clan. As a child, he was known as Koo-wi-s-gu-wi, meaning in Cherokee "Little White Bird."

Ross grew up in both frontier American and Cherokee environments. He was educated in English by White men. In 1814, during the War of 1812, he fought as a lieutenant of a Cherokee regiment, alongside Andrew Jackson's troops. They defeated the Creeks at the Battle of Horseshoe Bend in what is now central Alabama. Later, as a trader, he became one of the wealthiest members of the Cherokee nation. Ross's warehouse and landing on the Tennessee River became well known to both Cherokees and Whites. He established a ferry for supplies and passenger flatboats. The general area became known as Ross's Landing (present-day Chattanooga, Tennessee). Ross was also a successful planter and owned nearly 20 Black slaves who tended his land.

Given his ancestry and childhood, Ross might be considered an unlikely leader for the Cherokees. He spoke the Cherokee language only haltingly, and he preferred to communicate in English. However, he had a firm attachment to the ancient lands of the Cherokees, and he was devoted to the unity of the Cherokee Nation. The Cherokees did not want a leader who would barter away their land. They sought one who was savvy about treaty making with Whites and who was committed to protecting the Cherokee homeland. His bicultural background helped Ross represent the Cherokee Nation to United States government officials. Ross was elected principal chief of the Cherokee Nation in every election from 1828 to 1860.

Under Ross's leadership, the Cherokee government unanimously adopted a resolution in 1822. It pledged the Nation ". . . to hold no treaties with any commissioners of the United States to make any cession of lands, being resolved not to dispose of even one foot of ground."

Approximately 3,500 Cherokees had moved west to Arkansas under terms of an 1817 treaty. U.S. Secretary of War John C. Calhoun urged the Cherokees to cede land equal to that which had been occupied by those who migrated. John Ross steadfastly refused this inducement and several others like it from the U.S. government.

The Georgia state government refused to recognize the Cherokee constitution of 1827. The legislature claimed that Georgia had the right to extend its laws over all territory in the state and to coerce obedience to them from all people who resided within the boundaries of the state. In 1829, Georgia added a large portion of Cherokee land to the state and extended its laws to that region. In July of the same year, gold was discovered on Cherokee lands in northeast Georgia, attracting intruders from across the frontier region. A proclamation from the governor of Georgia intended to block the gold diggers had no effect.

The following year, President Jackson declared to the Cherokees that he would not challenge the authority of the state of Georgia. Those Cherokees who did not immigrate voluntarily to land west of the Mississippi must, according to the president, submit to state law. Chief Ross stiffened his resolve. He led numerous delegations to Washington to prevent the growing intrusion on Cherokee lands. The delegations were unsuccessful.

Failing to persuade the legislative and executive branches of the federal government, Ross turned to the judicial branch. The adoption of the Indian Removal Act convinced him to pursue a new strategy. A murder case provided an opportunity. The Cherokee General Council authorized Chief Ross to begin legal proceedings in the U.S. Supreme Court. The Cherokees intended to argue that they were a sovereign nation and that their laws and lands could not come under the authority of Georgia.

The 1831 case involved a Cherokee citizen named George Tassel. He was arrested by Georgia authorities for murdering another Cherokee within Cherokee territory. A Georgia court tried and convicted Tassel. The Cherokee Council claimed that Georgia laws were not valid within the Cherokee Nation. The Nation hired a former United States attorney general to challenge Tassel's conviction. Georgia executed Tassel before the case ran its course.

In *Cherokee Nation v. Georgia*, the Supreme Court dodged the main issue at stake in the case—enforcement of Georgia law within the Cherokee Nation. The court held that the Cherokees, as a "foreign nation," had no legal standing before the court. In its decision, written by Chief Justice John Marshall, the Court ruled that the Cherokees were in a special position as "dependent domestic nations." The meaning of the decision was unclear. With it, however, the Court left the door open for a future case brought by a U.S. citizen who did have legal standing.

Such a case soon arose. March of 1831 marked a legal deadline requiring all Whites on Cherokee lands to swear allegiance to the government of Georgia. Eleven missionaries, all White citizens of the United States, were arrested and convicted of refusing to comply with the Georgia law. They were all sentenced to 4 years of hard labor. Georgia released nine of the missionaries who agreed either to leave the state or take the oath.

Two of the missionaries refused to leave Georgia or take the oath. With legal support from the Cherokees, they appealed their convictions to the United States Supreme Court.

The stunning decision in the case, *Worcester v. Georgia*, also written by Chief Justice John Marshall, came in March 1832. The Supreme Court, in a vote of six to one, demanded the release of the two missionaries. The court declared that Georgia had no authority to extend its laws over the Cherokee people. In the majority opinion of the court, Chief Justice Marshall wrote:

> The Cherokee Nation, then, is a distinct community, occupying its own territory, with boundaries accurately described, in which the laws of Georgia can have no force, and which the citizens of Georgia have no right to enter, but with the assent of the Cherokees themselves, or on conformity with treaties, and with acts of Congress . . .

But the governor of Georgia refused to enforce the decision, and President Jackson declined to use federal powers to force the state to comply. The two imprisoned missionaries decided to end legal proceedings and were granted a pardon by the governor.

When the Supreme Court issued its decision, most Cherokees were jubilant. Elation soon turned to dismay when it became clear that the decision of the high court would not be enforced. The breach within the Cherokee Nation between the Treaty Party and those refusing removal intensified. The Treaty Party, representing no more than 10% of the tribe, was now convinced that the Cherokees, invaded by White Georgians and pressured by both state and federal authorities, had no alternative but to negotiate a treaty for removal.

Chief Ross, supported by the majority of Cherokees, insisted that the Cherokees must remain in their homeland at all costs. He urged his people to resist removal. He declared that any Cherokee who endorsed or participated in negotiating a removal treaty was a traitor and an enemy to the Cherokee people.

In 1835, the U.S. treaty commissioner called for a conference at New Echota, the capital of the Cherokee Nation, located near present-day Calhoun, Georgia. John Ross and the Cherokee Council did not attend; Ross was leading yet another protest delegation to Washington. Leaders of the Treaty Party were in attendance. Out of a population of approximately 16,000, just over 200 Cherokees met there. They ratified a removal treaty by a vote of 75 to seven. Major Ridge, one of the Treaty Party leaders, spoke in favor of the removal treaty. In a speech to the Cherokees assembled at New Echota, he said:

> Yet they are strong and we are weak. We are few, they are many. We cannot remain here in safety and comfort. I know we love the graves of our fathers, who have gone before to the happy hunting grounds of the Great Spirit. . . . We can never forget these homes, I know, but an unbending, iron necessity tells us we must leave them. I would willingly die to preserve them, but any forcible effort to keep them will cost us our lands, our lives, and the lives of our children. There is but one path of safety, one road to future existence as a

Nation. That path is open before you. Make a treaty of cession. Give up these lands and go over beyond the great Father of Waters.

The U.S. Senate ratified the Treaty of New Echota the following spring. It passed the Senate by only one vote more than the two-thirds required by the Constitution for ratification of a treaty. Under terms of the treaty, the Cherokees had 2 years to remove to their new western homes.

The treaty provided for the exchange of all Cherokee land east of the Mississippi River. Further, the Cherokees would receive $5 million (more than $130 million today) from the United States (to be distributed *per capita* to all members of the tribe), an additional $500,000 (approximately $13 million today) for educational funds, title forever to land in Indian Territory (west of the Mississippi River) equal to that given up, and full compensation for all property left behind.

Opposition to removal persisted. John Ross insisted that if the Cherokees held tight, they could outlast the Jackson administration. A new president, he was confident, would surely honor the Supreme Court decision. The Cherokee National Committee and National Council passed a resolution protesting what they considered an unauthorized treaty. In their view, it had been adopted without the confidence, advice, or consent of the regularly constituted authorities of the Cherokee Nation. The majority of Cherokees believed that the Treaty Party had violated the will of the people. The protest resolution, signed by 16,000 Cherokees, virtually every Cherokee in the East, was presented by John Ross to Secretary of War Lewis Cass.

Opponents of the treaty, led by John Ross, pressed on in insisting that the Cherokees had a right to their eastern homelands. It was argued that they were the original inhabitants, and that protection of their lands had been promised by earlier treaties with the United States. Further, the U.S. Supreme Court had recognized Cherokee sovereignty. In addition, they argued that the Cherokees were a peaceful people who had accommodated to White civilization in accordance with the vision of early American presidents. As evidence, they cited governing themselves under a constitution modeled on that of the United States; success at settled agriculture; literacy of their people; and reception of Christian missionaries and their religion.

The protests against the treaty were ignored in Washington. In 1838, President Martin Van Buren, Jackson's successor, ordered that all Cherokees who had not yet complied with the treaty be forcibly moved west. Their grueling journey has come to be known as the Trail of Tears.

In the spring of 1838, as the deadline approached, only about 2,000 Cherokees had moved west. Seven thousand federal troops ringed Cherokee territory. Along with Georgia militia, they rounded up the remaining Cherokees, sometimes dragging them from their houses as other soldiers stood by with rifles and bayonets. The Cherokees were confined in stockades, many herded into what were literally cattle pens, in preparation for their forced removal. Hundreds died of disease in the holding camps and thousands died later along the trail.

Chief John Ross had reluctantly accepted that further attempts to overturn the treaty would be futile and that removal had become unavoidable. He persuaded the secretary of war to allow the Cherokees to conduct their own removal. Conductors organized detachments of approximately 1,000 Cherokees each for the journey.

Along the trail, many women and children rode in wagons drawn by teams of mules or oxen. Some of the others rode on horseback. Most walked. The wagons were loaded with household belongings. Many cherished items, from pet dogs to furniture, were left behind.

One surviving Cherokee remembered the Trail of Tears with simple eloquence:

> Long time we travel on way to new land. People feel bad when they leave the Old Nation. Women cry and make sad wails. Children cry, and many men cry, and all look sad when friends die, but they say nothing and just put heads down and keep on go towards West. Many days pass, and people die very much.

Most detachments took 5 to 6 months to travel the 1,000 miles from the Cherokees' old home to their new one, and the whole process took about a year. The final detachments arrived in the western Cherokee Nation in late March of 1839. From stockades to final destination, at least 4,000 Cherokees perished, one-fourth of the entire Cherokee Nation.

John Ross's houses, farm, ferries, and other property were seized. He arrived in the western Cherokee Nation as part of the final detachment. During the journey, his Cherokee wife, Elizabeth "Quatie" Brown Henley Ross, with whom he had six children, died of pneumonia near Little Rock, Arkansas, where she is buried.

The new western Cherokee world simmered with discord. The wounds caused by removal festered. Angry talk, bitter accusation, and violent reprisal flared among the Cherokees for the next 30 years. Hostile conflict ensued between the supporters of the Treaty Party, and the anti-removal faction devoted to Chief Ross, erupting into violence and revenge killings. For example, the most prominent leaders of the Treaty Party—Major Ridge, his son John Ridge, and Elias Boudinot—were all assassinated in June of 1839 by extremist opponents of removal.

However, the Cherokees endured. Today, there are three federally recognized and sovereign Cherokee tribes living peacefully. The largest of the three is the Cherokee Nation. It comprises more than 300,000 members who trace their ancestors to the Trail of Tears. Seventy thousand of them live in Oklahoma. The United Keetoowah Band of Cherokee Indians (UKB), also headquartered in Oklahoma, is a second contemporary Cherokee tribe. It has more than 13,000 members, mostly descendants of Old Settlers who had emigrated before the Treaty of Echota. The third federally recognized Cherokee tribe, the Eastern Band of the Cherokee Nation, comprising approximately 11,000 people, lives in North Carolina. It descends from 800 Cherokees who refused to remove west. Nearly 900,000 Americans today claim Cherokee ancestry. All are American citizens.

The major sources for this chapter were:

Meacham, J. (2008). *American lion: Andrew Jackson in the White House*. New York, NY: Random House.

Moulton, G. E. (2004). *John Ross: Cherokee chief*. Athens, GA: University of Georgia Press.

Perdue, T., & Green, M. D. (2005). *The Cherokee removal: A brief history with documents*. New York, NY, and Boston, MA: Bedford/St. Martin's.

Smith, D. B. (2011). *An American betrayal: Cherokee patriots and the Trail of Tears*. New York, NY: Henry Holt and Company.

LEARNING ACTIVITIES FOR "THE WILL OF THE PEOPLE"

Facts of the Case

1. Which states in the East did the Cherokees inhabit?
2. What were the goals of the missionaries among the Cherokees?
3. Who was Sequoyah and what was the *Cherokee Phoenix*?
4. What was the nature of the conflict between John Ross and the Treaty Party?
5. What did the Supreme Court decide in the case of *Worcester v. Georgia*?
6. What were the provisions of the Treaty of New Echota?

Historical Understanding

1. What were the aims of the "civilization program"?
2. What was the policy of President Andrew Jackson regarding Native Americans?
3. What arguments against removal did the Cherokees offer?
4. Describe the Trail of Tears.

Expressing Your Reasoning

Should John Ross have opposed Cherokee removal? Why or why not?

Key Concepts from History

What do the following have in common?

1. The Vatican, also known as Vatican City, is the location of the Holy See, the papacy and those associated with the Pope in the government of the Roman Catholic Church. Vatican City is also the smallest country in the world, encircled

by a 2-mile border separating it from Italy. Its territory is just 109 acres, and its population is under 1,000. It operates its own legal system. The Vatican's territorial independence is guaranteed by the Lateran Treaty signed in 1929 with the Kingdom of Italy and revised in 1985. According to the terms of the Lateran Treaty, the Holy See has full ownership, exclusive dominion, and authority and jurisdiction over the city-state.

2. In 1898, as part of the peace treaty following the Spanish-American War, Spain ceded the Philippines, a group of islands in the Western Pacific, to the United States, which established it as a territory. The following year, Emilio Aguinaldo was elected president of the First Philippine Republic. His attempts to persuade other countries to recognize his government failed. An outbreak of general hostilities between U.S. and Filipino forces in February 1899 began the Philippine-American War. Aguinaldo's government effectively ceased to exist on April 1, 1901. He pledged allegiance to the United States after being captured by U.S. forces. The Philippines continued as a U.S. territory until July 4, 1946, when the United States recognized the independence of the Republic of the Philippines. Today, it is an independent country. In addition to membership in the United Nations, the Philippines is also an active member of ASEAN (Association of Southeast Asian Nations), an organization designed to strengthen relations and promote economic and cultural growth among states in the Southeast Asian region.

3. Canada is a country in the northern half of North America. It extends from the Atlantic to the Pacific and northward into the Arctic Ocean. It is the world's second-largest country by total area. The country's population is approximately 35 million. Formerly a British colony, Canada achieved independence from the United Kingdom, and in 1982 removed its last remaining ties of legal dependence on the British Parliament. The House of Commons, the lower house of the parliament, makes Canada's laws. Canadians elect representatives to the House of Commons. The prime minister is the head of government and is chosen by the political party with the largest number of members in the House of Commons. Like the United States, Canada has a federal system. The Canadian national government shares power with the provincial governments. Canadian national governments maintain active relations with other nations, mostly through multilateral organizations including the United Nations, the Organization of American States, and the North Atlantic Treaty Organization (NATO).

Historical Inquiry

The American Civil War posed special problems for the Cherokees in their new homeland. Using online and other sources, test the hypothesis that the Cherokees were disloyal to the United States during the war, and compose a short essay in which you accept or reject the hypothesis. Use evidence to support your decision.

To begin your investigation, the following search terms will be helpful:

- Cherokees and The Civil War
- Cherokees at Pea Ridge
- Chief John Ross during The Civil War
- Confederate Cherokees

CHAPTER 15

Foreigner in My Native Land

Juan Seguín and the Texas Revolution

Juan Seguín

Courtesy of the artist, Mark Barnett.

Texas is called "The Lone Star State." Its flag features three broad fields, one each of red, white, and blue—with a bold single star amid the blue. Unlike any other American state, Texas, before it became a state, was (briefly) an independent country, the Republic of Texas. Its nickname during those 9 years (1836–1845) was "The Lone Star Republic."

Before Texas became a country, it was part of Mexico, and before that, it was part of New Spain, the Spanish empire in North America. In 1519, when the first

Spanish conquistadors arrived in search of gold, what is now Texas was home to several Native American tribes, including the Comanche, Apache, Caddo, and Karankawa. Their ancestors had been there for many hundreds of years.

In the late 1600s, the Spanish settled Texas by establishing Catholic missions where they would teach the Native Americans about Christianity. In 1718, San Antonio was established with the building of a mission there. That mission would later become known as The Alamo.

In 1821, the Mexican War for Independence ended control by Spain over its North American territories. The new independent country of Mexico was formed from lands of the former New Spain. The Mexican Constitution of 1824 included Texas in the new nation as part of a joint state called Coahuila y Texas. To encourage settlement in Texas, the newly established Mexican government allowed immigration from the United States. That immigration policy was intended to promote settlement of sparsely populated Texas and to create a buffer against the Native Americans in the territory.

The first person to obtain permission to bring Anglo-American settlers into Spanish Texas was Moses Austin. The new Mexican government passed the grant to his 27-year-old son, Stephen F. Austin, often called "The Father of Texas," after whom the present-day capital of Texas is named. The families brought to Texas by Austin, known as the Old Three Hundred, settled along the Brazos River in 1822 with the approval of the Mexican government.

The colony grew rapidly. By 1834, 30,000 Anglos lived in Texas, compared to 7,800 Mexicans. Friction between Anglos and the government in Mexico City arose. Many of the settlers migrated from southern American states with their slaves. Some of them, as well as some of their financial supporters from the United States, wanted Texas to secede from Mexico and join the United States as a slave state, as did eventually happen.

During this time, there was intense political conflict in Mexico between centralists, who wanted strong control by the central government, and federalists, who favored decentralized power for the state governments. In 1835, the centralists, under President Antonio Lopez de Santa Anna, prevailed. He officially voided the Mexican Constitution of 1824 and assumed power in Mexico City. Mexico's Congress approved the centralized state and the laws Santa Anna proposed to uphold it.

Most Texians (as Anglo American Texans were called at the time) resented increased central control, and they organized conventions to adopt resolutions setting forth their grievances. They objected to customs duties (taxes levied on incoming goods), what the Texians considered unfair legal procedures, military rule, lack of protection from Indian attacks, and restriction of immigration from the United States (which had been halted in 1830). In one convention, the Texians also called for a state government of, for, and by Anglo-Texans, but they did not yet call for Texas to secede from Mexico.

A delegation led by Stephen Austin was sent by Texians to the Mexican capital to establish greater autonomy for Texas. Austin, though proclaiming loyalty to the Mexican government, was jailed for 18 months in Mexico City. He was suspected of treason for a letter he had written favoring a Texas state separate from the state of Coahuila y Texas. Soon after his release from prison in 1835, Austin radically changed his course. He put out a general call for Texians to stand to arms: "War is our only resource. There is no other remedy. We must defend our rights, ourselves, and our country by force of arms."

The Mexicans regarded the English-speaking Texians as foreigners, but the Texians viewed Mexican government troops marching into Texas as invaders. Clashes between the two erupted into armed conflict in October 1835. Texians fired the first shot of the Texas Revolution for independence during a skirmish with Mexican troops in Gonzales. Over the next 3 months, the Texian Army defeated all Mexican troops in the region.

After these initial victories, many of the Texas settlers were convinced the war was over. Those in the army drifted away, back to their farms and homes. Most of the remaining troops had recently arrived from the United States. Their presence contributed to the Mexican view that Texian opposition stemmed from outside influences. A harsh new policy of Santa Anna toward the Texians decreed that every person who had taken part in the revolt was to be executed or exiled. Other Texian colonists were to be removed to the interior of Mexico. No American settlers would be permitted to enter Texas in the future. Santa Anna was determined to extinguish forever what he considered the Anglo-American peril.

On March 2, 1836, Texians signed the Texas Declaration of Independence, proclaiming separation from Mexico and creation of the Republic of Texas. Sam Houston, protégé of American President Andrew Jackson and former governor of Tennessee, was made chairman of the constitutional committee of Texas. Already prepared, Mexican President Antonio Lopez de Santa Anna commanded a force of 6,000 that marched into Texas. Santa Anna led a large number of those troops to San Antonio to besiege The Alamo Mission.

About 100 defenders were then garrisoned at The Alamo. They had intelligence confirming that Santa Anna's forces were on their way. They also knew of his unforgiving policy toward Texians. The joint Texian and Tejano (Texans of Mexican origin) force of 100 at The Alamo grew with the arrival of reinforcements led by Alamo co-commanders James Bowie and William B. Travis. The folk-hero frontiersman and former Tennessee congressman, Davy Crockett, was also among those defending the Alamo. Several of The Alamo defenders brought their families into the mission for safety after Santa Anna's troops occupied San Antonio.

In the early morning hours of March 6, 1836, thousands of Mexican troops, led by Santa Anna, advanced on the Alamo. The defending frontiersmen from Kentucky and Tennessee, accurate though they were at firing their single-shot rifles, could not prevail against the professional Mexican cavalry and infantry. After repulsing two attacks, the defenders were overwhelmed by a third wave preceded by cannon fire. Mexican soldiers scaled the thick limestone walls of the fortress with ladders. Many of the defenders withdrew into interior buildings. Those unable to reach these points were slain by the Mexican cavalry as they attempted to escape. After the battle, a small number of survivors were shot by firing squad in a courtyard of the Alamo. Five hours after it began, the assault was over. The Alamo had fallen.

Approximately 200 defenders of The Alamo were killed. Of the Texians who fought during the battle, only two were spared: one a slave and the other a former Mexican soldier who claimed he had been captured and held by the Texians. In addition, several couriers who had been dispatched from The Alamo during the siege to get reinforcements were not present for the final assault. Other Mexican army forces defeated Texian resistance along the Texas Gulf coast, culminating in what was called "the Goliad Massacre," when Mexican soldiers at Goliad executed 300 prisoners of war.

News of these defeats sparked a rush by Texians to retaliate. "Remember the Alamo!" became the battle cry of the Texas Revolution. Many settlers rejoined the army, then commanded by General Sam Houston.

One defender of The Alamo who had been dispatched as a courier for reinforcements during the siege was Juan Seguín. He was born in Bexar (San Antonio) in 1806 into a prominent Tejano family. At the time of Juan's birth, Bexar, like all of Mexico, was part of the Spanish empire. His grandparents and great-grandparents had been settled in Bexar for a century.

Juan's father, Erasmo Seguín, was the local postmaster. He welcomed the more recently arrived Anglo-American settlers to the province. He was friends with Stephen Austin and personally conducted him across the border into Texas. Erasmo welcomed the first Anglo-American settlers (The Old Three Hundred) to the region, accepting that they would bring their slaves with them to Texas. Juan, like his father, developed a lasting friendship with Austin, the principal architect of Anglo-American settlement in the province.

The Seguín family was among the more affluent of San Antonio. Though he had little formal schooling, Juan learned to read and write (in Spanish), to tend cattle, and to work the family farm. While Erasmo Seguín was away in Mexico City representing Texas in the Mexican constitutional congress, 17-year-old Juan helped his mother run San Antonio's post office. At age 19, Juan married María Gertrudis Flores de Abrego, a member of one of San Antonio's most prominent ranching families; they eventually had 10 children.

Beginning in his youth, Juan Seguín was comfortable among Anglos who appreciated Tejanos and respected Mexican ways. Like his father, he came to believe that the best hope for the future of Bexar would be for Tejanos and Texians to be partners in its development. Both Seguíns supported establishment of a strong Anglo-American colony.

Seguín became involved in business, sometimes with Anglo-Americans. He was also a minor player in land speculation. Grants of land from the state government were bought and sold in hope of gain, but with risk. This speculation was later to become a grievance of Texians against Mexico.

Juan combined business with public service. He became involved in politics during a time of turmoil. At his birth, a Spanish monarchy ruled Mexico. He grew up during a period of revolutionary warfare. By the time he reached maturity, Mexico had become an independent nation-state.

At age 22, Juan was elected to his first political office as a San Antonio alderman (a member of the city council). There were tensions between the two factions we have already seen: centralists who supported a strong national government dominated by the military and the church, in which the states were mere administrative units; and federalists who supported a system of states' rights, where states exercised most authority. When Juan became mayor of San Antonio in 1833, he sided with the federalists. Juan also faced controversy over the status of Texas within the Mexican republic. Many Texians became vocal about separate statehood for Texas. They wanted to be separate from Coahuila y Texas, of which Texas was then still a part. Juan urged patience and compliance with federal and state laws.

Mexican authorities became alarmed at the separatist rumblings of the restive Texians. To bring them under control, a law was passed in 1830. It forbade further Anglo-American immigration into Texas, strengthened the military presence in the province, and prohibited further importation of slaves.

Juan continued to call for patience and compliance with federal and state laws. He urged that consultations be held in his state of Coahuila y Texas to quell the growing turmoil, but he was rebuffed by the national government. Juan was mindful of the letter by Stephen Austin advocating separation that landed him in a Mexico City prison in 1834. Later that year, the federalist-centralist struggle turned into open rebellion.

When the national government tried to disband local militias, Juan Seguín found new resolve. He issued a call to Tejanos and Texians "to use all our influence to rouse Texas against the tyrannical government of Santa Anna." At this point, he gave up his status as militia commander and joined the ranks of Stephen Austin's newly formed Federal Army of Texas. Austin commissioned Juan as a captain. In the fall of 1835, his company was involved in scouting and supply missions for the revolutionary army.

Juan and his comrades in arms joined the defenders of San Antonio who had withdrawn into the Alamo. At that time, he still considered himself a loyal Mexican. He believed that he was defending the revoked constitution of his country against the centrist rule imposed by Santa Anna.

Juan would have perished with the other defenders of the Alamo, except that he was dispatched from the fortress as a messenger. He was chosen to ride on horseback behind enemy lines with a call for reinforcements. As he departed The Alamo with a plea for help, he was still in the service of the Mexican state of Texas, albeit allied with the Texians. Very soon, however, he would fully embrace Texas independence.

When he returned with men to reinforce the Alamo, Juan listened in vain for the signal gunshot that was to be fired every 15 minutes for as long as the fort held. Finding The Alamo vanquished, he rode with his soldiers to join the Federal Army, now under the command of General Sam Houston. With his men, he formed the rear guard of San Antonio residents fleeing the Mexican army.

Juan's company was the only Tejano unit to fight with Houston at the historic Battle of San Jacinto on April 21, 1836. They were commended for their bravery, and Juan was promoted to lieutenant colonel. San Jacinto (not the Alamo) was the decisive battle of the Texas Revolution. Led by General Sam Houston, the Texian Army engaged and defeated Santa Anna's Mexican Army in a brief battle. Santa Anna surrendered and was held as a prisoner of war. Seguín stood alongside Houston at the formal surrender. Three weeks later, Santa Anna signed the peace treaty dictating that the Mexican Army must leave the region, paving the way for the Republic of Texas to become an independent country.

After the battle, Seguín supervised the withdrawal of the Mexican army from Texas. He then returned to San Antonio and was appointed military commander of West Texas. During this time, he directed burial services for the remains of The Alamo dead. As captain of a Texas force in 1839, he protected colonists in a campaign against Comanche Indians. Later that year, 30 miles from San Antonio, he was honored with a parade and celebration in a town newly named Seguin in his honor.

Juan Seguín was elected to the new Texas Senate. He was the only Tejano senator during the republic, and he served three terms. Despite his lack of English, he was chairman of the Committee on Military Affairs. As a legislator, he initiated efforts to have the laws of the new republic printed in Spanish.

Despite the treaty signed by Santa Anna after the defeat of his army at San Jacinto, armed conflicts continued between Mexico and the Lone Star Republic. In March 1842, Santa Anna's forces overran San Antonio. Colonel Seguín led a counterattack that chased the occupying Mexican Army from Texas.

At this time, there was an influx of Anglo-American newcomers into the new Republic of Texas, including adventurers and land-hungry Americans. Many were unaware of the Tejanos' history and their support of Texas. Remembering Santa Anna's cruelty, some Anglos sought reprisals against all Mexicans, including Tejanos who had fought alongside the Anglo-Americans. Tejano landowners appealed to Juan for protection, but he was unable to protect them.

Some of the newcomers challenged Seguín's loyalty and leadership. Others resented his enforcement of the law in San Antonio: Some Americans had illegally occupied city land. When, in his official capacity as mayor, Juan evicted them, they were resentful and threatened to take revenge against him personally.

Despite his military and political service, Juan, like other Tejanos, was increasingly suspected of disloyalty. He had raised a company of men and invested $3,000 to equip them as part of an abortive attempt to establish a Republic of the Rio Grande among the northeastern Mexican states. The leader of the failed attempt defected to Mexico. Juan was left with debt from the failed effort, and engaged in a smuggling operation to pay it. This brought him into contact with Mexican military men allegedly determined to recover Texas for Mexico. His contacts across the border brought more charges of disloyalty.

Branded a traitor, Juan was under increasing threat from Anglo-American newcomers who wanted to oust him as the most powerful man in San Antonio and the one who stood in the way of their land acquisition schemes. Fearing for his life and unable to get support from his friend Sam Houston, Juan resigned as mayor in 1842 and fled with his family to Mexico "to seek a refuge amongst my enemies." In his memoirs, he said: "Unable to suffer the persecution of ungrateful Americans, I had to leave Texas." He felt himself "a foreigner in my native land."

Juan claims in his memoirs that he was captured, arrested, and given a choice by Mexican authorities of enlisting in the Mexican Army or going to jail as a traitor to Mexico. He chose enlistment and organized a company of volunteers made up of Tejanos who had earlier chosen Mexico over Texas. Charges of treason followed quickly from Texas.

Not all Texans agreed. Sam Houston, then president of the Texas Republic, wrote to Juan's father, Erasmo:

> I pray, Sir, that you will not suppose for one moment that I will denounce Colonel Juan N. Seguín, without a more perfect understanding of the circumstances of his absence. I rely on his honor, his worth, and his chivalry.

Juan served as a staff officer in the Mexican Army. Under Mexican General Adrian Woll, Juan participated in operations against Texas. Later, he served under Santa Anna and fought against the United States during several battles in the Mexican-American War of 1846–1848. Texas joined the United States in 1845 as the 28th state, ending the brief existence of the Republic of Texas.

By the end of the war, Juan was weary and requested permission to return with his family to his native Texas. He returned to San Antonio, risking his safety at the hands of those convinced that he had been disloyal. He established a home near his father's house. He was elected justice of the peace and became a founder of the Democratic Party in Bexar County. He served as a judge in Wilson County. In 1883, he went to live in Nuevo Laredo, Tamaulipas, Mexico, to be near his son who was mayor there. In Nuevo Laredo, he and his wife, Gertrudis, lived out the remaining years of their lives. Juan's letters from that time portray him at peace with his life and his choices. He died in Nuevo Laredo in 1890, largely, but not entirely forgotten.

The remains of Juan Seguín were returned to Texas in 1974. As part of the American bicentennial celebration on July 4, 1776, those remains were reinterred in his namesake town, Seguin.

The major sources for this chapter were:

de la Teja, J. F. (2010). Juan N. Seguín: Federalist, rebel, exile. In J. F. de la Teja, (Ed.), *Tejano leadership in Mexican and revolutionary Texas* (pp. 212–230). College Station, TX: Texas A&M University Press.

Fehrenbach, T. R. (2002). *Lone star: A history of Texas and the Texans.* Boston, MA: Da Capo Press.

Seguín, J. N., & de la Teja, J. F. (2002). In J. F. de la Teja (Ed.), *A revolution remembered: The memoirs and selected correspondence of Juan N. Seguín.* Austin, TX: Texas State Historical Association.

Trevino, J. S. (Writer & Director). (1982). Seguín. *American Playhouse Season 1.* Arlington, VA: Public Broadcasting System.

LEARNING ACTIVITIES FOR "FOREIGNER IN MY NATIVE LAND"

Facts of the Case

1. What is the difference between Tejano and Texian?
2. What was the origin of the battle cry "Remember the Alamo"?
3. What military service did Juan Seguín provide to Texas?
4. Which public offices did Juan Seguín hold?
5. Why did Juan Seguín flee with his family to Mexico?
6. What military service did Juan Seguín provide to Mexico?

Historical Understanding

1. What was the Lone Star Republic?
2. Who was Stephen Austin?
3. How did federalists differ from centralists in Mexico?
4. What was the historical significance of the Battle of San Jacinto?

Expressing Your Reasoning

1. Should Juan Seguín have fled to Mexico? Why or why not?
2. Should Juan Seguín have joined the Mexican Army after fleeing to Mexico? Why or why not?

Key Concepts from History

What do the following have in common?

1. American territorial expansion to the Pacific coast had been a goal of U.S. President James K. Polk and his Democratic Party. They believed it was their God-given mission to extend the "boundaries of freedom." Mexico and the United States went to war in 1846. The war lasted 2 years and ended in the defeat of Mexico. Mexico lost almost half its territory to the United States. In the Treaty of Guadalupe Hidalgo that concluded the war, Mexico ceded land to the United States that included parts of present-day Arizona, California, New Mexico, Texas, Colorado, Nevada, and Utah.
2. Russia, Spain, Britain, and the United States vied for control of what Americans called "Oregon Country," the land west of the Rocky Mountains, including

present-day Oregon, Washington, Idaho, and portions of Montana, Wyoming, and British Columbia. By the 1820s, treaties were negotiated whereby Russia and Spain withdrew their territorial claims, leaving Britain and the United States to occupy Oregon Country jointly. Caravans of American pioneers, lured by the lush Willamette Valley, headed west on the Oregon Trail. Disputes over control of the region ensued between Britain and the United States. In the 1844 U.S. presidential election, Democratic candidate James K. Polk called for ending the Oregon boundary dispute by annexing all of Oregon Country. In 1845, highly influential journalist John L. O'Sullivan addressed the ongoing boundary dispute with Britain in his newspaper, the *New York Morning News*. He argued that the United States had the right to claim all of Oregon: "And that claim is by the right . . . to overspread and to possess the whole of the continent which Providence has given us for the development of the great experiment of liberty and federated self-government entrusted to us." The expansionist slogan "Fifty-four Forty or Fight!" alluded to an American idea of setting the border at that line of latitude. In 1846, the Oregon Treaty with Britain established the border between British North America and the United States farther south, along the 49th parallel.

3. As early as 200 A.D., a group of Polynesians, traveling by boat over thousands of miles of ocean, arrived on what are today the Hawaiian Islands. English Captain James Cook, the first European explorer to set foot on Hawaii, landed in 1778. To the British, and everyone who came after, it was paradise found. Great Britain, France, and the United States all eyed Hawaii as a potential addition to their landholdings. Americans came to Hawaii and established a powerful sugar industry there. Hawaii became the target of America's first imperial push when the drive for national expansion extended beyond the North American continent. In a note sent in 1893, the U.S. minister to Hawaii said, "The Hawaiian pear is now fully ripe and this is the golden hour for the United States to pluck it." Some Americans invoked the idea that America had a divine providence that was destined by God to expand its borders. Others believed that America simply had a mission, the right to extend its liberty to new realms. Advocating annexation of Hawaii in 1898, President William McKinley said that it was "destiny." The Hawaiian monarchy was overthrown. Hawaii was annexed in 1898. The Hawaiian Islands remained a U.S. territory until 1959, when they were admitted to statehood as the 50th state.

Historical Inquiry

On May 11, 1846, President James Polk reported to Congress that Mexico had attacked the United States. The president said that Mexican troops had "invaded our territory, and commenced hostilities by attacking our forces." He went on to say that Mexico was at fault for "commencing an offensive war and shedding the blood of our citizens on our own soil." Congress declared war.

The Whig opposition insisted that President Polk, a Democrat, provide ev-idence to support his claims about an invasion of U.S. territory. On December 22, 1847, 38-year-old, first-term Whig representative Abraham Lincoln of Illinois introduced what has come to be known as the Spot Resolutions. In a speech before the House, Congressman Lincoln demanded that President Polk submit evidence to Congress that the land on which the initial battle of the war occurred was indeed American territory. The resolutions required that the president specify just what "spot" it was on American soil that American blood had been spilled. Lincoln's obvious implication was that it had *not* been American soil.

Using online and other sources, test President Polk's claim that Americans had been attacked on American soil. Compose a short essay in which you accept or reject the truth of the claim. Use evidence to support your decision. To begin your investigation, the following search terms will be helpful:

- Lincoln and the Mexican War
- Start of the Mexican War
- James K. Polk and the Mexican War
- "Spot Resolutions"
- Whig opposition to the Mexican War
- Ashmun Amendment

CHAPTER 16

A Different Drummer

Henry David Thoreau

Henry David Thoreau

"If a man does not keep pace with his companions, perhaps it is because he hears a different drummer. Let him step to the music which he hears, however measured, or far away." These words were written by an American rebel and literary giant Henry David Thoreau. He was highly critical of the society around him during the 1830s and 1840s. He was not fond of the spread of factories and railroads in the North, or the expansion of slavery in the South. Thoreau deplored what he considered the greed and materialism of his times. What disturbed him most of all were events in the fastest growing section of the new nation, the West.

As the frontier pushed farther and farther west, Americans came to believe in what they termed their *manifest destiny*. Originally, this term represented a desire to spread democratic government to all people of the Western Hemisphere. By the 1830s, manifest destiny had taken on a slightly different meaning. According to many land-hungry Americans of the time, it was the destiny or historic duty of the United States to expand westward to the Pacific Ocean. Manifest destiny was soon to collide with the Mexican border.

During the 1820s, a democratic government in Mexico opened its land to settlers from the United States. By 1830, more than 20,000 Americans, many of them southerners, had entered Texas, at this time a part of Mexico. Many settlers brought their slaves with them, in violation of Mexican law.

In 1830, Mexico closed its doors to further settlers from the United States. A new military government feared the possibility of Texas becoming a U.S. state. Americans in Texas protested the new policy vigorously. Fighting broke out in 1835. The Mexican Army besieged a force of Texians and Tejanos (American and Mexican Texans) in an old Spanish mission called the Alamo. Those defending the mission were all killed. Soon thereafter, another force of Texans rallied behind the leadership of Sam Houston. Under the cry "Remember the Alamo," the Texans defeated the Mexican Army at the Battle of San Jacinto.

Meanwhile, in March 1836, a group of Texans declared their independence from Mexico. They drafted a constitution for a new independent republic of Texas, often called the Lone Star Republic. The United States recognized the new government, but Mexico did not.

When the new republic petitioned to join the United States as a state, strong opposition developed in the United States. Because Texas allowed slavery, northerners in Congress opposed admission to the Union of another slave state. Others feared that to admit Texas would lead to war with Mexico.

The Democratic presidential candidate of 1844, James K. Polk, called for the annexation of Texas. Soon after his election, Texas was admitted to the Union. The annexation of Texas was a major loss of territory for Mexico and a blow to Mexican national pride. It touched off war between the United States and Mexico (1846–1848).

Some northerners opposed the war against Mexico. They feared that slavery would spread into the vast new territories and that slave states might gain a majority in the U.S. Senate. This would reduce the chance that the federal government could prevent the spread of slavery. One northerner opposed to both slavery and the Mexican-American War was Henry David Thoreau.

Henry was born in Concord, Massachusetts, in 1817 and resided there nearly his entire life. His father, John, made pencils for a living. Henry's mother often kept boarders in the family house. Henry heard abolitionist views expressed at the dinner table by his parents and the boarders. Henry had a brother and two sisters. The Thoreau family enjoyed an affectionate home life. None of the four children ever moved away from Concord.

Henry's boyhood home was in Concord Village. He cherished the countryside surrounding the village. As a child he was attracted to the outdoors and the companionship of nature. He was homesick when away from Concord. While visiting New York as a young man, Henry wrote in a letter to his mother, "I would be content to sit in Concord, under the poplar tree, henceforth, forever."

He graduated from nearby Harvard at age 20. In college, he was a village boy away from home. He was not much impressed by the school, nor did he make much of an impression upon his professors. His life there was solitary and dull, but he loved the library. Though far from the top of his class, Henry was probably the most well-read Harvard graduate of 1837.

In a college essay Thoreau expressed his growing dislike of conformity. The essay urged independent thought and strong individuality. "The fear of displeasing the world," he wrote, "ought not in the least to influence my actions." He remained a nonconformist his whole life.

After college, Thoreau was troubled by how to make a living without sacrificing his individuality. He became a teacher in the Concord Public Elementary School. One day, while observing his class, a member of the school committee noticed that Thoreau did not flog (strike with a whip) his pupils when they did poorly in school. After class, he was ordered to use a cowhide switch on his pupils. Thoreau believed that physical punishment had no place in education. To express his view that physical punishment was senseless, he thrashed six good students as a perverse protest against the school policy and then resigned.

Later, Thoreau and his older brother, John, opened a successful private school in Concord. No flogging was allowed. Emphasis was placed on nature study. In their school the Thoreau brothers introduced "fieldtrips." They often took students boating on the river and had them search for arrowheads, birds, and flowers.

The private school closed in 1841 because of John's ill health. Henry was troubled anew about how to support himself. He earned some income manufacturing pencils with his father. Exceptionally practical and resourceful, Henry improved pencil lead by baking the graphite mixture into cylinders, and he invented a machine that drilled a hole in the wood of the pencil so the lead cylinder could simply be slipped in. John Thoreau & Company pencils were considered the best on the market. Once Henry had mastered their production, he moved on. The work did not leave him the freedom he wanted to study nature and write. "Life," he declared, "is too valuable to put into lead-pencils."

Around this time Thoreau made the acquaintance of Ralph Waldo Emerson, who also lived in Concord. Emerson was a world-famous scholar, 14 years older than Thoreau. The two developed a close and lasting friendship. Emerson saw in Thoreau an undeveloped genius. In Emerson's company, Thoreau's mind flourished.

Emerson was the leader of a group of Concord thinkers known as the transcendentalists. Their first principle was freedom of thought. The group's favorite meeting place was Emerson's house. Thoreau joined the group.

During the 1830s, transcendentalists in New England believed that there is a body of knowledge innate within people, beyond what they know from their senses of touch, sight, hearing, and smell. This knowledge, they believed, *transcends* the senses. For each person, it was the voice of God within—a conscience, moral sense, or inner light.

According to the transcendentalists, every child was born with an innate ability to distinguish between right and wrong. In their view, it was the duty of a good citizen to heed the voice within rather than the corrupting voices from the surrounding world. Everyone must be free to act according to one's conscience to find the truth buried within.

The transcendentalists were optimistic that a new American mind would emerge. They urged people to be self-reliant individuals, to free themselves from ignorance, and to think for themselves. They believed that, free of dead European ideas, the new American would discover eternal truths.

Emerson not only influenced Thoreau's thinking, but also helped Thoreau support himself. Thoreau agreed to work as a handyman around the Emerson household and to tutor Emerson's son in exchange for a room and meals in the Emerson house.

Thoreau fell in love with a young woman, Ellen Sewall, and proposed marriage to her. She refused him. Thereafter, his romantic feelings were channeled into a deep love of nature. Living and working at the Emerson household failed to provide Thoreau the solitude he craved. He took delight in his daily walks in the woods, but he wanted more privacy than he could get living with the Emersons.

As he wandered through the village or its surroundings, Thoreau was often mistaken for a farmer. His boots were never polished and his clothes were homespun. He ridiculed the manners of polite Concord society. Many in the Concord community considered him an eccentric loner or even a shiftless crank. He scoffed at their acquisitions of material possessions. In his quest to simplify life, material belongings had little importance. The mass of men, he said, lived "lives of quiet desperation," struggling to get rich and buy things.

Other than a rowboat and his books, Henry owned almost nothing. He boarded mostly with his family or with the Emersons. When he ran out of money, he took a paid job temporarily. He could find work as a surveyor, and he was a skilled carpenter. "He chose to be rich," wrote his friend Emerson, "by making his wants few and supplying them himself."

In 1845, at the age of 27, Henry decided to escape to Walden Pond, located on property owned by Emerson. He went there, he said, "to live deliberately, to confront only the essential facts of life, and see if I could not learn what it had to teach, and not, when I came to die, discover that I had not lived."

With his own hands he built a cabin near the pond. Into it he moved a bed, a desk, a table, a few utensils, three chairs, and a tiny mirror. He also planted a small vegetable garden. For 2 years he lived like a hermit at Walden, studying the natural environment and recording his thoughts at great length in a journal. At

Walden, Thoreau accepted his animal neighbors as they accepted him. For example, in his journal he reported that a mouse nested under his cabin and came to pick crumbs at his feet while he ate lunch.

Taking a walk with him, Emerson recalled, was like walking with an encyclopedia. Thoreau recognized animal tracks, wildflowers, and birdcalls.

Thoreau believed that it was wrong to take the life of any animal. Because of this belief, he had a strong preference for a vegetarian diet. He did catch fish for his meals now and then, but felt guilty about it.

One day he discovered that woodchucks were destroying beans in his Walden garden. He caught one in a metal trap and then let it go. The same woodchuck reappeared in his garden a few days later and was again trapped. Thoreau asked a veteran trapper whether there was any way to get woodchucks without trapping them. The reply was "Yes; shoot 'em, you damn fool." Thoreau carried the woodchuck 2 miles away, opened the trap, and set him free.

While at Walden, it was unusual for Thoreau to pay attention to what went on very far from Concord. The Mexican War, however, spurred him to protest. In late July 1846, Henry walked one evening from Walden into Concord. He was on his way to get a mended shoe from the cobbler's. In the village he was stopped by Sam Staples, the local constable, tax collector, and jailer.

Thoreau had not paid his poll tax for 3 years and owed $1.50 (about $42 today). The poll tax, also known as a head tax, was levied as a fixed sum on all eligible voters. It was an important source of revenue for the local Concord government. Staples insisted that Thoreau pay the tax due. Thoreau refused to pay. It was a government, he said, that buys and sells men, women, and children, referring to the enslaved. (The poll tax was local and its receipts went to neither the state nor federal government.)

Staples pleaded with Thoreau to pay the tax. Thoreau said, "If you call on me to pay for a rifle, Sam, it's the same as asking me to fire it. You're making me as much a killer as a foot soldier, who crashed the border into faraway Mexico." Sam thereupon locked Thoreau up in the Concord jail.

The Mexican War had stiffened Thoreau's opposition to the poll tax. He detested slavery. In his words: "when a sixth of the population of a nation which has undertaken to be the refuge of liberty are slaves, and a whole country is unjustly overrun and conquered by a foreign army . . . I think it is not too soon for honest men to rebel."

The morning after he was jailed, Thoreau's aunt paid the tax without his consent. Although Thoreau objected, the constable insisted on releasing him. Emerson believed that Thoreau's protest was in "bad taste" and that it was shortsighted to try to reform society by protesting an isolated evil. According to some accounts, he visited Thoreau in jail and asked, "Henry, what are you doing in there?" Henry's reply was "Waldo, the question is what are you doing out there?"

Thoreau is well known as the author of *Walden*, the book he wrote about the 2 years he spent living in the woods at Walden Pond. It continues to be widely read. The book is his spiritual reflection upon simple living in natural surroundings and self-reliance.

Two years after the night he spent in jail, Thoreau authored what was at first ignored but later became a historic essay entitled *Civil Disobedience*. The title has become a significant concept in political history. In the essay, Thoreau explains his defiance of the law and tries to justify peaceful resistance by citizens to the authority of government. Some of the enduring ideas expressed in this essay include:

"To be patriots, some citizens must serve the state with their consciences and resist the government."

"If [an injustice of the government] . . . requires you to be an agent of injustice to another, then, I say break the law."

"Must the citizen ever for a moment, or in the least degree, resign his conscience to the legislator? Why has every man a conscience then? I think that we should be men first, and subjects afterward. It is not desirable to cultivate a respect for the law, so much as for the right. The only obligation which I have a right to assume is to do at any time what I think right."

"It is the citizen's duty to obey the voice of God within rather than that of civil authority without. If he will go to prison rather than obey an evil law, he will through his courage and his martyrdom arouse the conscience of his people to rebel *en masse* and through their resistance they will clog the machinery of tyranny by filling the courts and the jails and thus bring about repeal of the offensive law."

More than a century later, American civil rights leader Dr. Martin Luther King, Jr., noted in his autobiography that his first encounter with the idea of nonviolent resistance was reading Thoreau's essay on civil disobedience while in college. In his autobiography, Dr. King wrote:

Here, in this courageous New Englander's refusal to pay his taxes and his choice of jail rather than support a war that would spread slavery's territory into Mexico, I made my first contact with the theory of nonviolent resistance. . . . I became convinced that noncooperation with evil is as much a moral obligation as is cooperation with good. No other person has been more eloquent and passionate in getting this idea across than Henry David Thoreau. . . . The teachings of Thoreau came alive in our civil rights movement. . . . Whether expressed in a sit-in at lunch counters, a freedom ride into Mississippi, a peaceful protest in Albany, Georgia, a bus boycott in Montgomery, Alabama, these are outgrowths of Thoreau's insistence that evil must be resisted and that no moral man can patiently adjust to injustice.

Thoreau was again aroused to civil disobedience during the early 1850s. In 1850, Congress passed the Fugitive Slave Law. The law granted slaveholders, or their agents, authority to seize and carry back to the South runaway slaves found in the North. Under the law, local citizens were prohibited from aiding runaways and could be ordered by a court to pursue fugitive slaves.

On September 30, 1851, Henry Williams, who had escaped from slavery in Virginia to Boston, learned there were warrants out for his arrest. He fled on foot to Concord, where he sought out the Thoreau family. They lodged the fugitive for the night and collected funds to help him along the way. The next morning Henry Thoreau went to the railroad station and bought a ticket for the runaway. By helping him get safely on his way to Canada, Thoreau risked prosecution for breaking federal law.

Most abolitionists distanced themselves from the antislavery zealot John Brown. In 1859, hoping to arm slaves and spark a violent rebellion against the South, Brown led an ill-fated armed assault on the federal arsenal in Harpers Ferry, Virginia, a holding place for approximately 100,000 rifles and muskets. Some of the rebels and local townspeople were killed, as was one of the U.S. Marines sent to suppress the rebellion. Brown was captured by federal forces, jailed, and later executed.

Thoreau composed a speech, "A Plea for Captain John Brown." In it he vigorously defended Brown and his actions. Thoreau's speech was influential. At first, most Americans condemned Brown's raid at Harpers Ferry. Soon, however, the abolitionist movement began to accept Brown as a martyr. By the time of the American Civil War, soldiers of the North were literally singing Brown's praises.

In 1862, Henry David Thoreau, age 44, fell victim to tuberculosis. He was buried in Sleepy Hollow Cemetery on the woody knolls that were his pleasure in Concord.

Thoreau's ideas about civil disobedience were not laid to rest with their author. In addition to their influence on Martin Luther King in his struggle for the civil rights of Black Americans, they influenced Leo Tolstoy in his opposition to czarist Russia and Mahatma Gandhi in his leadership against British colonial control of India.

The major sources for this chapter were:

Canby, H. S. (1939). *Thoreau.* Boston, MA: Houghton Mifflin.

Connor, S. V., & Faulk, O. B. (1971). *North America divided: The Mexican War 1846–1848.* New York, NY: Oxford University Press.

Derleth, A. (1962). *Concord rebel: A life of Henry D. Thoreau.* Philadelphia, PA: Chilton.

Harding, W. (1966). *The days of Henry Thoreau.* New York, NY: Alfred A. Knopf.

Thoreau, H. D. (1966) *Walden and civil disobedience.* New York, NY: W. W. Norton.

LEARNING ACTIVITIES FOR "A DIFFERENT DRUMMER"

Facts of the Case

1. Why did Sam Staples arrest Thoreau?
2. How did Thoreau justify refusing to pay his poll tax?
3. What did Thoreau do when Henry Williams arrived in Concord?
4. Why did Thoreau decide to live at Walden Pond?

Historical Understanding

1. What did manifest destiny mean to 19th-century Americans?
2. Why were some northerners opposed to the Mexican War?
3. What were the major beliefs of the New England transcendentalists?
4. What were the major provisions of the Fugitive Slave Law of 1850?

Expressing Your Reasoning

Should Thoreau have refused to pay his poll tax? Why or why not?

Key Concepts from History

What do the following have in common?

1. Civil rights activist Rosa Parks was born in 1913 in Alabama. In 1943, she became actively involved in civil rights issues by joining the Montgomery, Alabama, chapter of the National Association for the Advancement of Colored People (NAACP). She served as secretary to the chapter president, a post she held until 1957. Montgomery was racially segregated by law. As part of segregationist policy, bus drivers were required to provide separate seating for White and Black passengers. A sign, roughly in the middle of the bus, separated White passengers in the front of the bus from African American passengers in the back. When the seats in the front of the bus filled up and more White passengers got on, the bus driver would move back the sign separating Black and White passengers and, if necessary, tell Black passengers to give up their seats. On December 1, 1955, after a long day's work at a Montgomery department store, where she was a seamstress, Rosa Parks boarded the bus for home. She took a seat in the first of several rows designated for "colored" passengers. As the bus continued on its route, it began to fill with White passengers. When the bus became full, the driver noticed that a White passenger was standing in the aisle. He stopped the bus and moved the sign separating the two sections back one row and directed four Black passengers to give up their seats. Three complied, but Parks refused and remained seated. The driver demanded, "Why don't you stand up?" to

which Rosa replied, "I don't think I should have to stand up." The driver called the police. Rosa was arrested and fined. Later, she recalled that her refusal wasn't because she was physically tired, but that she was tired of giving in. She later said she couldn't have lived with herself if she had given in and stood up. The police arrested Rosa Parks at the scene for violation of the Montgomery city code.

2. Sam Houston is the only person to have become the governor of two different U.S. states. He was governor of Tennessee before moving to Texas when it was a Mexican state. He is best known as a leader of the Texas Revolution and for his role in bringing Texas into the union as a state. His victory commanding troops at the Battle of San Jacinto in 1836 secured the independence of Texas from Mexico. He was elected as the first and third president of the Republic of Texas. When Texas was annexed by the United States in 1845, Houston became a U.S. senator and, in 1859, he became the governor of the State of Texas. Although Houston was a slave owner and opposed abolition, he believed fervently in preserving the Union. At the start of The Civil War, he opposed the secession of Texas from the Union, but an elected convention voted to secede from the United States. Texas joined the Confederate States of America on March 2, 1861. Houston refused to recognize secession, but the Texas legislature upheld its legitimacy. The governor refused to take an oath of loyalty to the Confederacy. In an undelivered speech, he added:

> Fellow-Citizens, in the name of your rights and liberties, which I believe have been trampled upon, I refuse to take this oath. . . . I refuse to take this oath. I deny the power of this Convention to speak for Texas. . . . I protest against all the acts and doings of this convention and I declare them null and void.

Sam Houston was evicted from his office as Texas governor for refusing to take the loyalty oath.

3. Raoul Wallenberg was born in Sweden in 1912 to a prominent banking family. He attended the University of Michigan where, in 1935, he received a degree in architecture. His American degree did not qualify him to be an architect in Sweden, so, fluent in several languages, he took various jobs in business that involved international travel. Beginning in 1938, Hungary's fascist government, like its German counterpart, enacted laws restricting Jews' activities. Wallenberg's Jewish business associate found it increasingly difficult to travel between Sweden and Hungary for their import-export business. Wallenberg traveled to Hungary on his behalf. German troops occupied Hungary in 1944, and mass exportation of Jews to extermination camps in Poland began. Wallenberg was horrified by the atrocities committed by the Nazis. In the United States, the administration of President Franklin D. Roosevelt created the War Refugee Board to aid Jews being persecuted. Working with the Swedish government, the War Refugee Board sought someone to dispatch to Budapest to organize a rescue program for Hungarian

Jews. The Swedish Ministry for Foreign Affairs assigned Wallenberg to the task. Working with fellow Swedish diplomats, Wallenberg issued "protective passports" to Jews which identified the bearers as Swedish subjects awaiting repatriation and thus prevented their deportation. Although they were not strictly legal, these documents looked official and were generally accepted by German and Hungarian authorities. Through Wallenberg's efforts, tens of thousands of Hungarian Jews were saved from deportation to Nazi death camps.

Historical Inquiry

Thoreau's *Walden: Life in the Woods*, published in 1854, is a reflection upon simple living in natural surroundings. Some believe that the book marks Thoreau as the first American environmentalist.

Using online and other sources, test the claim that Henry David Thoreau was the founding voice of American environmentalism. Compose a short essay in which you accept or reject the truth of the claim. Use evidence to support your decision. To begin your investigation, the following search terms will be helpful:

- Thoreau
- In defense of Thoreau
- Walden
- Environmentalism

Part V

A HOUSE DIVIDED
1850–1865

CHAPTER 17

The Bloodhound Law

The Fugitive Slave Law and Northerners' Resistance

"Effects of the Fugitive-Slave-Law" by Theodor Kaufmann

Courtesy of the Library of Congress.

On a cold night in March 1854, someone rapped loudly on the door of a small cabin near Racine, Wisconsin. A few African American men were inside playing cards. One man was Joshua Glover, a fugitive (runaway) slave from Missouri. Another was Nelson Turner, a free man. "Don't open it until we know who's there," whispered Glover. There were rumors that slave catchers were in the area. Turner ignored the warning and opened the door.

Benjamin Garland (the slaveholder from whom Glover escaped), two federal marshals, and several other men burst into the cabin. They rushed toward Glover, knocked him to the floor, and pointed a pistol at his head. They then dragged him, now bruised and bleeding, out the door and took him straight to jail. Later, after a mob broke into the jail and rescued him, Glover escaped to Canada via the Underground Railroad. Sherman Booth, a local newspaper editor, had not participated in the rescue. However, because of his fiery speeches against the jailing of Glover, Booth was charged, tried, and convicted of instigating the rescue.

The Glover incident was only one of many such incidents. Glover's capture, rescue, and escape took place during a national debate on slavery. The debate raged around the legal position of fugitive slaves and the legality and morality of slave catching. Only a few years before the Glover incident, the U.S. Congress had passed the Fugitive Slave Law of 1850 (also referred to as the Fugitive Slave Act of 1850). The law required the return of captured runaway slaves to their owners.

Slavery had a long history in the United States. During the entire colonial period, slave traders brought captured people, mostly West Africans, to America where they were sold to work in the tobacco and cotton fields of the South and on farms in the North. Both northern and southern families used enslaved people for household work and childcare. There were never as many slaves in the North as the South, but slavery still existed in all the northern colonies. In fact, the slave trade center in the colonies was in New England.

A slave-owning household in New England and the Mid-Atlantic colonies, on average, had at least two enslaved persons. They worked on the farms in the growing and harvesting seasons and in households in the winter. The 1764 census listed 4,500 slaves in Massachusetts.

During and after the American Revolution, northern colonies began to abolish the practice of slavery. One reason was the support of African American enslaved people for the Revolutionary War. Many colonies paid slave owners to enlist their slaves in the military during the war with the British. Enslaved people who enlisted were promised their freedom at the end of the war. About 9,000 Black Patriot soldiers served in the Continental Army and Navy and in state militia units. Other enslaved people worked as spies. One-fourth of the militia soldiers from White Plains, New York, were Black slaves. The militia, led by General George Washington, was famous for its defeat of the British in the Battle of Yorktown in 1781. Many of these Black Patriots were freed after the war, but others were not. The question was then asked: If a man fights for his country, why can't he vote in his country?

Some northerners who opposed slavery called themselves "abolitionists" because they supported the abolition (that is, the end) of slavery. Some abolitionists were inspired by the sacrifice and loyalty of the Black soldiers during the Revolutionary War. Many others thought slavery was morally wrong. Still others thought slave labor was simply not economically practical.

Many of the Founding Fathers (including Washington, Jefferson, and Franklin) who signed the U.S. Constitution were slaveholders. Although some

Founding Fathers objected to slavery on principle, the Constitution did not reflect this objection. The Fugitive Slave Clause of the U.S. Constitution (Article 4, Section 2, Clause 3) states:

> No person held to service or labour in one state, under the laws thereof, escaping into another, shall, in consequence of any law or regulation therein, be discharged from such service or labour, but shall be delivered up on claim of the party to whom such service or labour may be due.

In short, fugitive slaves had to be returned to their masters. When the last state (Rhode Island) ratified the Constitution in 1790, questions remained. How was the return of fugitive slaves to be enforced? What was the punishment for helping fugitive slaves escape to freedom? To answer these questions, the U.S. Congress passed the Fugitive Slave Law of 1793 (full title: "An Act respecting fugitives from justice, and persons escaping from the service of their masters"). The act authorized local governments to capture and return fugitive slaves to their owners and levied fines ($500, or about $12,000 in today's currency) on people who helped fugitive slaves escape.

Bounty hunters and other civilians could now legally capture and return fugitive slaves to their masters. Children born of fugitive mothers in free territories and states, including Canada, were classified for life as the slave property of their mother's master. Even northern free Blacks who had their "free papers" (a certificate of manumission issued to freed slaves) risked capture and re-sale into slavery. Punishment of recaptured slaves by their masters was often harsh: Whipping and branding (burning a symbol into the flesh with a hot iron) were not uncommon.

The State of Massachusetts was a leader in the abolition movement. Quock Walker's story caused many citizens and politicians in Massachusetts to oppose slavery. Walker, who was enslaved in Massachusetts, had been promised his freedom. In 1781, when his owner refused to free him, Walker ran away. He was soon captured, returned to his owner, and beaten. There were two civil trials and one criminal trial related to the event. In the criminal trial, Walker was declared a free man at this trial. In his charge to the jury, the chief justice stated that under the Massachusetts Declaration of Rights, "all men are born free and equal." Massachusetts nonetheless did not legally abolish slavery until 1793, although no slaves were listed in the 1790 census.

Other states passed "gradual emancipation laws" that did not actually abolish slavery. Instead, such laws set out procedures for slowly phasing out slavery. In 1799, for example, the New York state legislature passed "An Act for the Gradual Abolition of Slavery." The act stated that as of the date of enactment, children born to enslaved mothers were free, but they had to work for their mother's master as indentured servants into their twenties. However, the act also established that existing slaves would remain enslaved.

Although the northern states began restricting slavery, in one way or other, the southern states took no such action. Southerners feared that national law would abolish slavery throughout the country, so they encouraged the idea that slavery was a good fortune to the enslaved. Articles, cartoons, and columns in newspapers and magazines promoted the fiction that slaves were childlike and dependent. Speakers in churches and lecture halls said enslaved people could not care for themselves. These articles portrayed plantation life in the South as happy evenings of songs and stories after days of work in the fresh air and sun. This life was contrasted with the life of northern workers, free men and women, who worked long hours in dirty, dangerous factories and lived in crowded and dark tenements.

The abolitionists tried to combat this false image of the enslaved and their lives. They found their spokesperson in Frederick Douglass, social reformer and author, who was born a slave in a shack in Maryland. In 1838, he and his future wife, Anna Murray, escaped from slavery by train and steamboat. They reached safety in New York City at the home of a well-known abolitionist. Douglass later wrote about his arrival in the North: "A new world had opened upon me."

As the movement to free slaves grew in the North, slaves in the South remained personal property of their owners, with no legal rights. For example, they could be sold, separated from their families, rented out, and used as wagers in card games. Evidence shows plantation life was far from the happy life that some southerners claimed. Some slaves revolted, while others ran away. They escaped to free states, Canada, and sometimes Mexico or other foreign countries. Assisted by abolitionists and other allies, the fugitive slaves followed a path to freedom called the Underground Railroad.

The Underground Railroad was a network of safe houses and secret routes that ran through 14 northern states to Canada. Former slaves, abolitionists, and church leaders, among others, helped the runaways escape via this network. Harriet Beecher Stowe's 1852 novel, *Uncle Tom's Cabin* (one of the most famous novels in American literature), featured the Underground Railroad.

Historians estimate that by 1850, between 40,000 and 100,000 fugitive slaves had traveled on the Underground Railroad. However, this number is only a small fraction of the total slave population in the United States at the time (roughly 3.2 million). The risk of capture and severe punishment was too great for many slaves.

Harriet Tubman was the most famous "conductor" on the Underground Railroad. In 1849, she ran away from her Maryland slave owner. Her family did not hear from her for 2 years. Then, in 1851, Harriet returned home to help her family, especially her 70-year-old parents who were too frail to escape by foot to freedom. She hired a wagon to carry them.

While enslaved people continued to run away, the issue of slavery and its abolition wound its way through the U.S. court system. On March 19, 1788, the Pennsylvania state legislature amended its "An Act for the Gradual Abolition of Slavery," originally enacted on March 1, 1780. The amendment stated, "No negro or mulatto slave . . . shall be removed out of this state, with the design and intention that the place of abode or residence of such slave or servant shall be thereby altered or changed."

On March 25, 1826, the Pennsylvania state legislature again strengthened its antislavery laws with the Pennsylvania Fugitive Slave Act of 1826, which stated in part:

> If any person or persons shall, from and after the passing of this act, by force and violence, take and carry away, or cause to be taken or carried away, and shall, by fraud or false pretense, seduce, or cause to be seduced, or shall attempt so to take, carry away or seduce, any negro or mulatto, from any part or parts of this commonwealth, to any other place or places whatsoever, out of this commonwealth, with a design and intention of selling and disposing of, or of causing to be sold, or of keeping and detaining, or of causing to be kept and detained, such negro or mulatto, as a slave or servant for life, or for any term whatsoever, every such person or persons, his or their aiders or abettors, shall on conviction thereof, in any court of this commonwealth having competent jurisdiction, be deemed guilty of a felony.

This law set the stage for a legal conflict with the Fugitive Slave Law of 1793 and the U.S. Constitution. In 1832, a former slave, Margaret Morgan, moved from Maryland to Pennsylvania. Her master, John Ashmore, had not emancipated her, but she had lived as a free woman for many years. When Ashmore died, his heirs decided to reclaim her. They hired a slave catcher named Edward Prigg. On April 1, 1837, Prigg and three men abducted Morgan and her children and took them back to Maryland. Prigg was convicted of violating the Pennsylvania Fugitive Slave Act of 1826. In his appeal to the U.S. Supreme Court, he argued that Pennsylvania law should not supersede federal law or the U.S. Constitution.

In *Prigg v. Pennsylvania*, the U.S. Supreme Court ruled that the Fugitive Slave Law of 1793 and the U.S. Constitution took precedence over the Pennsylvania Act. Prigg's conviction was thus overturned. In writing for the court, Justice Joseph Story, although a passionate supporter of abolition, said that the Pennsylvania Act was unconstitutional under Article IV of the Constitution and the Federal Fugitive Slave Law of 1793.

However, the court's opinion included a sentence that seemed to suggest the issue was not quite settled. (In a biography of his father, Judge Story's son wrote that this sentence was a deliberate attempt to destroy the practical enforceability of the Fugitive Slave Law of 1793.) The controversial sentence read:

> As to the authority so conferred upon state magistrates [to deal with runaway slaves], while a difference of opinion has existed, and may exist still

on the point, in different states, whether state magistrates are bound to act under it; none is entertained by this Court that state magistrates may, if they choose, exercise that authority, unless prohibited by state legislation.

State legislatures in Connecticut, Massachusetts, Michigan, Maine, New Hampshire, Ohio, Pennsylvania, Wisconsin, and Vermont took inspiration from these five words in the ruling: "unless prohibited by state legislation." It seemed the U.S. Supreme Court suggested that state legislatures had the authority to pass laws forbidding the capture and return of runaway slaves. These states soon passed "personal liberty laws"—laws that protected free Black Americans and fugitive slaves by prohibiting state officials from capturing and jailing them, leaving that responsibility solely in the hands of federal officials. Moreover, the personal liberty laws said fugitive slave cases could not be heard in the states, and no assistance could be given to people trying to capture slaves.

The Fugitive Slave Law of 1793 was still the law of the land. However, in some states, only federal officials could enforce it. State magistrates could not, if state legislation took away that authority.

Throughout the first half of the 19th century, political leaders continued to clash over the slavery issue. From 1846 to 1850, politicians and other leaders from the slave states and the free states angrily argued about the legality of slavery. The key question was whether slavery would be allowed in the new territories that were acquired after the Mexican-American War (1846–1848). Finally, a settlement was agreed on: the Compromise of 1850, which was a package of five separate bills. Whig Senator Henry Clay of Kentucky and Senator Stephen Douglass, Democrat of Illinois, brokered the compromise.

The most contentious of the five bills was the fourth, which was informally called the Fugitive Slave Law of 1850. This bill allowed federal officials in all states and territories to assist in the return of slaves to their masters in states and territories where slavery was legal. The law was nicknamed the "Bloodhound Law" because dogs were used to track fugitive slaves. This was the law that led to the capture of Joshua Glover in Racine, Wisconsin, in 1854.

Glover had escaped from slavery in Missouri in 1852. Under the Fugitive Slave Law of 1850, Glover should have been returned to his master in Missouri, Benjamin Garland. However, many settlers who opposed slavery and were active in the Underground Railroad lived in Wisconsin, a free state. Inspired by Sherman Booth, a group of these abolitionists broke down the doors of the Milwaukee County jail where Glover was imprisoned and freed him.

Sherman Booth, newspaper editor, politician, and abolitionist, often expressed his views on slavery at public meetings. When he was a student at Yale University, Booth taught English to imprisoned Africans who had seized the slave ship *Amistad*. This experience led to his interest in slavery and abolitionist issues. He wrote passionately against slavery and the Fugitive Slave Law of 1850 in his newspaper's editorials. On the morning of March 11, 1854, the day after Glover was jailed,

Booth received a telegram from the mayor of Racine, Wisconsin, about Glover's capture and imprisonment. Booth immediately rode a hired horse to Milwaukee, stopping along the way to urge people to attend a protest meeting at the Milwaukee courthouse. It was reported that he shouted, "Freemen to the rescue!"

Before a few thousand people in front of the courthouse in Milwaukee, Booth spoke against the kidnapping of a citizen without a legal hearing or a warrant for his arrest. He encouraged the protesters to obey the law but to express their opposition to it. After more speeches, meetings, various legal measures, considerable delay, and futile calls for the arrest of Garland and the U.S. deputy, the protesters lost patience. Twenty or so strong men seized a length of wood some 20 feet long and 8 to 10 inches in width from a nearby St. John's Cathedral construction site, and broke down the jail door. Glover was released and whisked away to safety in Canada.

Although Booth was not one of the 20 men involved in the jailbreak, and had not encouraged it, he was charged by federal authorities with "aiding and abetting" Glover's escape. He refused to appear in court and was arrested 4 days later. He was even burned in effigy by pro-slavery supporters.

Booth admitted he had spoken against the capture and imprisonment of Glover. Before his trial, he and his lawyer, Byron Paine, appeared before the Wisconsin Supreme Court where they argued that the Fugitive Slave Law of 1850 was unconstitutional. They based their argument on the fact that accused runaway slaves, imprisoned without trial, were denied due process of law as guaranteed by the U.S. Constitution. They also argued that Glover, who was considered "property" on the warrant, was exempt from the act because it referred to "persons held to service or labor" but not property. A third argument was that each state had the right to determine the constitutionality of federal laws. This was an example of the states' right argument that has often been used, and continues to be used, to oppose federal laws. In Booth's argument, the State of Wisconsin had the authority to rule on the legality of the Fugitive Slave Law of 1850.

When the jury acquitted Booth at his trial, abolitionists across the country cheered the decision. He was, however, soon rearrested and held for trial in a federal district court. The federal officials reasoned that the Wisconsin Supreme Court had exceeded its legal authority by declaring a federal law unconstitutional. This time Booth was found guilty, sentenced to a month in jail, and fined $1,000 (about $30,000 in today's currency).

Further legal controversy followed, and the case finally went to the U.S. Supreme Court. In *Ableman v. Booth*, the justices agreed with the federal position and overturned the Wisconsin Supreme Court's decision. Chief Justice Roger B. Taney, writing for the nine justices, declared that states had no authority to interfere with federal laws: State courts could not make rulings that contradicted or violated decisions of the federal courts, and thus Wisconsin did not have the authority to nullify federal rulings. In addition, the ruling stated that the Fugitive

Slave Law of 1850 was constitutional. According to the ruling, if people in a state tried to free a federal prisoner in the custody of a U.S. marshal, that marshal would have the "duty to resist it, and to call to his aid any force that might be necessary to maintain the authority of law against illegal interference." The decision suggested that all laws regarding the return of runaway slaves should be uniform throughout the country. As expected, abolitionists were outraged by the decision.

Further legal controversy ensued, and Booth spent more than a year in jail. Although Booth refused to ask for a pardon, President James Buchanan pardoned him in 1861 on his last day as president, 2 days before President Lincoln was inaugurated. Booth was released from prison and absolved of his fines.

Four years later, in 1865, the Thirteenth Amendment, Section 1, to the U.S. Constitution abolished slavery: "Neither slavery nor involuntary servitude, except as a punishment for crime whereof the party shall have been duly convicted, shall exist within the United States, or any place subject to their jurisdiction." As for Glover, when he arrived in Canada, he found work for the Montgomery family, who owned an inn, farms, and sawmill. He worked for them for 34 years. He died in 1888, a free man.

The major sources for this chapter were:

Clark, J. I. (1955). *Wisconsin defies the Fugitive Slave Law: The case of Sherman M. Booth.* Madison, WI: The State Historical Society of Wisconsin.

Foner, E. (2015). *Gateway to freedom: The history of the underground railroad.* New York, NY: W. W. Norton & Company.

Mason, V. (1895). *The Fugitive Slave Law in Wisconsin* (Bachelor's thesis). University of Wisconsin, Madison.

McDonald, W. T., & Jackson, R. W. (2007). *Finding freedom: The untold story of Joshua Glover, runaway slave.* Madison, WI: Wisconsin Historical Society Press.

Millstein, E. (2015). *The Underground Railroad: A movement that changed America.* Clarkston, MI: St. Clair Press.

Rapley, R. (2015). The abolititionists. In *American Experience.* Arlington, VA: Public Broadcasting System.

Wilder, C. S. (2001). *In the company of Black men: The African influence on African American culture in New York City.* New York, NY: New York University Press.

LEARNING ACTIVITIES FOR "THE BLOODHOUND LAW"

Facts of the Case

1. How did northern states abolish slavery within their borders?
2. What were the provisions of the Fugitive Slave Law of 1793 and the Fugitive Slave Law of 1850?

3. What was the Underground Railroad?
4. What was the decision in *Prigg v. Pennsylvania?*
5. How did Justice Story's decision in *Prigg v. Pennsylvania* inspire the abolitionists to protest the Fugitive Slave Law of 1850?
6. What was Wisconsin's personal liberty law?

Historical Understanding

1. Why was the Compromise of 1850 called a compromise?
2. Why did antislavery groups in the North oppose the Fugitive Slave Law of 1793 and the Fugitive Slave Law of 1850?
3. Explain the idea of states' rights with respect to slavery.
4. What reasons did Chief Justice Taney provide for ruling against Sherman Booth in *Ableman v. Booth?*

Expressing Your Reasoning

Should the Wisconsin protesters have broken Joshua Glover out of jail? Why or why not?

Key Concepts from History

What do the following have in common?

1. In the 18th century in New Jersey, fugitive slaves who had escaped and been caught were not permitted to sue for their freedom, so they used another means to try to achieve their freedom: They petitioned courts to issue an order to their detainers to provide a valid reason for their detainment.
2. Between 1882 and 1890, Judge Ogden Hoffman, Jr., of the U.S. District Court, Northern District of California, issued thousands of orders to immigration authorities who had detained Chinese immigrants upon entering the United States, requiring the immigration authorities to provide proof of a valid reason for the Chinese immigrants' detainment.
3. In January 2017, President Donald Trump issued an executive order that prohibited the entry of refugees or visa holders from seven Middle Eastern countries, resulting in the detainment of hundreds of travelers in U.S. airports. Two Iraqis, Hameed Khlaid Darweesh and Haider Sameer Abdulkhaleq Alshawi, were detained at Kennedy Airport on January 27, despite having been approved for travel and entry to the United States and having valid documentation. The Yale Law School Worker and Immigrant Rights Advocacy Clinic, together with the American Civil Liberties Union, the National Immigration Law Center, the International Refugee Assistance Project, and Kilpatrick Townsend & Stockton LLP, petitioned the court, arguing for release of the two Iraqi men,

claiming that there was no cause for the detainment. Judge Ann Donnelly ruled in favor of the petition and issued a nationwide temporary stay (halt) and ordered the government not to remove, among others, any "individuals from Iraq, Syria, Iran, Sudan, Libya, Somali, and Yemen legally authorized to enter the United States."

Historical Inquiry

Daniel Glover was a fugitive slave who gained his freedom, despite having been caught. Did most fugitive slaves gain their freedom? Using online and other sources, test the hypothesis that most fugitive slaves succeeded. Compose a short essay in which you accept or reject the hypothesis. Use evidence to support your decision. To begin your investigation, the following search terms will be helpful:

- Underground Railroad
- Fugitive slave
- Capture of fugitive slaves

CHAPTER 18

Blow Ye the Trumpet

Antislavery Zealot John Brown

John Brown in 1856

John Brown

The poet Julia Ward Howe's classic "Battle Hymn of the Republic" was inspired by and written to the same tune as the most popular marching anthem of Union soldiers during The Civil War, "John Brown's Body," of which a portion of one of the many variants is:

> John Brown's body lies a-mouldering in the grave; (3x)
> His soul's marching on!

(Chorus)
Glory, glory, hallelujah! Glory, glory, hallelujah!

Glory, glory, hallelujah! his soul's marching on!

He's gone to be a soldier in the army of the Lord! (3x)
His soul's marching on!
(Chorus)
Glory, glory, hallelujah!
His soul's is marching on!

Born in 1800 in Torrington, Connecticut, John Brown was the fourth of eight children. The Brown family was deeply religious. Its ancestry traced back to the 17th century English Puritans. John Brown claimed that one of his ancestors, on his father's side, arrived with the Pilgrims at Plymouth Rock.

Brown was true to his Puritan heritage. He studied the Bible constantly and was a strict Calvinist. Calvinism (also called Reformed Christianity) is a major branch of Protestantism that follows the teachings of 16th-century European theologian John Calvin. The Puritans were Calvinists. In America, Congregational and Presbyterian churches are Calvinist in origin.

Calvinists believe that all people are sinful and incapable of believing in God on their own. God elects (that is, chooses) people to be faithful. According to this belief, all those whom God has chosen, the elect, will come to faith, and only the elect receive salvation. This doctrine that all is foreordained is called *predestination*. John Brown believed that God predetermined everything.

Like other devout Calvinists, Brown believed that the elect could be known by their conduct. They would be faithfully vigilant against sin. Calvinist ministers preached that to hold humans in bondage was a sin against God. John Brown's father shared that view and became a fervent abolitionist. From early in his life, at church and at home, John Brown was taught to be zealous against the sin of slavery.

His zeal was deepened by a childhood experience. While traveling with his parents, he befriended a boy his own age enslaved by a family hosting the Browns. John was deeply disturbed when he witnessed the ways the boy was mistreated. His master beat the boy with household tools and made him sleep in the cold, wearing only rags. The experience was seared in John's memory. While still in his youth, he came to believe that battling the evils of slavery was his God-given destiny.

Later, Brown would use the promise of equality in the Declaration of Independence to justify his antislavery views. Tracing the Golden Rule to the Bible, he invoked it, too, against slavery: Do unto others as you would have them to do unto you. His parents taught him that the Golden Rule applied to people of all races.

When John was 5 years old, his family moved from Connecticut to Ohio. Three years later, his mother died. His father operated a successful tannery (a place where animal hides are tanned into leather), and John learned the trade. In his teens, he was sent east for schooling in New England. He wanted to become a minister. An eye inflammation interfered with his studies, and funds for school ran out. At age 17, he returned to Ohio and abandoned study for the ministry.

At age 18, John Brown was tall and lean with dark hair brushed straight back. His chiseled face, with hollow cheeks, sharp jaw, and glittering blue-gray eyes gave him a fiercely determined look. He had resumed working at his father's tannery, but would later go into business for himself. He worked hard and skillfully as a tanner, and later as a surveyor, farmer, land speculator (one who invests in land with the hope of gain but risk of loss), horse breeder, and wool dealer.

True to his convictions about slavery, John aided people fleeing enslavement. The first occasion was shortly after he returned to Ohio from school in the East. A fugitive approached him and begged for help in evading a band of Whites pursuing him. Brown hid the fugitive safely in his cabin. For the next 2 decades, John Brown chose this kind of direct aid to individual fugitives. He was an active worker in Ohio for the Underground Railroad (the network of secret links from the South to the North and Canada helping enslaved people flee to freedom).

In 1820, John married Dianthe Lusk, a quiet woman of deep piety, at the Congregational Church in Hudson, Ohio. She was a guiding influence in John's life during their years together.

In 1826, John moved with Dianthe and their three children to New Richmond, Pennsylvania, where three more children were born to them. They moved so that John could establish a tannery of his own and the family could work a new farm. New Richmond was a wilderness when the Browns arrived, filled with bears, wolves, deer, and wild turkeys. In 4 months, Brown created a homestead. He cleared 25 acres of timberland and built a log house, barn, and tannery. He founded a community at New Richmond, establishing its first church and school, and became its first businessman and postmaster.

Dianthe Brown died during childbirth in 1832 at age 31. Already grieving over the death of his 4-year-old son the previous year, John was deeply grief-stricken by the loss of his wife and unborn child. He was left to tend to five surviving children while running the tannery. In 1833, he married a second wife, 16-year-old Mary Day. The daughter of a nearby blacksmith, Mary had little education. She impressed John as a practical, hardworking woman. She proved to be a rock of stability for John. They were married until John's death and had 13 children together, only six of whom survived to adulthood.

Mary cared for her own children and her five stepchildren. Families were large in America at the time. The average household had nine children. At a time before modern medicine, many died young of childhood illnesses, as did six of the Brown children. Four of the youngest died from dysentery (a bacterial infection of the intestines) in a single year, and Brown's son reported that his father never fully recovered from those deaths. Many children did not survive long after birth, and some died from accidents. One of the Brown children, for example, was scalded to death in a kitchen accident.

Although Brown was a stern and strict father, he was beloved by his children. He would sing with them at bedtime, recite fables to them, and he cared for them when they were sick. He was gentle to animals. His children both respected and feared him. He punished them severely for lying, speaking sacrilegiously, and for disobedience, sometimes lashing them. Brown's strict Calvinistic religion, un-wavering belief in racial equality, and antislavery passion were all instilled in his children.

The Brown family rose before sunrise. Each morning after breakfast, John led the family in a religious service, often reciting from memory sayings from the Bible. One of his favorites was: "Remember them that are in bonds as bound with them." While in New Richmond, Brown built a special room in the barn that served as a hiding place for fugitive slaves fleeing north along the Underground Railroad.

John Brown did not approve of the methods of leading abolitionists such as William Lloyd Garrison, the Boston editor of the *The Liberator*, an influential abolitionist weekly. The most prominent abolitionists believed in nonresistance, that by persuasion alone slaveholders would abandon slavery. They rejected vio-lence. If persuasion failed, Garrison and other abolitionists favored separation of the North from the South. John Brown favored preservation of the Union, and he did not reject the possibility that violence might be necessary to end slavery.

Slave revolts inspired John Brown. Most admired by him were the revolts of Nat Turner and Cinques. Both were designed to terrorize Whites through vio-lence as a means of liberation from slavery.

Nat Turner's rebellion in 1831 was the most violent of the many slave revolts. Enslaved on a Virginia plantation, Turner spread a plan among nearby slaves for a violent takeover of Southampton County. The revolt began the last Sunday night of August. Turner, along with six others, armed with swords and axes, went from plantation to plantation, killing men, women, and children, some while they slept. After more than 50 had been killed, Whites organized a pursuit. Hundreds of enslaved people, many of whom took no part in the revolt, were slaughtered in the chase. Turner was captured 2 months later, tried, and hanged, along with 16 other enslaved people who had joined the revolt

Cinques led a rebellion in 1837 of 53 enslaved people who were being trans-ported from Cuba to Spain on the Spanish ship *Amistad*. The slaves broke free of their chains and killed the captain and three crewmembers. The ship was then directed to America and came ashore on Long Island. The rebels were brought to trial, and the U.S. Supreme Court exonerated them on the basis of America's prohibition of the international slave trade.

In 1835, after 9 years in New Richmond, the Brown family moved back to Hudson, Ohio. A wealthy businessman had invited John Brown to run a tannery there with him.

The remote village of Hudson was a hub of antislavery activity. For many fugitives, the road to freedom passed through Hudson. Fines for helping fugitive slaves were high—$1,000 (around $25,000 today) for each one assisted. John

Brown became a busy conductor for the Ohio branch of the Underground Railroad. He established a new station in Hudson, again constructed a hiding place in his barn, and regularly transported fugitives to stations farther north.

Brown was not content to confine his antislavery efforts to the Underground Railroad. Events on the national stage during the mid-1830s spurred him to greater militancy. Leading abolitionist William Lloyd Garrison had tried to deliver an antislavery address in Boston. He was seized by a proslavery mob, bound, and pulled by a rope through the city's streets to a chorus of "Lynch him!" In 1837, the Illinois antislavery editor Elijah P. Lovejoy was murdered by a mob.

John Brown heard about the murder of Lovejoy at a prayer meeting in his Congregational church. There were several speeches condemning the murder. When they ended, Brown stood and loudly proclaimed, "Here, before God, in the presence of these witnesses, from this time, I consecrate my life to the destruction of slavery." His children recall that shortly thereafter, he openly declared his commitment to antislavery violence, and he persuaded family members to pledge themselves to armed warfare against slavery.

At first, Brown was successful in business, but he lacked tact and flexibility. Those shortcomings and steep economic downturns kept him from prospering. He borrowed huge sums to speculate in land shortly before the Panic of 1837, a major economic depression that caused land values to plummet. Brown defaulted on his debts. Lawsuits were filed against him in four states, and they plagued him for the rest of his life. His farm tools, furniture, and livestock were auctioned off. His farm was taken away. By the end of 1842, Brown was bankrupt.

For a fresh start after declaring bankruptcy, Brown moved his family to Springfield, Massachusetts. In 1847, the famous writer Frederick Douglass, who had escaped slavery 9 years earlier to become the era's leading Black abolitionist, visited John Brown at his family home in Springfield. After dinner, Brown revealed to his guest a plan to emancipate the slaves of the South.

Brown's plan called for a group of 25 men to be stationed in small groups in the Appalachian Mountain range of Virginia. These small groups would raid nearby plantations, liberate enslaved Blacks, arm them, and retreat with them to mountain hideaways. From there, the revolution would spread to major slave plantations southward through Tennessee, Alabama, Mississippi, Georgia and other slave states. Brown insisted that he intended to reform, not overthrow, the government of the United States. Mindful of Nat Turner, whom he greatly admired, John Brown's goal was to weaken the institution of slavery by terrorizing slaveholders. Brown told his visitor that he was "not averse to the shedding of blood."

Douglass admired Brown, but he considered Brown's plan doomed to failure. He declined to participate in carrying it out. Two years after their meeting, however, Douglass expressed a kind of endorsement. In 1849, he said that he would welcome news that Blacks had arisen in the South, and were engaged in spreading "death and destruction there."

Brown's commitment to Black people and his opposition to slavery fascinated Douglass. The prominent Black abolitionist wrote, "Brown believed that slave holders had forfeited the right to live and that the slaves had the right to gain their liberty in any way they could."

John became interested in a large area of land in upstate New York. A wealthy antislavery reformer, Gerrit Smith, set aside a huge area there for an experiment. He hoped to establish a community of freed slaves and had opened the area to settlement by free Blacks and fugitive slaves. At very low cost, Brown purchased 244 acres from Smith. The settlement was in the isolated village of North Elba, below the Adirondack Mountains near Lake Placid.

Brown moved his family to North Elba. He built a house for them there and, with Black settlers, established a community. He surveyed the settlers' properties and guided them in farming.

Although a harsh, isolated place, North Elba was a kind of paradise to John Brown. There he could support and be the head of his family. He could live as an equal among free African Americans, while also working actively for the overthrow of slavery.

White visitors were struck by the respect and dignity he showed toward his Black neighbors. He addressed them as Mr., Mrs., or Miss and dined with them in his house and in theirs. All of this was extraordinary for a White person in the middle of the 19th century. Even most White abolitionists held to racial stereotypes of the time and lived apart from Black people. Not John Brown. His Black neighbors grew fond of him.

While in North Elba he created a new station for the Underground Railroad. With his Black neighbors, he helped fugitive slaves flee to safety in Canada.

Brown had not, however, abandoned his plan for a rebellion that would bring down slavery. In 1850, he focused on Virginia as the key location for his plan. Harpers Ferry was a town of some 2,500 people, located where the Potomac River meets the Shenandoah in what is now West Virginia.

A hub of the Baltimore & Ohio Railroad, Harpers Ferry was the site of a major federal armory that produced weapons used by the military forces of the United States. The arsenal contained 100,000 muskets and rifles. Brown planned to raid the armory and to seize rifles and munitions for liberated slaves who would join him in carrying out his plan to abolish slavery.

Meanwhile, the national conflict over slavery was heating up. As part of the Compromise of 1850, Congress passed, and President Millard Fillmore signed into law, a new and much tougher Fugitive Slave Law. The law gave slave catchers the authority to hunt down runaway slaves anywhere. Moreover, law enforcement officials were required by the new law to aid in the capture and return of runaways.

The Fugitive Slave Law infuriated John Brown. It seemed to him that the "Slave Power" ruled the nation. In Washington, proslavery advocates controlled the Senate, the White House, and the Supreme Court. Slavery was expanding in the Deep South. "King Cotton" had become wildly profitable, due in part to the cotton gin and slave labor. Southern cotton production boomed, supplying most of the world's demand. The value of cotton exports was greater than all other American exports combined. Abolitionists despaired, and John Brown fumed.

A new term had emerged for slavery: "the peculiar institution." It implied that slavery was "peculiar" or distinctive to the South. In 1850, President Fillmore said, "We must endure it and give it such protection as is guaranteed by the Constitution."

Brown's rage grew in response to another federal law: the Kansas-Nebraska Act, signed into law by President Franklin Pierce in 1854. The Missouri Compromise of 1820 had excluded slavery from the North, including the vast territories (lands owned by the United States but not states) of Kansas and Nebraska. The Kansas-Nebraska Act repealed the Missouri Compromise and gave settlers in Kansas and Nebraska the power to decide by vote whether to be slave or free. This new authority to choose was called *popular sovereignty.*

In response to popular sovereignty, proslavery and antislavery forces competed for supremacy in Kansas. Proslavery settlers went there to cast election ballots for slavery. They were thwarted by 5,000 Missourians, known as "Border Ruffians," who crossed into Kansas Territory, seized the polling places, and created their own proslavery legislature.

Abolitionist settlers, known as Jayhawkers, then flocked from the East for the purpose of making Kansas a free state. Five of John Brown's sons decided to homestead in Kansas, joining other abolitionist settlers in efforts to bring an end to slavery there.

Exhausted from his travels to settle persisting lawsuits over his debts, Brown remained in North Elba. Events in Kansas, however, were soon to beckon him.

The antislavery forces in Kansas were outnumbered and outgunned. John Brown, Jr., sent an urgent plea to his father asking for weapons to arm the Kansas antislavery settlers; John Brown gathered every weapon he could and departed for Kansas. In October 1855, Brown arrived at his sons' Kansas homestead, a place called Brown's Station, located along Pottawatomie Creek. He was dismayed at the desperate conditions. His sons were ill with fever and starving. They had little shelter. Brown swiftly built sturdy log cabins and brought order to Brown's Station.

The Kansas winter that year was especially snowy and bitter. In January, a Free State (antislavery) man was hacked to death. The murderers tossed his body on the man's icy doorstep. News of the murder and of other proslavery violence brought money and guns into Kansas from all over the North. The fight between proslavery and antislavery forces intensified.

In May 1856, hundreds of Border Ruffians marched on Lawrence, Kansas, and sacked the town. The antislavery inhabitants did not fight back. Very soon afterward, news from Washington spread. After delivering an impassioned antislavery speech entitled "The Crime Against Kansas," abolitionist Senator Charles Sumner of Massachusetts had been attacked on the floor of the United States

Senate. Offended by the speech, a South Carolina congressman, Preston Brooks, beat the senator nearly to death with a heavy, gold-handled cane.

The sack of Lawrence and the beating of Sumner motivated John Brown to act. Believing that he was an avenging instrument of God, he took revenge. He said that it was time to "fight fire with fire" to "strike terror in the hearts of the proslavery people." Brown directed his four sons, son-in-law, and two others to sharpen their swords on the grindstone. Late on the moonlit night of May 24, 1856, he led the men, armed with their swords, rifles, and revolvers, to nearby cabins along Pottawatomie Creek. They were headed for the residences of men who were not slaveholders but were known to be advocates of Kansas as a slave state.

Brown banged on the door of one of those cabins while those inside were asleep. He ordered the men to come out. As women and children watched from inside the cabin, Brown's men split open heads and cut off arms, killing three of the men. John Brown watched as the men were hacked to death, and he fired a single bullet into the head of one of the men after he was dead. Brown's men proceeded to two more cabins. With Brown watching, they dragged out and murdered two more men. With horses and other property confiscated from their victims, Brown's party departed.

News of these events, referred to as the Pottawatomie Massacre, spread quickly, sparking an all-out war between proslavery and antislavery factions in the territory, earning it the nickname "Bleeding Kansas." In August of 1856, a force of proslavery Border Ruffians attacked the antislavery town of Osawatomie. John Brown led 40 men in defending the town. Outnumbered, they were forced to withdraw and the town was burned to the ground. John Brown's son, Frederick, was killed in the fighting. For his valiant, albeit unsuccessful, stand, Brown became known as Captain Brown of Osawatomie and Osawatomie Brown.

In 1857, news from Washington bolstered Brown's conviction that slave interests controlled the U.S. government. The Supreme Court issued a landmark decision in support of slavery. Known as the Dred Scott case, it affirmed the legal right of slave owners to take their slaves into western territories.

Conflict over slavery persisted in Kansas. The steady buildup of northern settlers ultimately succeeded in excluding slavery by ballots rather than bullets. Kansas was admitted to the Union in 1861 as a free state.

For John Brown the battle against slavery extended beyond Kansas. By this time, 4 million people were enslaved in the United States. Osawatomie had stiffened his resolve to liberate them. He said then, "There will be no more peace in this land until slavery is done for."

Brown's exploits in Kansas drew national attention to him. A reporter interviewed him in Kansas after Osawatomie. The newspaper reports made Brown famous in the North. He became legendary as a ferocious enemy of slavery—a northerner who fought back. A New York play entitled *Osawatomie Brown* celebrated him on Broadway.

In John Brown's mind, the Fugitive Slave Law was God's trumpet calling him to military action. His favorite hymn was "Blow Ye the Trumpet, Blow." In the Bible story, Gideon is inspired to take up his sword when the angel of the Lord blows his trumpet. God then instructs Gideon to have his small force go into battle against the wicked Midianites while blowing their trumpets. Frightened by a deafening sound, the enemy scatters in fear, and Gideon triumphs. The Bible story embodied John Brown's belief that a small band of the righteous could bring divine wrath upon the wicked.

The fighting in Kansas had temporarily diverted Brown from his plan to attack Harpers Ferry. He now sought help to carry out that plan. For the next 2 years, he traveled widely to raise money and weapons for a direct assault on slavery in the heart of the South. He met with wealthy abolitionists, pillars of eastern society, who opposed violence, but nevertheless supported him financially. Learned men, novelists, and prominent clergymen idolized him and gave him money for guns. They were ready for what many called "The Second American Revolution."

By the summer of 1859, Brown was ready to act on his plan to attack the federal armory at Harpers Ferry. In July, he rented a farmhouse across the Potomac in Maryland, five miles from the town. The 198 rifles and 200 revolvers Brown had acquired were stored at the farm, as well as nearly 1,000 wooden pikes. Brown had procured the pikes as practical weapons for the slaves he expected to join him, but who would be unaccustomed to handling firearms.

Brown recruited 21 men, including fugitive slaves, college students, free Blacks, three of his sons, and a neighbor from North Elba. One of the insurgents, a free Black man named Dangerfield Newby, had a personal reason to join Brown. Virginia born, he had been freed in 1858 when his owner moved to Ohio. His wife and children, however, remained enslaved near Harpers Ferry. Newby feared that they would soon be sold farther south and that he would never see his family again.

In August, Brown met again with Frederick Douglass in hopes of convincing him to join the war. To the brilliant writer and abolitionist, John disclosed the details of his imminent plan to raid Harpers Ferry, capture the guns at the arsenal, and prompt an army of nearby slaves to join him.

Douglass refused Brown's invitation to join the raid on Harpers Ferry, tried to dissuade him, and criticized it afterward. He believed that by attacking the federal government Brown was headed into "a trap of steel" from which escape would be impossible. His admiration for Brown, however, was affirmed. Later he wrote, ". . . though a white gentleman, [Brown] is in sympathy a black man, and as deeply interested in our cause as though his own soul had been pierced with the iron of slavery."

Harriet Tubman, another prominent Black abolitionist, attempted to support Brown's raid. Brown had met with her in Ontario, Canada, in a community of Black people, many of whom had fled to freedom along the Underground Railroad. From Canada, Tubman tried and failed to recruit Black Canadians for Brown's little war.

Several of the 21 men that Brown had recruited waited at the Maryland farmhouse near Harpers Ferry. They hoped for more recruits, but none came.

Late into the chilly, drizzly night of October 16, 1859, John Brown, fiery-eyed and now with a long, white beard, formed his recruits into pairs and marched them into Harpers Ferry. At first, they were successful. The arsenal had only one guard, who quickly surrendered.

Soon, however, things went awry. While approaching town, a train stopped. The baggage master at the Harpers Ferry train station ran out to find out why the train had stopped. Brown's men shouted at him to halt. When the baggage master did not stop, they shot him dead. He, a free Black man, was the first victim of the raid.

News of the raid traveled immediately by telegraph to Richmond, the Virginia capital, and to Washington. Local townspeople took up arms against the invaders. Virginia militia approached the arsenal where the raiders were now scattered. On the way, they shot and killed Dangerfield Newby. An angry mob mutilated his dead body. In his pocket there was a letter from the wife he had hoped to set free. Two other insurgents were also shot and killed. John Brown's revolution was quickly unraveling.

Brown gathered those of his men who were left and took refuge, with 11 hostages, in the small fire-engine house of the armory. The mob and militia surrounded the fire-engine house and fired their weapons at its windows and brick walls. Two of Brown's sons, Oliver and Watson, lay mortally wounded on the floor of the engine house. Oliver, curled up in great pain, begged his father to kill him. Brown replied, "You must be a man. You must die like a man." Twenty-year-old Oliver died before sunrise. His older brother Watson died 2 days later.

By morning, a company of 90 U.S. marines, commanded by Colonel Robert E. Lee, was lined up in the armory yard. The engine house was completely surrounded. Brown was told that the lives of the insurgents would be spared if they surrendered. Brown refused. Marines stormed the building. Brown was wounded and struck unconscious. The marines took control of the engine house. The raid had lasted 36 hours.

As Brown lay wounded on the stone floor of the engine house, reporters were allowed to interview him. Their reports transformed him into an instant celebrity. He now had the attention of the world, and he understood the value of that attention. He seized the opportunity to get his ideas out to the public through the reporters.

Seven days after the raid, the wounded Brown was carried to the courthouse in nearby Charlestown, the county seat, for a trial that lasted less than 5 days. Brown's lawyer recommended that he plead not guilty by reason of insanity. Believing that plea would be false, Brown refused. He pleaded not guilty to all charges against him. During the trial, he lay on a cot because of his wounds, standing only when he addressed the court. There was no dispute over the facts of the case. Under Brown's leadership, the insurgents had seized the armory, taken hostages, armed slaves, killed five men, and wounded many others.

It took the jury only 45 minutes to reach a unanimous verdict. They found Brown guilty of murder, treason, and inciting slave insurrection. He was sentenced to death by hanging.

In an interview before the trial, Brown was asked, "How do you justify your acts?" He replied:

> I say my friend you are guilty of a great wrong against God and humanity . . . It would be perfectly right for anyone to interfere with you, so far as to free those you willfully and wickedly hold in bondage. . . . I think I did right, and that others will do right who interfere with you at any time, and at all times. I hold that the golden rule, do unto others as you would that others should do unto you, applies to all who would help others to gain their liberty.

The day before John Brown's execution, his wife, Mary, visited him in jail for a final, tearful farewell. The next day, December 2, 1859, John Brown sat atop a long wooden box in the back of a horse-drawn wagon rolling to the gallows. Brown was escorted up the scaffold. A hood was placed over his head and a noose around his neck. The trap door of the gallows was released and he dropped to his death.

The wooden box contained his coffin. He was transported north in it and, on December 9, he was buried in North Elba. As the coffin was lowered into the grave, Brown's African American friend, Lyman Epps, sang Brown's favorite hymn: "Blow Ye the Trumpet, Blow."

John Brown's hanging became much more than the execution of a criminal. To some, he was a bloodthirsty madman. To others, he was a hero who had killed for a just cause. The South rejoiced in his execution. In the North, church bells tolled for him. The raid on Harpers Ferry and Brown's execution polarized Americans on opposite sides of the slavery divide and was among the events that propelled America to civil war.

After The Civil War, Frederick Douglass gave a rousing speech celebrating the legacy of John Brown. He told his audience that the Union's armies "found it necessary to do on a large scale what John Brown attempted to do on a small one." In Douglass's view, John Brown began the war that ended slavery.

The major sources for this chapter were:

Banks, R. (1998). *Cloudsplitter*. New York, NY: HarperCollins Publishers.

Chowder, K. (Writer) & Kenner, R. (Director). (2000). John Brown's Holy War. *American experience*. Arlington, VA: Public Broadcasting System.

Horwitz, T. (2011). *Midnight rising: John Brown and the raid that sparked The Civil War*. New York, NY: Henry Holt and Company.

Reynolds, D. S. (2005). *John Brown, abolitionist*. New York, NY: Alfred A. Knopf.

LEARNING ACTIVITIES FOR "BLOW YE THE TRUMPET"

Facts of the Case

1. What was John Brown's religious background?
2. How did John Brown's views about racial equality differ from those of most other abolitionists?
3. What did John Brown do in North Elba, New York?
4. What was the Pottawatomie Massacre?
5. What was John Brown's goal in attacking Harpers Ferry?
6. What were some major effects of John Brown's conviction and execution?

Historical Understanding

1. What was popular sovereignty?
2. How did the Kansas-Nebraska Act repeal the Missouri Compromise?
3. What were the major provisions of the Fugitive Slave Law of 1850?
4. What is meant by "Bleeding Kansas?"
5. What was the Dred Scott decision?
6. What did the U.S. Supreme Court decide in the case about the *Amistad*?

Expressing Your Reasoning

Was John Brown justified in attacking Harpers Ferry? Why or why not?

Key Concepts from History

What do the following have in common?

1. The Boston Tea Party was a protest by the Sons of Liberty (a secret society formed to protect the rights of the colonists and to fight taxation by the British government) in Boston, on December 16, 1773. A group of men, some disguised as Native Americans, in defiance of the Tea Act of 1773, destroyed an entire shipment of tea sent by the East India Company. They boarded three British East India cargo ships in the Boston Harbor and threw 45 tons of tea into the harbor. The British government responded harshly, and the episode contributed to the American Revolution. The Tea Party was the culmination of a resistance movement throughout British America. Colonists objected to the Tea Act because they believed that it violated their rights as Englishmen to be taxed only by their own elected representatives and not by a British parliament.
2. On the morning of September 11, 2001, a series of four coordinated suicide attacks against the United States was carried out by the extremist group Al-

Qaeda. The attacks killed nearly 3,000 people, injured more than 6,000 others, and caused at least $10 billion in property damage. Four passenger airliners operated by two major U.S. airlines were hijacked. The hijackers were from Saudi Arabia and other Arab countries, and they were affiliated with Al Qaeda. Two of the planes were crashed into the North and South towers of the World Trade Center complex in New York City. Both towers collapsed, with debris and the resulting fires causing partial or complete collapse of all other buildings in the World Trade Center complex as well as significant damage to 10 other large structures. A third plane was crashed into the Pentagon (Defense Department headquarters), leading to a partial collapse of the building. The fourth plane initially was steered toward Washington, D.C., but it crashed into a field near Shanksville, Pennsylvania, after passengers attempted to overcome the hijackers. The attackers were allegedly acting in retaliation for America's support of Israel, its involvement in the Persian Gulf War, and its continued military presence in the Middle East.

3. On December 2, 2015, 14 people were killed and 22 were seriously injured in an attack at the Inland Regional Center in San Bernardino, California. The attack consisted of a mass shooting and an attempted bombing. The attackers, Syed Rizwan Farook and Tashfeen Malik, were a married couple. They had stockpiled thousands of rounds of ammunition and a dozen homemade pipe bombs in their home. According to the director of the FBI, they were "homegrown violent extremists." Their target was a San Bernardino County Department of Public Health training event and employee Christmas party. Farook was an American-born U.S. citizen and an employee of the county health department. Malik, born in Pakistan, was a lawful permanent resident of the United States. She posted a pledge of allegiance to ISIS (also known as the Islamic State of Iraq and Syria) on Facebook while the attack was happening. ISIS has called for people worldwide to launch attacks in its name. Its goal is the creation of a "global caliphate" (an Islamic empire ruled by a leader called a caliph) secured through a global war. To that end, it aims to replace existing borders across the Middle East and to take its war to Europe and America, and ultimately to lead Muslims toward a battle against the "unbelievers." Four hours after the attackers fled the scene of the attack in San Bernardino, police pursued their vehicle and killed them in a shootout.

Historical Inquiry

After they launched their attack on Harpers Ferry, John Brown and his men were pursued by Virginia militia. A state militia is a military force that is raised from the civilian population to supplement a regular army in an emergency. The Second Amendment to the U.S. Constitution states:

A well regulated Militia, being necessary to the security of a free State, the right of the people to keep and bear Arms, shall not be infringed.

Modern debates about the Second Amendment have focused on whether it protects a personal right of individuals to keep and bear arms, or a right that can be exercised only by those belonging to a state militia. Using online and other sources, test the hypothesis that the Second Amendment to the U.S. Constitution permits individuals to own and keep firearms for their personal use. Compose a short essay in which you accept or reject the truth of the claim. Use evidence to support your decision. To begin your investigation, the following search terms will be helpful:

- The Second Amendment
- James Madison and the Second Amendment
- The right to bear arms
- *District of Columbia v. Heller*
- Firearm case law in the United States

Note: During World War I, Congress passed the National Defense Act of 1916, which required the use of the term *National Guard* for the state militias and further regulated them.

CHAPTER 19

Tears of Blood

Robert E. Lee and The Civil War

Confederate General Robert E. Lee, 1864

Courtesy of the Library of Congress.

On a mid-April morning in 1861, a lone horseman rode slowly over the Potomac Bridge that linked Virginia with Washington, D.C. In his military officer's uniform he looked majestic on horseback. Beneath his appearance of calm dignity, he was inwardly tormented.

Colonel Robert E. Lee felt the dampness from the river as his horse clopped heavily upon the planks of the old bridge. He had been summoned to Washington for an interview with General Winfield Scott, general-in-chief of the U.S. Army. Lee's earliest army service had been under Scott. His affection for the old soldier was deep. As Lee approached Scott's office, he knew that the struggle raging within him was about to reach a climax. He would have to make a choice.

Events that burdened the lone horseman that April day were moving very quickly. Six days earlier, Confederate guns had opened fire on the federal soldiers of Fort Sumter, near Charleston, South Carolina. Two days afterward, the commander of the fort surrendered to South Carolina militia units.

A civil war had been threatening since the end of 1860. On December 20, in response to the election of Abraham Lincoln as president, South Carolina had seceded from the Union. The states of Mississippi, Florida, Alabama, Georgia, and Louisiana soon followed South Carolina's lead and withdrew from the Union. A Texas convention overrode that state's governor, Sam Houston, and joined the other states that had seceded.

Early in 1861, delegates from six of the seceding states met and drafted a constitution for the Confederate States of America. The Confederate Constitution resembled the Constitution of the United States. There were, however, two major differences. The Confederate Constitution stressed the "sovereignty and independent character of each state." It also guaranteed the right to own slaves, implied but not explicitly guaranteed in the U.S. Constitution. In response to the bombardment of Fort Sumter, President Lincoln had asked Congress for 75,000 troops. War between the states had come. Would Virginia, largest of the southern states, join the Confederacy? A Virginia convention was debating this issue at the moment that Colonel Lee rode into Washington.

The future of his home state weighed heavily on Colonel Lee. As he approached General Scott's office in the War Department building, he wondered what he would do if Virginia seceded. Entering the building, he drew some comfort from the fact that General Scott was a fellow Virginian.

Scene 1 of the play by John Drinkwater entitled *Robert E. Lee* presents a dramatic account of the meeting between these two soldiers. The characters in this part of the play are:

The Officer (Perrin): A major of the general's staff
The Orderly: A soldier attached to the general's staff
Scott: Winfield Scott, general-in-chief, U.S. Army
Lee: Robert E Lee, lieutenant-colonel, U.S. Army

The Officer (indicating paper): The recruiting reports are good this morning, sir. Over half the President's 75,000 in 3 days.
Scott (consulting the papers on his table): Yes-yes. What's the time?
The Officer: Just on twelve o'clock, sir.
Scott: If Virginia goes, we shall lose Lee.
The Officer: Surely not, sir. A soldier all his life.
Scott: I hope not, but I think so.
(The Orderly comes in.)

The Orderly: Colonel Lee is here, Sir.

Scott: Ask him to come in.

(The Orderly goes.)

Scott: You needn't go, Perrin. Take notes.

Perrin: Yes, sir.

(The Orderly shows in ROBERT E. LEE, at this time a Lieutenant-Colonel in the U.S. Army. The ORDERLY goes.)

Scott: Good-morning, Colonel.

Lee: Good-morning, sir.

Scott: This is Major Perrin. You've no objection to his hearing what we have to say?

Lee: No, certainly.

Scott: Sit down, please. *(They sit.)* It is at the President's suggestion that I asked you to come.

Lee: I am honoured, sir.

Scott: The problem is at the moment common—lamentably common. But we felt that your case was a special one, or rather, in a special sense a representative one. The esteem in which you stand in Virginia, and your personal record in the army, make your views of particular—as I say of representative—importance. We considered that a personal interview was the proper way of learning them.

Lee: I welcome your confidence.

Scott: You are aware that six states have already declared for secession from the Union?

Lee: I understood five.

Scott: Alabama's decision comes this morning.

Lee: I had not heard.

Scott: Do you approve?

Lee: If I were a mere spectator of events, I should say no.

Scott: A spectator?

Lee: It can hardly be an abstract question with me, you see, sir.

Scott: You mean Virginia?

Lee: Being a Virginian, yes, sir.

Scott: Your state, you mean, right or wrong?

Lee: Right and wrong are such dangerous words for men to use, ever.

Scott: Duty is a plain thing, Colonel Lee.

Lee: It should be, sir. But for it we may have to forfeit the good opinion of men that we cherish. My duty may not seem to me, for example, what you consider it should mean.

Scott: Your mind is fixed?

Lee: No—it is very gravely troubled.

Scott: Virginia's decision is not yet announced.

Lee: The Convention was sitting late into the night, I hear.

Scott: I gather that the indications are that she will follow the others.

Lee: In view of what has happened, I fear so.

Scott: You fear so?

Lee: Yes. I am opposed to secession on principle. More, I do not think the issue upon which it is proposed is a sufficient one. I would gladly see every slave freed rather than the Union should be broken.

Scott: You hold your commission under that Union.

Lee: I know, sir. It has made my life a fortunate one.

Scott: Then where can be the difference in opinion of which you speak?

Lee: I am two things, sir. I am not a statesman, nor do I in any other way control public policy. I am a soldier. But before that I am a citizen of Virginia. If my state decided to dispute the authority of the service in which I have for so long had the honour to be, I may regret the decision, but I may feel it my duty to respect it in my action.

Scott: Then let me put it more explicitly. The Government, as you know, has declared war on the rebel states.

Lee: The seceding states.

Scott: The rebel states, Colonel Lee. Be plain about that. Major Anderson has been forced to surrender at Fort Sumter. The President's appeal for 75,000 men is being answered eagerly. We are facing no holiday campaign. Other states will doubtless join the rebels. Two years will hardly see it through.

Lee: I should have said four, sir.

Scott: I was discussing the situation as a whole with President Lincoln yesterday evening. You were much spoken of. There is no officer in the army of whom he has a higher opinion, and I was privileged to say how just I considered that opinion to be. He instructed me to offer you the command of all Union forces in the field. I may say for myself that I think that even so great a distinction has been fully earned, Colonel Lee, and I could make the offer to no one with so much satisfaction.

Lee: The President's confidence, and yours, sir, are very much above my merit. I cannot express my sense of this. But what am I to say?

Scott: To say? How do you mean, to say?

Lee: Virginia has not spoken.

Scott: The army that you serve calls you to lead it. And you ask what you shall say.

Lee: To lead it against whom?

Scott: Against rebels to their country.

Lee: It may be against Virginia.

Scott: Then still against rebels.

Lee: Against my own people.

Scott: You are a soldier, you say. You are under orders.

Lee: I have been allowed to serve under you, sir. I know what discipline is—I do not need to be reminded. There have been times when I have obeyed orders with no very light heart. When I arrested John Brown at Harper's Ferry, I could have wished that the duty had fallen to another. For I believed that the old man had conscience in him. But then obedience was against my private feelings only. Now it may be against my public loyalty to the soil that made me. My Virginia.

You may be asking me to invade, perhaps to destroy my own homeland. Do you wonder that I answer "What am I to say"?

Who was this lieutenant colonel being offered command of the entire Union Army at such a critical hour? How did this Virginia soldier come to face such an agonizing decision? The answers to these questions can be traced to the early years of the American republic.

Like Washington and Jefferson, Lee was a product of the Virginia gentry. In 1799, John Adams wrote to a friend that the Lee family had "more merit in it than any other family." Two Lees had stood with Adams at the signing of the Declaration of Independence.

Robert was born, the fifth of six children, in 1807 when his father, "Light-Horse Harry" Lee (Henry Lee III), was 51 years old. It was said of Robert's father that he had "come out of his mother's womb a soldier." Light-Horse Harry was a military hero of the Revolutionary War and a man of expansive charm. He played a major role in defeating the British at Yorktown. He was present when Lord Cornwallis surrendered his army to George Washington, the historic moment marking the effective end of the American Revolutionary War. Congress voted Henry Lee a medal. After the war, he served three terms as governor of Virginia.

In his later years, Henry Lee, a loving but absent father, followed a path to ruin. His failed land speculation schemes wrecked his family financially. He suffered the disgrace of being arrested and jailed for debt. In 1811, when Robert was 4 years old, Harry became involved in a violent fight. The beating he took left him crippled and disfigured. He never regained his health. When Robert was 11 years old, his father died a broken man.

Robert, however, chose to remember his father as a hero of the Revolutionary War and as George Washington's friend. That legacy shaped Robert E. Lee as he became a soldier himself.

Following the death of his father in 1818, with his two older brothers away, Robert helped his mother run the family's modest brick house in Alexandria, Virginia. He served as housekeeper, supervised the marketing, and managed the garden and stable. He was devoted to his sickly mother.

Tall, physically strong, disciplined, and an able horseman, Robert decided to join the army, like his father. In 1825, at age 18 he secured an appointment to West Point, the U.S. military academy. There, he was a model cadet. He received no demerits and graduated second in his class. His record at West Point earned him the right to choose a commission in the Engineer Corps (today the Army Corps of Engineers). At the time, it was the most prestigious and intellectually demanding arm of the U.S. Army. Lee left West Point with the technical knowledge that would make him an accomplished civil engineer.

Robert's mother had instilled in him a precise sense of right and wrong and a strong spiritual belief. She pressed upon him her deep Protestant faith. Lee became a religious man with a firm, lifelong belief in the goodness of God's purpose, the need to submit to it, and the certainty of those who did so of a place in heaven. His mother also taught him self-denial, self-control, and frugality in all financial matters. In his later years, Robert said that he "owed everything" to his mother.

Following graduation from West Point in 1829, Robert began courting Mary Custis. Mary was elegant, quiet, and religious. She was also the granddaughter of George Washington: Mary's father, George Washington Custis, was the adopted son of the first president. George Washington Custis had built an estate called Arlington, high in the hills above Alexandria, Virginia. That imposing white-pillared mansion is now the centerpiece of Arlington National Cemetery.

Robert and Mary were married in 1830. They and their children lived comfortably at Arlington. Robert loved the vast Arlington mansion that had become a national shrine to the Father of the Country. Many of the first president's belongings were kept there. Lee also felt a measure of the respect and affection for his father-in-law that his own father had not been home long enough to receive. Arlington inspired in Lee an even deeper reverence for George Washington. All seven of Mary and Robert E. Lee's children were born at Arlington and grew up there.

As a junior officer in the Engineer Corps, Lee successfully undertook some of the largest and most difficult public works projects of the time. The Corps deepened and maintained harbors, built canals and locks, drained marshes, dredged channels to make rivers navigable for steamboats, built levees to prevent rivers from flooding farmland and cities, drew maps and constructed barriers to protect the American coastline. One project that Lee directed was creation of a safe deep-water channel on the Mississippi River that opened St. Louis to shipping. Lee was hailed by the mayor of St. Louis as the man "who brought the Father of Waters under control."

Army life deprived Robert of spending much time at home. During the Mexican War (1846–1848) he was gone for 22 months. It was in Mexico that the then 40-year-old son of Light-Horse Harry Lee made his mark as a soldier.

Despite his misgivings about the cause of the Mexican War, Lee's ability as a military engineer contributed to major U.S. victories. His competence, tact, grace, and quiet manner won the favor of his superiors. During the war, Lee was promoted rapidly to captain, then major, and then brevet lieutenant colonel. He served on the staff of the commanding general and hero of the Mexican War, Winfield Scott. Scott said that his success in Mexico "was largely due to the skill, valor, and undaunted energy of Robert E. Lee."

No other officer in the Mexican War received such high praise or won such widespread admiration. Lee, however, had no real taste for war. In the aftermath of the Battle of Vera Cruz, he rode around on his horse among the wreckage of the city. In a letter to Mary, he wrote: "It was awful! My heart bled for the inhabitants. The soldiers I did not care that much for, but it was terrible to think of the women and children." During his long tour in Mexico, he was homesick for Mary, the children, and Arlington.

Following the Mexican War, Lee had several assignments as a career army officer, often supervising construction of military forts. Then, in 1852, he began 3 of the most pleasant years of his life in upstate New York. He was appointed to take command as superintendent of the U.S. Military Academy at West Point, then, as now, a hallowed institution. His family settled in the superintendent's house. Lee tightened discipline and raised academic standards at the military academy.

After his years at West Point, Lee was transferred to the Texas frontier, where the army was assigned to maintain order in the recently annexed state. He was pleased with his new rank of lieutenant colonel, but camp life on the frontier was lonely. He was assigned to pursue Mexican bandits and resistant Comanche Indians, far from Arlington, and places much less appealing to Lee than West Point. He began to think that his life was being wasted, that his military career was drawing to its end with no hope of further promotion.

In 1857, Lee received news that George Washington Custis had died. Mary Lee inherited most of the Custis estate, and Robert E. Lee was named executor. He was granted leave to come to Virginia to settle the estate of his father-in-law. Lee had long cherished Custis, perhaps in part as his last living link with George Washington. He would now take charge of the Custis estate, including Arlington.

Upon his arrival, he faced two serious problems. The first was that Mary, at age 49, had become an invalid and was continually in pain. She could hardly move around the house without assistance.

The second problem was the disarray of the Custis estate. It was a tangled mess, and Lee took on the responsibility of unraveling it. The estate should have been a prize for the Custis heirs. It was rich in land, buildings, and possessions of great historical value. Lee soon discovered, however, that everything was burdened by debt and years of mismanagement.

The Custis estate included 65–70 slaves. Lee had first come to slave ownership when he inherited several slaves from his mother's estate upon her death in 1829. The exact number is not known. To provide additional cash for his household, Lee hired out the slaves he inherited to work elsewhere, a practice common among some slaveholders. He divested himself of slaves sometime between 1847 and 1852. The record is unclear about when he either sold or freed them.

Had Lee sold a small number of the slaves inherited from the Custis estate in nearby Alexandria, he would have been able to settle all the estate's debts. The terms of his father-in-law's will, however, called for emancipation of the slaves within 5 years. Lee felt obliged to fulfill the terms of the will. He never sold any of the enslaved to raise money, but he hired some of them out to work elsewhere, and the estate was paid for their labor. The Lees met their obligation to free the Custis slaves within 5 years. Over time, Lee managed to put the estate in order.

Lee could impose severe punishments on slaves, especially those who attempted to run away. One of those enslaved at Arlington, Wesley Norris, recounted how he had been treated by Lee. Norris recalled that it had been the general impression among the slaves at Arlington that they would be freed upon Custis's death. Lee informed them that they must remain slaves for 5 years. After 17 months, Norris ran away to Maryland with his sister. They were apprehended, jailed, and then sent back to Arlington.

Upon their return, Norris reports that Lee ordered that the runaways be tied firmly to posts, stripped to the skin, and whipped. According to Norris, Lee, standing by, frequently enjoined the overseer giving the lashes to "lay it on well."

In 1859, while in Arlington on leave from his posting in Texas, Lee was shopping in Alexandria one morning. A young lieutenant handed him a message. It said there had been a disturbance at Harpers Ferry. Virginia marines were being sent to the scene of the trouble. Lee was ordered to command them.

A man named John Brown had led a band of followers in seizing the federal armory at Harpers Ferry. Brown had fought against the extension of slavery in Kansas. He intended to free slaves of Virginia and then of the whole South through armed rebellion.

When Lee arrived at Harpers Ferry, he learned that Brown and about 20 of his followers had been driven by Virginia militia into a stone fire engine house on the armory premises. Brown's followers had earlier shot and killed two men. Several hostages had been taken into the engine house by the insurgents.

Colonel Lee sent a message to those in the engine house demanding surrender. Those who surrendered, he promised, would be turned over to civilian authorities. The message warned that the armory was surrounded and that escape was impossible.

An officer carried the message under a white flag to the engine house. As he approached, the front door was opened a crack. Through the crack the face of a gaunt and grimy old man appeared. It was John Brown holding a carbine.

Brown wanted to make a deal. He asked to be allowed to pass through the army lines with his followers until they reached Maryland. There, the hostages would be released. Some of the hostages called out, urging the militia not to use force on Brown. "He will kill us," one shouted.

Lee, seeking surrender of the insurgents, would strike no bargain. He gave the signal for the marines to storm the engine house. Carbines crackled inside and smoke drifted outside. Two marines were shot, one mortally. Two of Brown's followers were killed by bayonet thrusts. Injured himself, Brown was taken prisoner, tried for treason and murder, convicted, and hanged. Many northern opponents of slavery considered John Brown a hero and a martyr. In Lee's opinion, Brown, though conscientious, was a fanatic who had incited rioters to insurrection.

Although he did not approve of John Brown's methods, Lee himself expressed opposition to slavery. In an 1856 letter to Mary, Lee wrote that "slavery as an institution, is a moral & political evil in any Country." Lee's attitude was one of gradualism. Slavery, he believed, would best be ended by allowing it to fade gradually away. Christian charity and not force, he thought, would convince people eventually to free the slaves. In his letter to Mary declaring slavery a "moral and political evil," he added:

> I think it (slavery) however a greater evil to the white man than to the black race, & while my feelings are strongly enlisted in behalf of the latter, my sympathies are more strong for the former. The blacks are immeasurably better off here than in Africa, morally, socially & physically. The painful discipline they are undergoing, is necessary for their instruction as a race, & I hope will prepare & lead them to better things. How long their subjugation may be necessary is known & ordered by a wise Merciful Providence. Their emancipation will sooner result from the mild & melting influence of Christianity, than the storms & tempests of fiery Controversy. This influence though slow, is sure.

In the presidential election of 1860, Lee voted for John C. Breckinridge, the extreme proslavery candidate. (A more moderate southerner, John Bell, carried Virginia in the election.) Lee would forever oppose political rights for former slaves.

After Harpers Ferry, in 1860, Lee was again assigned to Texas. The spirit of secession was then spreading through the South. Lee was upset to discover that it had crept into the army command. He strongly disapproved of states' breaking away from the Union. In a letter to his son, Lee wrote: "It [the Constitution] was intended for 'perpetual union' so expressed in the preamble, and for establishment of a government, not a compact, which can only be dissolved by revolution, or the consent of all of the people in convention assembled." Lee dismissed secession as "silly" and wrote that he "could anticipate no greater calamity for our country than a dissolution of our union."

Lee did not think preserving slavery was a goal worth fighting for. He kept his opinions to himself while stationed in Texas, where enthusiasm for secession grew when Abraham Lincoln was elected president in 1860.

As civil war threatened, Lee qualified his commitment to the Union. He said: "A Union that can only be maintained by swords and bayonets, and in which strife and civil war are to take the place of brotherly love and kindness, has no charms for me."

When he entered West Point as a young man, Lee had taken an oath "to support and defend the Constitution of the United States against all enemies, foreign and domestic." Yet his loyalty to Virginia was intense. It was bolstered by Virginia's role as the "cradle of the Revolution" and his deep roots in the state. Asked in 1860 "whether a man's first allegiance was due his state or the nation," Lee replied that his first obligations were to Virginia. Considering himself first and foremost a Virginian, Lee put devotion to his state above national patriotism.

On April 17, 1861, days before Lee's meeting with General Scott, and just 3 days after the surrender of Fort Sumter, President Lincoln asked his trusted associate, Francis Blair, to sound out Colonel Robert E. Lee regarding command of the Union Army. Lee visited Blair across Lafayette Square from the White House. According to Blair's son, Lee said: "Mr. Blair, I look upon secession as anarchy. If I owned the four millions of slaves at the South, I would sacrifice them all to the Union; but how can I draw my sword upon Virginia, my native State?"

Lee's distaste for abolitionists was increased by the recent clash with John Brown at Harpers Ferry. Lee believed the South would be better off without slavery. Like most southerners, however, he also believed that the federal government had no business imposing northerners' views on the slave states.

After the Mexican War, promotions had not come quickly to Lee. He began to think his military career had stagnated. He was also burdened by being far from Mary as her disability worsened. He longed to return home to Virginia. The opportunity came with the unexpected order to report to Washington, D.C., where he was to have an interview with General Scott.

The morning after the interview, Lee returned home across the Potomac to Arlington. Along the way he stopped at John Mosby's drugstore in Alexandria. There, he glanced at the newspaper. The headline read: "VIRGINIA SECEDES."

War would mean that Arlington, because it was so close to the capital, might soon be occupied by federal troops. The mansion might be seized and perhaps destroyed. Lee needed to decide which side he would stand with. The next morning, April 20, 1861, he submitted his letter of resignation from the United States Army. In a letter written later that morning to his sister in Baltimore, he said:

> I had to meet the question whether I should take part against my native state. With all my devotion to the Union and the feeling of loyalty and duty as an American citizen, I have not been able to make up my mind to raise my hand against my relatives, my children, my home.

Over his decision to resign from the U.S. Army, Lee's wife, Mary, remarked: "My husband has wept tears of blood."

Having resigned from the U.S. Army, Lee would now accept command in the Army of the Confederate States. On April 22, 1861, Robert E. Lee left for the capital of the Confederacy, Richmond, Virginia, leaving Arlington forever. In May, 13,000 federal troops occupied the Custis-Lee estate in Arlington, pitching their tents on the lawns and chopping down the trees around the mansion for firewood. Lee's family abandoned their home, never to return.

Lee accepted command of the Army of Northern Virginia, the primary military force of the Confederate States of America. His three sons also joined the Confederate Army. Robert E. Lee was to become the most accomplished and revered general of the Confederacy during The Civil War.

General Lee achieved battlefield success against Union forces despite the many disadvantages hindering the Confederacy. The North had a much larger population, productive industry for weapons and supplies, greater wealth, better transportation facilities, and naval superiority. Nonetheless, Lee prevailed in battle after battle against larger, better-equipped Union armies. Some of these Civil War battles have become legendary: for example, Manassas, Fredericksburg, Chancellorsville, Cold Harbor, and Spotsylvania.

By 1863, General Lee decided to change the war for the South from defense to offense. He moved his army north into Pennsylvania. His aim was to inflict on the Union a defeat so complete and so humiliating that northerners would lose heart and give up the war.

The decisive and historic battle was fought during the first 3 days in July 1863 at Gettysburg, Pennsylvania. They were the bloodiest 3 days in American history. Lee's narrow defeat at Gettysburg was the major turning point of The Civil War. The battle, like so many that preceded it, was horrific. Casualties at Gettysburg totaled 23,049 for the Union (3,155 dead, 14,529 wounded, 5,365 missing). Confederate casualties were 28,063, more than a third of Lee's army (3,903 dead, 18,735 injured, and 5,425 missing).

After Gettysburg, the defeat of the Confederacy was only a matter of time. Lee was able to prolong the war for almost 2 more years, but with no further offensive campaigns.

The end finally came on April 9, 1865, at Appomattox Court House, Virginia, where Robert E. Lee surrendered to Union commanding general, and future president, Ulysses S. Grant. After signing the surrender document, Lee rode quietly off on horseback, impeccable in his dress uniform, to inform the men nearby who had so loyally served him, tipping his hat to the Union generals saluting him.

The death toll from The Civil War is estimated to have been between 620,000 and 750,000, more than 2% of the population of the United States. Nearly as many died fighting The Civil War as in all other American wars combined.

Shortly before war's end, Lee had been named general-in-chief of all Confederate armies. Venerated by his men during the war, Lee would be admired after it ended. Especially in the South, he became a symbol of courage, courtesy, dignity, and lack of self-interest. He is honored on three U.S. postage stamps, and in 1959 a navy ship, the USS *Robert E. Lee*, was named for him. His image has been carved into the granite of Stone Mountain in Georgia. There are monuments honoring him, both in the South and the North, and in Statuary Hall of the U.S. Capitol. At the time of this writing, there have been protests against some of these monuments and some are being taken down.

After the war, Lee accepted federal rule, although he never expressed support for the equal rights of African Americans. Former Confederates who participated in the rebellion against the United States were pardoned by a Proclamation of Amnesty and Pardon issued by President Andrew Johnson in 1865. Lee, however, as a military leader of the Confederacy was excluded from the provision of amnesty and pardon of the proclamation. The proclamation required him, and categories of other Confederates, to sign an amnesty oath and to make special application to the president for pardon. Lee signed the oath and submitted his special application, complying in full with the requirements of the presidential proclamation. His amnesty oath, however, was lost among federal records and he was not pardoned, nor was his citizenship restored. One hundred years later, his amnesty oath was discovered in the National Archives, and in 1975, a joint resolution of Congress posthumously restored his full rights of citizenship, retroactively effective June 16, 1865. President Gerald Ford signed the joint resolution in a ceremony at Arlington House, the former Custis-Lee mansion, now part of Arlington National Cemetery..

In 1796, George Washington had endowed a college in Lexington, Virginia, with a generous gift. In gratitude for the gift, the college changed its name to Washington College. In October 1865, Lee was inaugurated as president of the college, a post he held until his death in 1870. Lee and his wife, Mary, who was by then crippled by arthritis, lived happily on campus. They are buried on the grounds. Soon after Lee's death, the college was renamed Washington and Lee University.

The major sources for this chapter were:

Dowdey, C. (1865). *Lee.* Boston, MA: Little, Brown.
Drinkwater, J. (1923). *Robert E. Lee.* Boston, MA: Houghton Mifflin.
Freeman, D. S. (Harwell, R., Ed.) (1961). *Lee.* New York, NY: Charles Scribner's Sons. (Original work published 1935.)
Korda, M. (2014). *Clouds of glory: The life and legend of Robert E. Lee.* New York, NY: HarperCollins.
Miers, E. S. (1956). *Robert E. Lee: A great life in brief.* New York, NY: Alfred A. Knopf.

LEARNING ACTIVITIES FOR "TEARS OF BLOOD"

Facts of the Case

1. Prior to The Civil War, what important contributions did members of the Lee family of Virginia make to their country?
2. What effects did the Mexican War have on the military career of Robert E. Lee?
3. What was Lee's view of slavery?
4. What was Lee's position on secession of states from the Union?
5. What offer did General Scott make to Colonel Lee in the name of President Lincoln?
6. What was Lee's family relationship to George Washington?

Historical Understanding

1. What did Confederate forces in South Carolina do in response to the election of Abraham Lincoln in 1860?
2. How did the Constitution of the Confederate States of America differ from the U.S. Constitution?
3. Describe General Lee's effectiveness as commander of the Army of Northern Virginia.
4. What was the significance of the Battle of Gettysburg?
5. How did casualty totals of The Civil War compare to those from other American Wars?

Expressing Your Reasoning

Should Robert E. Lee have declined command of the Union Army and accepted command of the Army of Northern Virginia? Why or why not?

Key Concepts from History

What do the following have in common?

1. Benedict Arnold began the American Revolutionary War in the Continental Army, but later secretly switched sides. As a general on the American side, he became commander of the West Point fort in New York, and offered to surrender it to the British. After the surrender plot came to light, in September 1780, Arnold joined the British Army as a brigadier general, with a sizeable pension and a signing bonus. Arnold led British raids in Virginia and in New London and Groton, Connecticut, before the war ended with the American victory at Yorktown. Arnold died in London.
2. Tomoya Kawakita was born in California to Japanese parents and grew up in Calexico, California. In 1939, after high school, he traveled to Japan with his father to visit his grandfather. His father returned to the United States, leaving Tomoya in Japan to attend a preparatory school. After the outbreak of war with the United States, he was stranded in Japan, holding dual citizenship in both the United States and Japan. He found employment as an interpreter at a prisoner of war (POW) camp that included about 400 captured Americans. After the war, Kawakita returned to the United States and enrolled as a student at the University of Southern California. One day in 1946, while shopping at a Sears department store in Los Angeles, army veteran William Bruce spotted the man who had brutalized him as a POW in Japan. Recognizing Kawakita, he reported him to the FBI. Kawakita was arrested, tried, and convicted of collaborating with the Japanese during World War II and mistreating American prisoners of

war. During his trial, former POWs testified how Kawakita had forced prisoners to beat one another and mistreated them in other ways. Kawakita claimed he could not be found guilty of the charges against him because he had lost his U.S. citizenship while in Japan. This argument was rejected by the Supreme Court, which ruled that he had in fact retained his U.S. citizenship during the war. The opinion of the court stated, "An American citizen owes allegiance to the United States wherever he may reside." At age 27, Kawakita was sentenced to death. His sentence was commuted to life imprisonment. He was eventually released from prison, deported to Japan, and barred from ever returning to the United States.

3. Nidal Malik Hasan was a U.S. Medical Corps psychiatrist and a U.S. Army major. On November 5, 2009, 1 month before he was to be deployed to Afghanistan, Major Hassan opened fire on his fellow soldiers at Fort Hood in Texas. Prior to the shooting, Hasan had repeatedly expressed extremist views and had been communicating with Anwar al-Alwaki, an American who was a senior recruiter and motivator involved in planning terrorist operations for the Islamist militant group Al-Qaeda. During the attack at Fort Hood, Hasan shot his unarmed victims while shouting the Arabic phrase "Allāhu akbar," usually translated as "God is [the] greatest." It is a common Islamic Arabic expression, used in various contexts by Muslims: in formal prayer, in the call for prayer, as an informal expression of faith, in times of distress, or to express resolute determination or defiance. Hassan was court-martialed and convicted of 13 counts of murder and 32 counts of attempted murder. Sentenced to death, he awaited execution in the military prison at Fort Leavenworth, Kansas, while his case was reviewed by appellate courts. As of this writing, Hasan's death sentence has not been carried out. The U.S. Senate released a report describing the mass shooting at Fort Hood as "the worst terrorist attack on U.S. soil since September 11, 2001."

Historical Inquiry

The defeat of Confederate forces commanded by Robert E. Lee at Gettysburg marked the turning point of The Civil War (along with the Union victory at Vicksburg, Mississippi, the following day, July 4, 1863). Had the Confederates won the battle, General Lee might have accomplished his goal of convincing the Union to give up prosecution of the war and negotiate a peace between the North and South. There are various opinions about who is responsible for the Confederate defeat in this historic battle. (Four months after the battle, President Lincoln, in what has become one of the most memorable speeches in American history, used the dedication ceremony for the Gettysburg National Cemetery to honor the fallen Union soldiers and to redefine the purpose of the war.)

Some believe that Robert E. Lee is responsible for the defeat at Gettysburg. Others claim that the blame rests with Lee's subordinates. Using online and other sources, test the hypothesis that General Robert E. Lee is responsible for the defeat of Confederate forces at the Battle of Gettysburg. Compose a short essay in which you accept or reject the truth of that hypothesis. Use evidence to support your decision. To begin your investigation, the following search terms will be helpful:

- Battle of Gettysburg
- J. E. B. Stuart
- Richard S. Ewell
- A. P. Hill
- Pickett's Charge
- General Longstreet and the Lost Cause

CHAPTER 20

Rich Man's War, Poor Man's Fight

Andrew Carnegie and The Civil War Draft

Civil War Draft Riots in New York City in 1863

Courtesy of the New York Public Library.

In 1835, Andrew Carnegie was born in Dunfermline, Scotland. His father, Will, was a weaver who had fallen on hard times. In order to make ends meet, Andrew's mother, Margaret, assisted her brother, who was a cobbler. She also sold potted meats in a small shop. Technological advances in the weaving industry made it difficult for independent weavers, such as Andrew's father, to make a living. Will and Margaret, along with Andrew and his younger brother by 8 years, Thomas, emigrated to the United States in 1848. They borrowed money from relatives to make the transatlantic journey. Andrew's parents hoped America would offer the family an opportunity to improve their lives.

While establishing themselves in the new country, the family settled in Allegheny, Pennsylvania, where they lived with relatives. Andrew's father could not get steady employment in a cotton mill, so he peddled his own linens door to door. Margaret found work mending shoes. When he was only 13 years old, Andrew found work in a cotton mill as a bobbin boy changing spools of thread for workers operating weaving looms. His starting salary was $1.20 per week ($35 in today's currency).

In 1850, Andrew took a job as a telegraph messenger boy in the Pittsburgh office of the Ohio Telegraph Company. Besides doubling his weekly earnings, the job allowed Andrew to travel the city delivering telegraph messages and getting to know business owners. He had a remarkable ability to remember locations of businesses and the names and faces of the business owners. His hard work and good memory helped him develop influential business contacts.

While waiting for messages to be delivered, Andrew developed the unusual ability of translating the different telegraph sounds by ear. He could record messages without using the traditional cable code that was printed on a paper slip. This ability helped him land a job as a telegraph operator. During this time, Andrew demonstrated his passion for self-education by availing himself of a large personal library open for lending to working boys.

Andrew's hard work and determination paid off in 1853, when Thomas A. Scott of the Pennsylvania Railroad Company hired him as a secretary and telegraph operator. Andrew quickly learned the inner workings of the railroad business that was growing rapidly as the nation became more dependent on transportation by rail.

Andrew was soon noticed by the president of the company, John Edgar Thomson. Both Scott and Thomson held the young Carnegie in high regard. They included him in investments that were made on inside information not available to the general public. Andrew benefited financially from these investments. His gains from them would later serve as a foundation for his many successes in business.

Carnegie was an abolitionist and supporter of President Lincoln and the Republican Party. By the time of Abraham Lincoln's 1860 election as president, Carnegie was well placed to benefit from the conflict that was brewing between the northern and southern states. He would gain financially from his connections within the railroad and telegraph businesses. Both industries would profit if war broke out.

The slave states maintained that neither the president nor Congress had the constitutional authority to abolish slavery. In his Inaugural Address, Lincoln stated that he did not wish to abolish slavery, and he agreed he did not have the authority to abolish it where it already existed. The president, though not an abolitionist, opposed the westward expansion of slavery. He believed it could be legally prohibited in states and territories where it did not already exist. He also believed that slavery would gradually end, and that slave owners would be compensated financially for losing slaves who were legally considered property.

Lincoln, like his presidential predecessor, James Buchanan, rejected secession as illegal. Like many others, they believed the Constitution called for the perpetual union of states. When nominated in 1858 as the Republican candidate for United States Senate in Illinois, Lincoln warned, however, that "A House divided against itself cannot stand. I believe this government cannot endure permanently, half slave and half free." From the point of view of most northerners, the war was intended to preserve the Union, not to end slavery.

In 1861, 11 states seceded from the United States and formed the Confederate States of America. The Civil War (1861–1865) broke out in April 1861 with the Confederate attack on Fort Sumter in South Carolina. Leaders of the Confederate states believed the election of Abraham Lincoln would lead to preventing the extension of slavery into western territories and new states, and eventually to the abolition of slavery.

The first years of The Civil War did not go well for the Union. What some thought would be a quick victory by the North turned into the bloodiest war in the history of the United States. Before the war ended, between 620,000 and 750,000 soldiers would be dead, one-third of them from battle and two-thirds from disease. The war claimed the lives of 10% of all northern males ages 20 to 30. Thirty percent of southern White males ages 18 to 40 died in the war.

For the first years of battle, enlistments and recruitments by states were high for both the North and South. The war continued longer than expected. The brutality and horror of battlefield deaths, wounds, and disease were reported by newspapers and by letters home from soldiers. As a result, enlistments fell and desertions rose.

In January 1863, President Lincoln signed the Emancipation Proclamation. The presidential order declared that all enslaved persons living in areas of rebellion were to be freed. Slaves who escaped to states not in rebellion were to be declared free and under the protection of Union forces. The law applied to 3 million of the 4 million enslaved persons in the United States. (The enslaved living in states that were not in rebellion were to be freed in future actions of states and the federal government, but were not freed by the Emancipation Proclamation.)

The proclamation was based on the President's war powers as commander-in-chief. In 1862, Lincoln had warned that he would issue such an order if the Confederate states did not end their rebellion. The proclamation was a war measure intended to improve the Union's efforts to win The Civil War. It also foreshadowed the eventual abolition of slavery. Once the proclamation was issued, the North was fighting not only to preserve the Union, but also to end slavery. This additional goal was an important factor influencing both Britain and France not to interfere in the war on the side of the Confederacy.

In 1862, to meet the demand for more Union troops, free Black men were finally permitted to enlist in the military. Initially, Lincoln was reluctant to approve this decision. He feared that the use of Black troops might cause border states to secede. The Emancipation Proclamation gave a needed boost to Union recruitment and enlistments.

In all, 179,000 Black men served in over 160 Union units of the army, navy, and support groups. The number included free Blacks from the North and fugitive slaves from the South (only 36,000 of those who served were from the North; the remainder were fugitive slaves from the South). In the Confederacy, Blacks served in noncombat labor positions. In 1865, just weeks before the end of the war, the Confederacy allowed Black males to enlist, but very few did. By the end of the war, 40,000 African Americans had died, three-quarters of them by disease. In July 1863, after the decisive Battle of Vicksburg, Union commander Ulysses S. Grant commended Black troops. He said, "All that have been tried have fought bravely."

When The Civil War broke out in 1861, Andrew Carnegie helped organize the transportation of Union troops by railroad. His boss at the Pennsylvania Railroad Company, Thomas Scott, had been appointed under secretary of war in charge of military transportation. Working closely with Scott, Carnegie helped provide military transportation and restore telegraph lines that had been cut by Confederate forces. Before long he would also acquire an interest in the iron and steel industry that resulted in his businesses obtaining lucrative contracts to provide materials for the building and repair of bridges that were essential for the war effort to be successful.

Although the Emancipation Proclamation spurred enlistments in the North, there remained an unmet demand for more Union troops. Voluntary enlistments were declining in all states. In March 1863, Congress passed the Enrollment Act of Conscription (EAC). Conscription, also known as a "draft," required those selected to serve in the armed forces.

The EAC required all able-bodied male citizens, and those applying for citizenship, between ages 20 and 45 to enroll. Married men were not to be called to service until all eligible unmarried men had been drafted. Federal agents determined the quota to be drafted by lottery based on the population in each congressional district. There is no evidence that Black men living in the North were specifically excluded from the draft.

There is uncertainty as to how many African American men were drafted under the EAC. The number of Black draftees was likely in the thousands. In 1864, when Congress amended the EAC and specifically called for the enrollment and drafting of "all able-bodied male colored persons between the ages of 20 and 45," the number certainly increased. This meant both free and enslaved Black men were eligible to be enrolled and drafted. The new law provided for compensation to slave owners who had one or more slaves drafted.

Various states had used draft measures to require military service in previous wars and in the current Civil War. The EAC marked the first time a draft was used nationally. Under the law, each U.S. congressional district had a federally appointed provost marshal authorized to enforce the new law and arrest those who avoided serving once called to duty. State and local governments lost most of their authority to decide who would and who would not be required to serve.

The EAC contained provisions that permitted a person, once drafted, to avoid serving. Draftees could find a substitute to replace them—perhaps a younger son serving for an older son deemed more essential to a family's business. Some volunteered to be a substitute for family reasons, while others were paid a fee to serve in place of a draftee. Substitutes were paid as much as $1,000 ($19,500 in today's currency).

Another option was for a draftee to pay a commutation fee of $300 ($5,500 in today's currency) and avoid serving altogether. In 1864, to discourage commutations, Congress amended the commutation provision to limit its life to only 1 year, after which the draftee himself would be required to serve. Commutation favored the wealthy and was unpopular among those who could not buy their way out of serving.

Only about 2% of Union forces were draftees. Six percent were substitutes. The rest were volunteers. Many enlisted in order to collect a bonus payment, or serve as a substitute, rather than take the chance of being drafted with no compensation. The draft directly or indirectly provided the additional forces needed by the Union.

Andrew Carnegie, at age 28, was drafted in March 1864 in the state of Pennsylvania. He hired a draft broker whose job it was to find someone willing to serve as a substitute. The broker found John Lindew, an Irish immigrant who had not yet enlisted or been drafted, who was willing to serve in Carnegie's place for a fee of $850 ($15,500 in today's currency). Carnegie thereby received a certificate of nonliability that exempted him from the draft until July 1867. If he had paid a commutation fee he would have been exempted for only 1 year.

Robber baron is a term for industrialists who in the latter half of the 19th century made their fortunes using questionable business practices. Among the most powerful of those who later became known as robber barons were J. P. Morgan, George Pullman, John D. Rockefeller, Andrew W. Mellon, and Andrew Carnegie, all of whom, along with many others, avoided the draft during The Civil War. Although they had not yet been given the "robber baron" title, Carnegie and the others were wealthy men when the war began. The economic opportunities the war presented served to further increase their wealth.

Some northerners resented the Emancipation Proclamation and the Enrollment Act of Conscription. What began as a war to keep the Union intact was now also considered by many as a war to abolish slavery. It was one thing to volunteer and fight to preserve the Union, but quite another thing to be drafted to fight, and perhaps die, to help free slaves. Added to concern over this change in war aims was the popular view that it was "a rich man's war and a poor man's fight." Wealthy men could pay to avoid serving, while those of lesser financial means could not.

Some wealthy industrialists who did not serve were benefitting financially from contracting to provide Union armies with fuel, uniforms, shoes, rifles, ammunition, provisions, transportation, and financing. Many of those who did serve chose to do so as a patriotic duty. Others, who could not afford to buy a substitute or pay a commutation, were compelled to serve. Resentment simmered in the North toward those who escaped death, wounds, and disease in battle because they could afford to pay their way out.

The EAC was the spark that ignited the New York City draft riots. Many White people believed that the draft did not apply to Black men and were resentful. Further, some Whites feared that the Emancipation Proclamation would result in newly freed slaves flocking to New York to compete for jobs with recently arrived immigrants, or to take the jobs of Whites who had been drafted. Compounding resentment toward the draft was the belief of many New Yorkers, especially those who were Democrats, that Lincoln and his Republican Party had changed the aim of the war from preserving the Union to abolishing slavery.

New York City was a stronghold for the Democratic Party. Many of those who were eligible for the draft had hoped the state and local Democratic Party would find ways of protecting them from the draft. The EAC, however, was administered through the federal government, which was under the control of the Republican Party.

Although thousands of New Yorkers fought and died for the Union, there were those who sympathized with the South. Cotton textiles were the leading export from New York, and cotton processing mills and plants employed thousands of people, so that there were New Yorkers who had a financial interest in the cotton picked by enslaved people in the South.

Opposition to the new federal draft reached a peak with the New York City draft riots that began on July 13, 1863. Rioting also occurred in Portsmouth, New Hampshire; Boston, Massachusetts; and in Ozaukee County, Wisconsin. The New York City draft riots are considered possibly the largest civil insurrection in American history. At least 120 were killed, 11 Black men were lynched, over 2,000 people were injured, and property damage was estimated at $97 million in today's currency.

New York City police could not control the rioting. To stop it, President Lincoln had to order federal troops to New York City from Gettysburg, where the decisive battle had ended several weeks before. The riots lasted 4 days. Black residents of New York City became the targets of the violence. Thousands of African Americans were driven from the city or fled out of fear. Three thousand Black residents were left homeless.

Initially, the State of New York and New York City had both been strong supporters of The Civil War, as evidenced by the numbers who had voluntarily enlisted and by financing of the war by New York banks. The Emancipation

Proclamation and the Enrollment Act of Conscription diminished, but did not end, support for the war in New York. One month after the rioting, the draft resumed under the watchful eyes of more than 1,000 Union soldiers.

The Civil War ended at Appomattox Court House 2 years later, when Confederate General Robert E. Lee, the commander of the Army of Northern Virginia, surrendered the last major Confederate army to General Ulysses S. Grant. The Union victory at the Battle of Gettysburg in July 1863 had become the major turning point in the war. The 3-day battle resulted in the death of over 50,000 men and thousands more injured. On November 19, 1863, President Lincoln eulogized the fallen soldiers during his address at the dedication of the Soldier's National Cemetery at Gettysburg. The Gettysburg Address is considered one of the most important speeches ever given by an American president. In the final paragraph of the address, Lincoln said,

> It is rather for us to be here dedicated to the great task remaining before us—that from these honored dead we take increased devotion to that cause for which they gave the last full measure of devotion—that we here highly resolve that these dead shall not have died in vain—that this nation, under God, shall have a new birth of freedom—and that government of the people, by the people, for the people, shall not perish from the earth.

Andrew Carnegie was one of the robber barons who had legally avoided The Civil War draft through substitution. He did not risk his life fighting for the Union, but he did profit from the war, and did significantly advance his career. Some of his wealth stemmed from the investments he made based on inside information that was not available to the general public.

The steel processing innovations Carnegie adapted from the inventions of others helped enable the United States to become the most powerful industrial nation in the world in the decades after The Civil War. His steel mills were the most efficient in the industry. Skyscrapers and bridges became affordable. For many people, this meant more jobs and higher pay. For Carnegie's employees, however, cheap steel meant lower wages and less job security.

Carnegie and his partners sold the Carnegie Steel Company to J. P. Morgan in 1901 for $480 million ($310 billion in today's currency). For a time, Carnegie was the richest person in the world.

Carnegie became a self-educated scholar and activist. He wrote and spoke out about wealth, forms of government (criticizing royalty in the United Kingdom), and the need for world peace. He counseled various American presidents against war and imperialism (extending the rule or authority of an empire or nation over foreign countries). After selling his steel company in 1901, Carnegie turned to philanthropy (helping others by generously donating money for good causes).

Carnegie believed that the first third of a person's life should be devoted to obtaining education, the second third to making money, and the last third to devising the means of giving the money away to worthwhile causes. By the time of his death in 1919, he had contributed over $350 million ($495 billion in today's currency) to libraries, museums, educational institutions, and other charitable foundations. During his lifetime he funded over 2,500 libraries in 47 states and countries around the world. By 1911, he had given away 90% of his fortune.

The major sources for this chapter were:

Bernstein, I. (1990). *The New York City draft riots, their significance for American society and politics in the age of The Civil War*. New York, NY: Oxford University Press.

Carnegie, A. (2006). *The autobiography of Andrew Carnegie and the gospel of wealth*. London, UK: Penguin Books, 2006. (Original work published 1920)

Cruz, B. C., & Patterson, J. M. (2005). In the midst of strange and terrible times: The New York City draft riots of 1863. *Social Education 69*(1), 10–17.

Nasaw, D. (2006). *Andrew Carnegie*. London, UK: Penguin Books.

LEARNING ACTIVITIES FOR "RICH MAN'S WAR, POOR MAN'S FIGHT"

Facts of the Case

1. Why did Andrew Carnegie's family emigrate to the United States?
2. How did Carnegie become successful?
3. How did Andrew Carnegie avoid serving during The Civil War once he was drafted?
4. What contributions to the steel industry were made by Carnegie?
5. What did Carnegie do with his fortune?

Historical Understanding

1. How did the North and the South view the causes of The Civil War differently?
2. What was the Emancipation Proclamation and how did it change the goal of The Civil War?
3. Why was the Enrollment Act of Conscription controversial?
4. What caused the New York City draft riots?
5. How did Black soldiers contribute to The Civil War?

Expressing Your Reasoning

Should Andrew Carnegie have served in the Union Army during The Civil War? Why or why not?

Key Concepts from History

What do the following have in common?

1. "We utterly deny all outward wars and strife and fighting with outward weapons for any end or under any pretence whatever; this is our testimony to the whole world." In 1660, George Fox, the founder of the religious sect known as Quakers, made this declaration. This declaration is known as the group's "peace testimony." The Quakers, also known as the Religious Society of Friends, vowed not to engage in war. Their belief is based on their understanding of the teachings of Jesus as holding that we should love our enemies and that non-violent confrontation of evil is superior to war. Within their religious community there was great opposition to slavery, a strong patriotic feeling toward the United States, and a fervent desire to preserve the Union. When The Civil War began, many Quakers honored the peace testimony and refused to go to war. Many other Quakers broke from the peace testimony and served in the Union Army and Navy. Those who were true to the opposition of their faith to war refused to volunteer or report for duty if drafted. Paying a commutation fee was viewed by many Quakers as an unacceptable way of contributing to the war effort.

2. Muhammad Ali is best known for being the all-time greatest boxer in the world. He won an Olympic gold medal in 1960 and world heavyweight titles in 1964, 1974, and 1978. Ali is also known for refusing induction into the army when drafted in 1966. He objected to being drafted on the grounds that it would violate his Muslim beliefs and that he opposed war, especially the war in Vietnam. He said,

   > My conscience won't let me shoot my brother, or some darker people, or some poor hungry people in the mud for big powerful America. They never called me nigger, they never lynched me, they didn't put dogs on me, they didn't rob me of my nationality, rape and kill my mother and father. Shoot them for what? How can I shoot them poor people? Just take me to jail.

   Having refused to be inducted, he was arrested and convicted for refusing to be inducted into the U.S. Army. His appeal of that conviction was decided in his favor by the Supreme Court in 1971.

3. Bernard Sanders was first elected as a U.S. Senator from Vermont in 2007. In 2016, he unsuccessfully ran for the Democratic Party's nomination for president, losing to Hillary Clinton. He was a civil rights and peace activist during his college years and became an outspoken opponent of the Vietnam War. He sought to avoid the draft as a pacifist on moral grounds. His application to avoid service was turned down. By that time, his draft lottery number had come up, but he was too old to be drafted.

Historical Inquiry

Lincoln's Gettysburg Address is considered one of the most memorable speeches ever made by a president of the United States. Did the address have a historical impact beyond honoring the brave soldiers, on both sides, who died in that battle?

Using online and other sources, test the hypothesis that the Gettysburg Address had a future historical impact beyond honoring the soldiers who had died in the battle. Compose a short essay in which you accept or reject the hypothesis. Use evidence to support your decision. To begin your investigation, the following search terms will be helpful:

- The Gettysburg Address
- Words that remade America
- Lincoln at Gettysburg by Gary Wills
- The Declaration of Independence and the Gettysburg Address
- All men are created equal

Permissions

Chapter 1

Father Junípero Serra © 1985 United States Postal Service. All rights reserved. Used with permission.

Chapter 2

Judge Samuel Sewall, 1729 Photograph © 2018 Museum of Fine Arts, Boston. Art Object by John Smibert.

Dawn of Tolerance in Massachusetts: The Public Repentance of Judge Samuel Sewall for his Actions in the Witchcraft Trials, mural by Albert Herter, 1942. Courtesy Commonwealth of Massachusetts, State House Art Commission.

Excerpt from *The Crucible* by Arthur Miller, copyright 1952, 1953, 1954, renewed © 1980, 1981, 1982 by Arthur Miller. Used by permission of Viking Books, an imprint of Penguin Publishing Group, a division of Penguin Random House LLC.

Chapter 3

Courtesy, Winterhur Museum, Engraving: THE BLOODY MASSACRE perpetrated in King-I-Street Boston on March 5th 1770 by a part of the 29th Reg\t by Paul Revere, Jr. 1770, Boston, MA, Ink, Watercolor, Laid paper, Bequest of Henry Francis du Pont, 1955.500.

Chapter 4

Isaac Jefferson courtesy of Memoirs and Daguerreotype, 1847, in the Tracy W. McGregor Library, Accession #2041, Special Collections, University of Virginia Library, Charlottesville, VA.

From *1776: A Musical Play* by Peter Stone and Sherman Edwards, copyright © 1964 by Sherman Edwards, copyright © 1969 by Peter Stone. Used by permission of Viking Books, an imprint of Penguin Publishing Group, a division of Penguin Random House LLC.

Chapter 5

Courtesy of the Massachusetts Archives. Massachusetts Archives Collection.239: 11-14, Petition of Belinda, February 1783. SC1/series 45X. Massachusetts Archives. Boston, Massachusetts.

Chapter 9

The masthead for *The New York Journal & Patriotic Register* is provided with permission of Photography © New-York Historical Society http://www.nyhistory.org.

Chapter 12

Tecumseh portrait (AL00198) courtesy of the Ohio History Connection (OHC).

Chapter 13

Winslow Homer, "The Bobbin Girl," Mill Girls in Nineteenth-Century Print, accessed November 6, 2017, http://americanantiquarian.org/millgirls/items/show/77.

Chapter 14

"The Trail of Tears," an oil painting by Robert Lindneux reprinted courtesy of Woolaroc Museum, Bartlesville, Oklahoma.

Chapter 16

Henry David Thoreau. Artist: Benjamin D. Maxham, 1856. Ninth-plate daguerreotype. National Portrait Gallery, Smithsonian Institution; gift of anonymous donor.

Chapter 18

John Brown in 1856, photograph courtesy of West Virginia State Archives, Boyd B. Stutler Collection.

Chapter 19

Excerpt from *Robert E. Lee* by John Drinkwater, copyright 1923 by Houghton Mifflin reprinted with permission by Curtis Brown, London.

About the Authors

David E. Harris is a retired professor of teacher education at the University of Michigan. Before holding that position, he was the social studies education director for the school districts of Oakland County, Michigan, and an American history teacher at James Madison Memorial High School in Madison, Wisconsin. With Alan Lockwood of the University of Wisconsin, he coauthored the first edition of *Reasoning with Democratic Values*. He lives in northern Michigan adjacent to the Sleeping Bear National Lakeshore with his wife, Marcia, a retired kindergarten teacher. Their children and grandchildren visit often. David wrote several of the chapters of this book while overlooking the splendor of the lakeshore.

Anne-Lise Halvorsen is an associate professor in the Department of Teacher Education at Michigan State University. Her research and teaching interests are elementary social studies education, historical inquiry, project-based learning, the history of education, the integration of social studies and literacy, and teacher preparation in the social studies. Her publications have appeared in *Journal of Curriculum Studies, Teachers College Record*, and *Theory and Research in Social Education*. She is the author of *A History of Elementary Social Studies: Romance and Reality* (Peter Lang, 2013) and the coauthor of *Powerful Social Studies for Elementary Students* (Cengage, 2012). In 2017, Anne-Lise won the Michigan Council for the Social Studies College Educator of the Year Award. She is a former kindergarten teacher and a former curriculum writer for the State of Michigan. She resides in Detroit, Michigan, with her husband, Bil Lusa, and their three children.

Paul F. Dain is a retired teacher from Bloomfield Hills, Michigan, where he taught American government, Advanced Placement American government, and Advanced Placement comparative government at Andover High School. He received his undergraduate degree in political science from Western Michigan University and his master's degree in the teaching of social studies from Wayne State University. In 1983, he received the Outstanding Social Studies Teacher Award from the Michigan Law-Related Education Organization. In 1987, he received the Master Teacher designation by Bloomfield Hills Schools. In 1997, he received the Newsweek-WDIV Michigan Outstanding Teacher Award. In 1984, he authored the *Detroit Free Press Elections Workbook*, an advanced-level workbook for high school teachers to use in teaching about presidential elections. Paul resides in Florida with his wife, Jane, where he continues to be engaged in educational, community, and civic activities.